THE
GOD HOLD
ON ME

THE OUTPOURING POWER OF

THE HOLY SPIRIT

By Joseph Harris

THE GOD HOLD ON ME

By Joseph Harris

A SPIRIT-FILLED LIFE IN CHRIST

GOD FULFILLING OUR LIVES WITH HIS LOVE

Destiny House Publishing, LLC

The God Hold On Me by Joseph Harris

Published by Destiny House Publishing, LLC

Copyright April 2012 Joseph Harris

International Standard Book Number:

ISBN-13: 978-1936867981

Unless otherwise stated, all scripture quotations are from the Holy Bible, King James Version. Scripture references that do not have the Bible version noted are the author's paraphrase.

Original printing 2012

Cover design. Editing and Publication Layout:

Destiny House Publishing, LLC. ALL RIGHTS RESERVED

All rights reserved under International Copyright law. No part of this book may be reproduced or transmitted in any form or by any means: electronic, mechanical, including photocopying and recording, or by any information storage and retrieval system, without written permission from the publisher.

Printed in the United States of America

For information:

Destiny House Publishing, LLC

www.destinyhousepublishing.com

P.O. Box 19774 - Detroit, MI 48219 - 888.890.4555

This book is designed to help overcome spiritual battles and principalities by getting into the presence of God, accepting Jesus Christ as Lord in your life. The God Hold is for you right now! If you have turned away from God or never accepted Him, or if you are facing all kinds of challenges including spiritual challenges, this book is for your life to get on track with Jesus Christ. There is no one like Him! All power is in Jesus Christ who blesses us through eternity.

CHAPTER 1   THE GOD HOLD ON ME……………………….…..1

CHAPTER 2   GOD CAPTURES THE HEART ……………….…38

CHAPTER 3   COMPLETELY UNDER GOD'S AUTHORITY…....64

CHAPTER 4   GOD HOLDS THE ABUNDANT LIFE……………..86

CHAPTER 5   COUNT ON GOD'S HOLD ……………….….…111

CHAPTER 6   THE GOD HOLD ON PRIEST……………….……128

CHAPTER 7 GRACE WATCHING OVER ME…………….……..148

CHAPTER 8 THE PRAYER HOLD………………………………..171

CHAPTER 9   THE POWER OF SALVATION ……………..…….196

CHAPTER 10 LORD, ORDER MY LIF……………………….…..224

CHAPTER 11 BLESS ME …………………………………….....249

CHAPTER 12 PEOPLE ON FIRE………………………….…......273

CHAPTER 13 GOD HOLD MY TONGUE……………….……......301

CHAPTER 14 THE GOD HOLD ON DESIRES……………..…...325

CHAPTER 15 SEEK FIRST THE KINGDOM OF GOD……...…..347

PRAYER TO GET IN TOUCH WITH GOD

Father, thank you for allowing me to write these passages and to give you glory. Thank you for the many blessings in my life. Thank you for my family and how you continue to watch over us. Thank you for the blessings that your word will deliver to people throughout the world.

Father, we thank you that your word will touch those that are facing difficulties in life and various circumstances. Father, we pray that you touch those that are facing difficult challenges. We pray that millions will be converted and that the pressures of life will not hold you back from being God's Servant. We pray that the word of God will penetrate every heart to the extent they will come to know you today and expect to reign and live eternally with you.

We pray that the quality of life changes for the better in each person's life. It is because of your love and kindness that we have life and have it more abundantly. Lord, we pray that these words will draw us near and help add to us closer to you It is your goodness and grace that sustain us. Father, may these readings in the God Hold deliver the reader and may each person discover the love of Christ Jesus in their lives. May these help each person lead them to know help and allow him to hold them each and every day. It is the God Hold that will sustain every man and every woman and child. Today, help the reader ask God to use the word of God to remove their spiritual scales so that each reader's visions will be clear for God's purpose and they will know that God has predestined this moment for their life.

Today, I surrender to your will and your way. I surrender all to you and acknowledge my sin before you. I pray repentance of my sin to you Father because you are the only true and wise God. There is no one like you. You are the only one who can set men free from bondage and sin that so easily entangles each person. Lord, give me understanding in your truth as I encounter these readings.

Help me to rightly divide this word and meditate day and night on your goodness as I glorify you. Your word is sharper than a two-edged sword and can penetrate the soul and spirit and me as God's creature. I pray that your word will go out and not return void. Father, help me not to be ashamed of the gospel. It is because of the power of the word of God that salvation and deliverance is given to those that ask. I need the God hold on me inside and out. Father God, take hold on my life.

DEDICATION:

This book is inspired and dedicated to my Father in Heaven, my parents, wife, children and siblings. Thank God for my parents for introducing me to Jesus Christ. My prayer is that my parents rejoice in Heaven before God's throne. My father and my mother were responsible for my first baptism. I thank God that both of them had vision to get their children in relationship with the Lord, Jesus Christ. They knew the importance of relationship. My mother ensured each son and daughter went into the water, fully immersed, baptized in the name of the Father, the Son, and the Holy Ghost.

My first church was Midway Baptist Church. I will never forget the late Reverend M.B. Bass who baptized me that day as a young boy around eight years old. Praise God! It was an experience for me that I never forgot. There was something about that moment that was embedded spiritually in my heart. My mother truly believed that God would bless us and keep us. She knew in her heart that God was and is the God of glory and eternal grace and mercy. She knew of His touch. And I believe she sought sound counsel from the Lord and my Father regarding her children's spiritual future.

I believe both of them knew the power of God. I credit them for guiding me in the right direction of life. This helped me then and now to avoid snares and walk away from the dark side of life. I could have been dead and gone if it had not been for the Lord on my side. If it had not been the Lord in the life of my parents, who knows which direction I would have taken. God led my parents to train me and guide me to Him.

We can't explain everything in life that happens, but we do know that God has His way of directing our lives. So I am grateful that He gave me parents to care for me. It was their care that led to my blinders being removed at those set times in my life even to this day. It was the discovery of His everlasting grace that I never understood then and still to this day I am puzzled at the remarkable, incomprehensible love and grace that He alone gives to me and to all the people of the world.

I was baptized again because later I understood better who God is in my life and the requirement of obedience regarding baptism. I am now aware of the symbolic meaning, sacredness, and solemnity in baptism. My parents have since departed to be with the Lord, but I thank God and bow before Him in worship and the highest exaltation and praise. I thank God for all of my siblings who had a role in helping their little brother grow up in those early years of life. They played a crucial role in family love and trust. It is a blessing to have siblings that love and respect each other. Chris, Craig, Linda, Jacqueline, Joann, and Mary, you all are appreciated and loved. You all have always been in my heart. Thanks to each one of you for your love and prayers. I pray the peace of God and the blessed communion of the Holy Spirit touches each of your lives.

This book is also dedicated to the soldiers of the United States Army who served throughout the world past, present, and future. I pray God's blessings and arm of protection be with all soldiers and families during war and peace. I pray they cling to the power of God's word in Psalms 91. I pray that all of God's Saints and those who know the power of prayer continue to lift up our soldiers. I pray for God's intervention in this world, that His peace, love, tranquility, healing, and the power of restoration be in their lives.

We pray that God always be the center of our lives and this country. I pray that the power of God's plan for our lives continue to manifest and be pleasing in His sight and lead us in our faith walk. Father, I thank you for family and friends. I thank you for all the soldiers that dedicate themselves for the defense of this nation. I thank God for the priest that prays daily for peace throughout the world. In Jesus Name, Amen.

PURPOSE: This book is for those who need salvation, deliverance, to the love of God, and to know the power of God in their lives. This book is for those who need someone to call on right now! This is for those who need to know that God can hold onto you in your worst moments of life. Whatever you are going through, God can hold you. You need the God that can hold you in the midnight hour. People need to understand that God has a hold on our lives. He holds His people in His perfect will because it is His way and His will. No other will compare to His. We belong to Him. He moves perfectly in our lives for His glory. Allow the word of God to change your heart as it has the power to take hold of all of your spirit, soul, and being. This book is for everyone to see God as the head of their lives. This serves to depend on His awesome power to be transformed and delivered into His Kingdom. God helps in all kinds of life situations. The intent is to not only witness for Jesus, but that you will be renewed in Christ. He alone can perform in our lives amazing and blessed things. In this book, Jesus immediately and continuously transformed people who came to Him and will do the same for those that call upon His name. This book shares His power of love as a priority in our lives. This book will challenge you to see with new vision that God has given you. It is a book used for your future and generations to come. You will be encouraged in every scripture to live a better life knowing that God has a hold on you and expects for you to seek Him. Readers will be enabled to immediately start grabbing hold to God for every situation in their lives. The God hold takes you into the presence of

His glorious blessings. This is also designed to bless those of the Church of Jesus Christ, the one who died and rose from the dead.

This book is designed for you to get into the church for worship services, accept Jesus as Lord and know your purpose as you grab hold to God. Our Lord has so much that he offers us. Go and get what is yours. Walk by faith in the blessings that are laid up for you. Get the God hold for your entire family. It is an emergency for your family! Think of rush hour! How everyone really wants to get somewhere. God wants you and your family to get somewhere in life and stop living the same tired way with no success and lost dreams.

REGINA'S STORY

Regina Golden pulled over to the side of a highway in tremendous fear of what just took place at work in the conference. She was shaking all over like her nerves were extremely bad. She began telling herself to be cool and calm down. Just a few minutes prior Regina had been in with a co-worker arguing viciously over a financial project that was scheduled to be completed—deal closed. The deal was not closed and Janet claimed that it was Regina's fault. Janet needed to file a report and send it to Mr. George Ruin. They did not discuss particular reasons for this unfortunate finance broker. It was clear to Regina in her mind that Janet and George were a click. She also believed that Janet was clicking with every other woman in that business office. To her surprise, she would discover that Janet also was in her personal life. Janet knew her husband as well. Meanwhile, the issue at hand was Regina's growing attitude of jealousy.

The Lord had spoken to Regina about her attitude of jealousy in regard to her co-worker several months prior. Instead of praying about it, she continued her cycle of gossip about Janet, belittling and demeaning her. She did not realize that she was tearing her down and scandalizing her name all because of her jealous heart. The truth was that she told herself about it, heard herself even after God spoke to her, but continued to sin. In her mind, the more she meditated on it, and talked about it to herself, and even to Loretta Hayes, her best friend, she sank deeper and deeper.

That is exactly what the sin life does to you. It causes you to sink in sin that creeps into your life. The more she talked about her, the more her resentment grew. To add to the matter, Janet had gained a new male friend who looked better than Regina's male friends. She even forgot the fact that she was married for a moment. Regina had discovered something through all of this. She finally realized that she did not have a real problem with her co-worker. She knew that the problem was sin. Her question to God was, "Lord how do I get free from the sin of jealousy and bitterness in my life? Release me from feeling this terrible way. I need you Lord to help me deal with this consuming sin, which is a strategy from the enemy. He was the liar in the beginning and is the liar now." Regina confessed and said to herself that God was her truth and her shield. It is her confession in Him who holds her future and every step she makes that will deliver her from sin, but she allowed it to attack.

Today trust in the Lord with all your heart and lean not to your own understanding. Acknowledge Him and He will direct your path

CHAPTER 1

THE GOD HOLD ON ME

Jeremiah 29:11: "For I know the thoughts that I think toward you, saith the Lord, thoughts of peace, and not of evil, to give you an expected end."

There are many fathers who invest early in their children's lives with IRA accounts, and money markets, and stocks, and bonds. The purpose behind it is to secure a prosperous future for that son or daughter. The father's intent is to set them up for success. His entire plan and thought process is to bless those in whom he invested.

God's thoughts consist of a plan for the lives of all of His people. He is the first person to invest and activate a success plan for each for his children. His plans for His people are set in stone. Notice that his plan started in his marvelous thoughts for his children. In fact and even better, God has a hold on His plan and His people. God has a hold on his own thoughts, his plans and his children. There is no failure in God thoughts and plans. God holds a plan for each person's life and there is no one capable of changing God's plans. Every plan is in His possession and orchestrated in His will for your life.

The enemy can't take it away from God because God has His own personal grip on every plan that He made for our lives. His plan for your life is more secure than being in a volt locked by dozens of locks and combinations. The level of security is beyond the highest measure. No one can break in and take it away. God knows all plans inside out. So, imagine God having a plan for your future. Imagine that God has already planned out a successful life for you. The believer has a life filled with outpouring blessings. God may have a plan for you to become a millionaire here on earth.

We know he has plans for you to be rich in heaven. So definitely being rich here is also granted to those who want it. God thinks good thoughts about us. He is not concerned with someone else's thoughts about you. Get rich and let other people try to figure it out. Don't get caught up with people getting jealous. Just get rich and live with a big smile and thank God every day. God does not think as man thinks, nor does He see as man sees. Just when you start thinking about giving up because you put your trust in someone else, God steps right in and reminds you that we are to worship Him alone and not be caught up in other people's opinions. It only adds to confusion. God is not a God of confusion.

You must trust God because His opinion is what counts. Listen, God has a hold on each of us in His personal way. It is a divine hold that no other person can have. Even when it seems like the enemy has such a grip on you. God has the power to release the enemy's grip and torment in your life at a moment's notice. Don't give up on God. It is exciting to experience God's power because it is the only power that sets people free. He holds our future and gives us hope. We can keep dreaming of things that we believe God for in our lives. God has a hold on our mind, heart, soul, and spirit. God knows our weaknesses and our relationship with Him.

The word hold implies a firm grip, holding on tight to someone or something. Hold means having possession of it and being secured by God. Jesus Christ has secured our salvation. We rely on God's strength to hold us and not let go. Hold also implies a passion to grip something or a person for the purpose of comfort. Love relationships also tend to be of such meaning behind hold and passion. In every marriage there should be a sense of passion that requires each person to hold one another. This reassures the bond in the marriage. Today is your opportunity to tell a family member and a friend that God's hold on them is far more valuable than anything else. You have just stepped into the life of success when you put God first. Please understand what the scripture is saying in Jeremiah. He said, *"For I know the plans I have for you..."* in Jeremiah 29:11. We are being told that God already knows what you will be successful in and how the plan will unfold. The best part about this plan that God has for his saints is that they are good plans and prosperity is in the plan. The best part of the plan is that God never runs out of His love and blessings. There is nothing negative about His plan. Whatever obstacles get in the way, they will not last nor block you because God has already put in motion for your success to be manifested. He also knows that your future will be prosperous and your hope is surely destined to come to reality. Our hope is powerful because it reminds us not to give up on things that are worth something. Ask God to strengthen your faith.

THE GOD HOLD ON ETERNAL LIFE

John 19:1-3: "Then Pilate therefore took Jesus, and scourged him. And the soldiers platted a crown of thorns, and put it on his head, and they put on him a purple robe, And said, 'Hail, King of the Jews!' And they smote him with their hands."

If you were in the enemy's camp and they had chained you down and locked you up behind doors, or in a chamber or prison, what would you do? Some people might go into a severe panic attack. Why? Because the isolation affects many people every day. We need God's intervention. The darkness affects you as well because you cannot see anything. You have no vision or any light to see. You would definitely be eager to break the chains and get up out of the prison, dungeon and darkness. You would do your very best to get out of that situation.

In fact you would strategize to get out of the camp and the bondage probably immediately. The problem is that the enemy had such a hold on your life for so many years that you are struggling to comprehend reality so you can make a new commitment. It is time for God now. You are blocking God's voice with your struggles. God has a unique way of dealing with those who do not listen and take action. As you are reading this, God wants you to take on a new "attitude."

The good news is that God somehow always manages to get a front row seat in your tragedy and testing times with the enemy. When God gets ahold of someone, it is for blessings and growth. Sometimes, it might be for chastisement. Ultimately, God's hold on you and I is to get us each to a point of acknowledging God and recognize His power and authority. God is the answer for us to walk right before Him.

God is the one who allowed us to have this present life. It took the God who had been rejected by millions of people to send His only begotten Son to set things right in God's sight. He sent His precious Son, Jesus Christ, to become a sacrifice for the sin of man. He became the lamb that was slain on the cross. So for all of humanity and life itself, God has a hold on us. The God hold for us is when Jesus paid the penalty of sin for us and bridged the gap to the Father. This happened when God determined it necessary to save mankind from its own self-destruction—sin. Love is what God gives as we remain in Him.

Creation was made by the love of God. Sin came by the pride and disobedience of Adam and Eve. It also came by Satan. Why did He do it? It was love that drove Him to rescue all people from His wrath. The only cure for pride and disobedience is the love of God. God used His method of sacrifice to set order and break the sting, stench and spell of sin by His Son, Jesus Christ. This would be the only way to please God and rescue a disobedient, self-destructive world. Jesus is pleasing and satisfying in God's sight. Make a choice today to love God back because He first loved each one of us.

GOD'S HOLD ON THE CROSS

John 19:16-20: "Then Pilate turned Jesus over to them to be crucified. So they took Jesus away. Carrying the cross by himself, he went to the place called Place of the Skull (in Hebrew, Golgotha). There they nailed him to the cross. Two others were crucified with him, one on either side, with Jesus between them. And Pilate posted a sign over him that read, 'Jesus of Nazareth, the King of the Jews.' The place where Jesus was crucified was near the city, and the sign was written in Hebrew, Latin, and Greek, so that many people could read it."

Nothing in all of history, nor things in this lifetime, compares to what Jesus did for the life of all of his people—even those that were lost and against Him. He blessed the whole world by saving everyone. He spared everyone's life by giving His on the cross. There could be no other sacrifice or substitute to save a dying world that was living in sin. It had to be Jesus Christ, the anointed one and Son of the living God to save us from God's wrath. His sacrifice atonement is what we all see as God's hold on our lives. Jesus was the sacrificial lamb, the course could not be changed. God the Father had set it in motion. He kept us alive when we should have been destroyed. We could never survive without the God hold on our lives through Jesus Christ. It was Jesus' death and resurrection that paved life. He brought us back to Him through His Son—the enemy has no power in that.

Have you ever been in a situation or the hands of someone else that called all of the shots over your life for whatever the situation was about? Was it a time in the military on the battlefield? Maybe you can recall that high authority figure whom thousands recognized and even bowed down to give him respect. Hundreds of years ago, Great Britain had rule over thousands of people, including early America until they broke away. You may remember the basic American history story of breaking away from Great Britain. It took the Revolutionary War to break away from that vicious rule of government. It took a ragged army of men to stand up and break away from tyranny.

The point is that it took power and blood to break away and be free forever from man's self-destructive bondage on the lives of others. A small army of Americans fought against Great Britain and won their freedom with blood, sweat, and bravery. It was the beginning of never being in bondage again by man. The only problem was that man still was not free. America had built a slave system and remained in bondage until another war happened. It seemed that war had to happen to set people free from the stain and poison of sin. In our spiritual condition, it took Jesus to battle men of great authority and surrender to them so He could die and break the grip and stain of sin in the lives of humanity—the lives of all mankind.

Thank God that He has the power to control everything from heaven. Thank God that he sent Jesus to war for us. Jesus' war was not like war on earth. It was a spiritual war that only God could resolve through a sacrificial lamb, His precious Son, Jesus. To this day, my heart rejoices and worships Him because He loved me enough to die for me and cleanse me of sin. He still loves you and I today the same—he has never stopped loving us. The God hold on us is through His death on the cross and His resurrection from the grave. He defeated death and the grave. There is no one like Him. His love is infinite and His power is everlasting to everlasting. He washed us in the power of His blood so that Satan would have no power over us. We accept Jesus as Lord of our lives because of His love that saved us from the death of sin.

CREATING THINGS

Genesis 1:15 -17: "The Lord God placed the man in the Garden of Eden to tend and watch over it. But the Lord God warned him, 'You may freely eat the fruit of every tree in the garden—except the tree of the knowledge of good and evil. If you eat its fruit, you are sure to die.'"

Creating the new garden in my backyard was probably one of the most important and biggest projects that I have had the pleasure to almost complete. It took at least seven years to see the outcome of those small trees turn into huge, full-grown trees. I used to be able to reach the top of the tree. At one time I was able to dig up the tree and move it to another location that my wife desired. One of things that fascinates me with the garden in the backyard is its beauty during the four seasons. It is as if I had never seen such beauty outdoors. I would always look with awe and amazement and state, "Look what God created." No one else can do what He has done.

We find in Genesis that God first expressed to us how important we are to Him when He created Adam and the world. God poured out every ingredient that man needed at that moment to perfect Adam and His creation. God simply reveals His power through His creation. God's creation is proof that He has all power. If you ever had doubts about God's power, look at His creation because He has already proven Himself.

Please understand that He did not prove Himself based on someone's request. It already exists through His almighty power. There is nothing that can change the fact that God created everything. He is the author and designer of creation just like He is the author of faith. His creative power is beyond all imagination. It is simply amazing. He expressed His love and creative power when He formed the first man—Adam was formed from the dirt. Before creating Adam, God created various necessities and gifts that He wanted Adam to have. He fulfilled all of

Adam's needs and desires before Adam could even make a request to him, except woman.

Later, God would give him a woman to be his helper. He knew that Adam would need someone to support him and stand beside him through his life. He knew Adam would need someone to love. God's plan of seed and reproduction had been established through man and woman. God valued both man and woman then and today, so he created the institution of marriage.

In Genesis chapter 2: 22-23, we read that God brought Eve to Adam as his wife and gift to him. God had already laid the foundation for everything that Adam needed in the garden. God had made the garden a paradise for Adam. Adam had a paradise to share with his wife. They lived in a perfect environment and atmosphere. All he needed to do was to be obedient. God gave all dominion and authority to Adam.

So really when you look at God giving Adam everything on earth, He was intentionally entrusting his creation to Adam. He also intended that Adam would take care of the garden and all things that were under his authority. God made it to where nothing could pluck Adam out of the hands of God because of his authority. At that time, the only harmful sin that could destroy Adam's blessings that God had given was the act of disobedience, and lack of humility. Adam was created with obedience. If he had not been created perfectly by God, then dominion would never have been under his authority.

Adam was also supposed to commune daily with God. His relationship with God was to be perfect. He was the image of God in the flesh, though not a comparison to Jesus Christ. He was given dominion, too, as an expression of His love to Adam and all humanity—the first man, and all men for generations to come. God has a hold on us that blesses us each and every day. I would rather God hold me than anyone else. I see in respect to His perfect creative power forming man by breathing inside of Him and providing all of his needs.

His love and creative power reflects in our lives today. God has proven that He has a hold on our lives. He is the one who keeps life inside of us. No one can breathe nor function without the power of God in our lives. He blessed all the things after He had created them. He ordained life and all things under His authority and divine power. God has mysteries that mankind has not unlocked yet and some that God only reveals as He deems it necessary.

The last thing we need to see is someone on earth getting cast down to hell like Satan, who used to be employed got cast down from heaven to hell for pride. Man was not created to reflect that pride and arrogance as the enemy displayed in heaven. We are not making ourselves high like we are gods. God desires that we walk in humility and love. We must worship in obedience; serve in obedience the only true and wise God. Today, it is important that we still search God's word and we seek God for our life's purpose. God knows all about what pleases Him most.

SEARCH FOR GOD IN YOUR LIFE

Job 11:7-9: "Can you search out the deep things of God? Can you find out the limits of the Almighty? They are higher than heaven—what can you do? Deeper than Sheol—what can you know? Their measure is longer than the earth and broader than the sea."

God gave us His grace through Jesus Christ to save us from the grips of the enemy. God knew exactly what to do for His people against the enemy's infiltration and man's acts of disobedience. What really touches us most is the fact that in all of God's power, He decides to keep man alive and help him through his devastation, deprivation and sin's contamination in his life. God decided in His infinite wisdom and loving kindness to have a grace hold on man.

This means that enemies cannot break God's favor in your life, especially when you submit to God and not to the enemy. The Lord is in essence opening channels of love that is so great, you could not miss it even when you walk blindly because He wraps His love and grace around each person. His love is a guide for our lives. The enemy desperately wants to kill you and steal all of your joy. God's grace is stronger because his firm grip and mighty power will not let you go! Today you can easily make up your mind to accept Christ because, quite frankly, you either get ahold on your life by God, or you allow the enemy to take over your life and destroy you and your family.

Your best option is obvious. That best option is asking God to put the God hold on you. You can even ask God what is His God hold on you. The God hold on your life is God's will for your life. God's power is working in your life right this very moment. God has a complete hold on the believer's life. See, in this passage you don't have to worry about searching out the deep things of God. He already has all the answers and knows all things. Let me put it this way: nothing can be hidden from God. No secrets, no things done in the dark can be hidden from God. Can you imagine God asking you that question in this passage? There are many that think they can answer. In reality, no man can answer. We must humble ourselves and submit to him as we worship Him for His goodness.

He purposed Himself to bless all people. His unlimited grace has no barriers because of the love of God that is inside it. Grace is eternal and never exhausted. Grace refreshes and grace is the deepness of God. We cannot fully grasp the height, width, or any kind of measure, of His grace, but we can experience spiritually the effects of His grace. His grace is always working.

He made grace for life to be sustained eternally for those who love Him and are called accordingly for His purpose. God is full of grace. Thank Him over and over. His grace is needed. Grace actually has a hold on me. I pray that you allow God's hold on you in every area of your life. His love will not miss any area. You just believe and have faith that God will work it out. I enjoy this tight hold on my life, as you should also.

There is no power on Earth that can remove God's grace. You and I can count on receiving His grace no matter what the circumstances are in life. Today, I urge you to form a relationship with Him who is above all creation and life itself. Move into the grace hold factor. I prefer to be in that kind of hold. Wrestlers do the headlock techniques on opponents. We have God on our side. Nothing can hold God for anything. He has a grip on us. I prefer a more deliberate and permanent grip.

We might as well say to our Father in Heaven, "I give in to you. I surrender to you because there is no way I can search out the deep things of you, Lord God, and know everything. I need to put my life in your hands so that you will deliver me out of darkness and deceit. I am reminded of Moses' attitude when he was allowed to speak to a burning bush. The burning bush was your presence in power that allowed Moses to step on holy ground in your very presence. Yet bow before you, Almighty Lord. I thank you, Father, that you allowed Moses to come before you and become a servant used to save your people in Egypt. In the mountains you dwell, in our homes you dwell. How you do it? I shall never know except that you are God all by yourself and your word says that 'nothing is impossible for you.'"

We live in an era where education and technology is moving and evolving at a high speed of finding new opportunities, and inventions, and discoveries. God wants us to prosper in His Kingdom. We must learn to trust that He knows all and decides when to reveal His mystery to those of the household of faith. He will reveal it to those that seek Him and find Him. God is the loving God of our life that will not be moved. In technology, those that are educated know how to examine systems for their fullest potential.

They know mathematics, trigonometry, and calculus. They have the scientific touch. They have that knowledge to dissect and explore different ranges and facts rather than an assumption of various equations. They are always looking for new ways to improve and process units. Some have the skills to develop new inventions. They can discover a vast number of chips that will make you rich. One of our friends discovered a new chip for a company and made millions for that company. When you get that smart, there is an advantage of earning a higher financial gain. You can step in another blessing of abundance.

Not only does money talk, you begin to be sharpened in your confidence and hope increases in your life. Your mind opens to a dimension that you never thought could happen to you.

Then it finally hits you. God is alive. God is real. God is the reason I prosper and walk in blessings. Even when I took His blessings for granted, He still blessed me. We can trust God to bless us in areas of lives that we cannot even imagine we need Him to work on. There is no one like Him neither in the earth nor in existence.

Suddenly, you begin to act like me and run to the nearest Pastor and say help me to find my calling. God uses men to help men to witness and glorify His righteous name. We need to always be reminded that our God is the God of creation. This is also means that God is the center of man developing new technologies and new discoveries. He gave man the ability to discover the computer, operating systems, computer chips, new hardware, new processing capabilities, and much more. We should be thankful that God allowed us to discover and advance in all areas of life. Praise His Righteous name. God put some things in the chip that will last for a long time—at least until the end. One thing that He wants all of His people to know is that He holds the future and all the deep things are in the palm of His hand. He is God and His love has no limits. Blessed be the name of the Lord.

A CHILDLIKE ATTITUDE

MATTHEW 18: 1-5: "At that time the disciples came to Jesus, saying, 'Who then is greatest in the kingdom of heaven?' Then Jesus called a little child to Him, set him in the midst of them, and said, 'Assuredly, I say to you, unless you are converted and become as little children, you will by no means enter the kingdom of heaven. Therefore whoever humbles himself as this little child is the greatest in the kingdom of heaven. Whoever receives one little child like this in my name receives me.'"

Humility is the key attitude that God wants in us. It is foundational. During Jesus' mission on earth, He walked with humility. He never displayed a prideful spirit. So demonstrating the right attitude impresses our Lord. The right attitude to possess is a humble spirit toward God and people because it changes things in your life and others. This kind of humble spirit is what pleases God.

In this passage, Jesus specifically tells us to be converted as little children. He wants us to have that kind of humble attitude when we approach Him and when we deal with other people. We need this attitude to enter the kingdom of heaven as He stated. Pride will not work, arrogance will not work, and self-sufficiency will not work. Boasting will not work. Humility is what He wants because it works for God. Jesus was using humility when He was talking to his disciples in this story.

Humility helps us in worship, teaching, preaching, and the entire Christian walk. When we submit to God, He will hold onto us and help us develop in many ways. Humility is one area of life that the Holy Spirit will help us to develop. It is important to God, so the operation of the Holy Spirit will work on us. God loves to hold onto those who walk in humility. Blessings are poured out in abundance. Look at the life of Jesus—his entire life was blessed and he spent his time pouring out blessings. He is still doing it today. Most children walk in this world with open hearts and feeling free. Jesus sees the innocence and love in the heart of a young child coming to Him and it pleases Him. These children came knowing that He was the Lord. In Jesus' eyes, they came with an open spirit and an open heart to get close to Jesus because they knew He was, and is, Holy. These children knew that Jesus was Lord and He could be trusted. So they opened themselves to Him. Humility is opening yourself up and submitting to God, knowing that He has all power. It is a deep feeling of surrender to know that God knows you don't walk high and mighty but lowly under His authority.

Who is the greatest does not impress the Lord. How about who can be a humble and willing servant of the Most High God? Jesus is not looking at who could sit in a high seat of authority. He is looking for men and women with a heart of God. We impress God with acts of obedience and worship for Him, not ourselves. There is no personal makeup, pretense, substance, or any show of a person that impresses God—it is simply being humble, obedient, blameless, fruitful, and a true worshiper of God.

God wants us to demonstrate that kind of attitude and innocence like a little child. Young children in this scripture displayed just that to Jesus. We must strive to protect young ones and support them because they are precious in God's sight. We actually have many missions in life as a Christian. Another thing is that God wants us to provide programs, a lending hand, and resources to support those who are having difficult times.

Our priority is helping the homeless, orphans, those in jails, and those who are struggling at home. God has a hold on our lives to help others to move from one condition to a better condition. He also shows us in the lifestyle that we can help and make a difference in the lives of others. Let us take that stand together. Let's walk in humility and help others survive on this battlefield. Jesus moves with compassion, and humility, and holds us in the palm of His hand. He keeps on blessing us because of who He is.

THE ANOINTING CONNECTION

The anointing is God's Spirit touching our lives. You can't see the anointing because He is Spirit, not flesh and blood. Nevertheless, He can reflect or reveal Himself through people. Look at Deacon Stephen in Acts 7—his face was glowing with the anointing on his life. The Holy Spirit sanctifies us, which connects us to God with the right attitude, spirit, and heart. The anointing that God gives us helps us to change and walk in the ways of God. The anointing equips us in power and makes us productive.

Only God anoints people for His purpose. He knows each person already. The anointing is the power of God that enables us to do works of faith. The true Christians preach under the anointing, sing under the anointing, and above all, worship and serve under the power of the Holy Spirit. If we did not preach under the anointing, all preaching would be in vein, and of Satan. There would not be any truth in the sermon and teaching. If we did not sing under the anointing, then it's just worldly and has no Godly effect. If it is just man's word alone without the anointing, then it's Satan at work delivering false words and lies.

The scripture reminds us in *1 Corinthians 2:14: "But the natural man received not the things of the Spirit of God; for they are foolish unto him, neither can he know them, because they are spiritually discerned."* We know the enemy to be the author of lies. He has no truth and we discern his motives and attacks in Jesus' name. All truth is in Jesus Christ and He passes His truth to His Saints and all who believe in Him.

God wants us to walk as born again believers under His anointed power. You must have Jesus as the head of your life and the Lord of your life to operate in the anointing. God already blessed us to receive the anointing on our lives. We block out everything in our lives and end up blocking out the very anointing. We must open our hearts and minds and allow the anointing to flow through us. We have power struggles and attacks on our entire family that seem unstoppable. But there is help. We have the power of the Holy Spirit on our side.

There was another hard downpour today here in Texas. It was rain in abundance and seemed as though a flood could have come any moment. The rain to me was symbolic of the anointing flowing in the life of the believer. It did not matter how long it rained today because God was giving more insight to the power of His anointing.

This rain was special to me because it reminded me of how God pours out His Spirit onto one person. He allowed me to see that He fills a person so completely, just how he wants them.

BECOME IMMERSED IN THE SPIRIT

Usually we think of getting soaked and wet to the max, and end up changing out of wet clothing because of that feeling of being soaked and unbalanced. We are so used to being dry. It rained so hard that it seemed as though the sky had burst open and released billions of tons of water to revive this planet. That probably was an understatement because God does send so much down. God waters this planet with more than you or I can imagine. Even though it sounds ridiculous, you will be surprised at what He can do in your life with a downpour.

That's right, God is in heaven doing some things we can't see. He pours down from heaven and blesses us. He rains on the just and the unjust. He is no respecter of persons when He rains down. He can out pour anything He wants at any given time. In Malachi 3, He says, when referring to tithing, "I will pour out blessings that you will not have room enough to receive."

Believers know that God has the power to control everything from heaven and any place on earth that He controls. He owns an operation center in every country, in every nation, in every city, in every state, in every house and in every temple, every church, and on every mission. No one can stop Him from controlling all things. That's right, He controls the waters, the skies, the valleys, the rivers, the oceans, men, women, children, spiritual things, life on Earth, death, and everlasting life—anything the imagination can think of.

As I watched the rain come down on my roof and observed the overflow of the water in my gutters, I was a little concerned for a moment because there should have been a perfect flow from the gutters to the down spout then to the ground. I thought something was going to get backed up or find a crack or an opening to get into and create a devastating leak. When it rains that hard (thunder showers), you definitely want to have a good roof and water flow. If the roof leaks there is potential for something in your house to cave in and get destroyed. Things do get expensive and inconvenient.

I want to remind us of what God said in His word. There is a latter rain that only God can pour out on us. God is saying let it rain because you will experience prosperity. Let the rain blanket me in the fullest of blessings. He wants us to experience the rain because the rain is an expression of abundance. All over the world, crops and people who were thirsty received the blessing of God's power to quench their thirst. People are tired of feeling the dryness and emptiness in their lives.

God has a way of allowing us to know that the rain is symbolic of blessings flowing in our lives. Rain signifies that there will be some fruit that will get watered. There is some fruit that has been stable and stagnant and burdened because it has not been nourished by essential nutrients. God can immerse us with His power raining down on us.

God can even immerse with waters that can cover us and wash us new. The God hold immerses us over, and over again.

In Joel 2, He says, I will pour out my Spirit. God will pour out His Spirit in such a magnified intensity than the rain we experience flows on when we are soaked and wet. Ask God to do an outpouring of the Spirit in your life. Start a new walk in Christ when God fills you with His Spirit. You will experience the love of Christ and gifts that God gave you. You may start speaking new tongues. Start the fivefold ministry gifts that you possess. Watch it come to pass. I tell you that God has such a downpour of ministry that exist that we as Christians all over the world cannot keep up. Do you want to start ministering? God's ministry is open and available twenty-four hours, seven days a week. You can become a servant anytime. He will equip you for His ministry. He will be glorified through all of His ministers.

GOD FORMED YOU

JEREMIAH 1:5: "Before I formed thee in the belly I knew thee; and before thou camest forth out of the womb I sanctified thee, and I ordained thee a prophet unto the nations..."

There are many people who still suffer from identify crisis. Those that suffer are usually those who lack confidence in themselves. They usually are blinded to the fact that God had formed them before life began on the earth. The God hold was on you and I before time even begin. God had already blessed us before we could identify with ourselves. This scripture was written to remind us that God sees you the way He made you. God did not change anything except what He wants for you. He ordered my life and yours for His purpose. So you do not have to have an identity crisis. He is there for you. You can cast your cares on Him because He cares.

One of the major problems with most people is that they try to carry themselves through life. They try to live without Jesus Christ. Life is broken without Him. Sin causes the separation and the identity crisis because sin separates a man from the one Lord you can be restored by. God is looking to bless you and me more and more each day.

I knew you before you were in your mother's womb. How can you know someone before the seed had even been developed? God is the one who decides what the seed will be because He made the seed in man. We existed in God's eyes even before our time could be manifested on earth. That is a reason to shout because no one else can express such power and make creative miracles come to existence.

God wanted Jeremiah to be encouraged about the mission he would be faced with. He was called and set apart by God as his prophet to the nations. He wanted Jeremiah to know that all power is in His hand and that He would be with Him in delivering messages from God. So to express His power, He wanted Jeremiah to know that He knew Jeremiah before He was conceived.

The Lord has already thought about us before we could even know ourselves, before we even came into the world. He knew everything about each person individually and accurately before we could know anything about ourselves. That is enough to shout about! God knew our hearts, and minds, and soul, and strength before we knew anything about it. What a reason to praise Him and serve Him the rest of your life.

Everyone that God calls has a specific purpose for Him. No one should live life without knowing his or her purpose. If you do not know, ask God. Seek Him with all of your heart and soul and He will answer. The word of God is also the answer. God will bless you through His word. Seek ye first the kingdom of God and His righteousness. When you seek Him everything else that He desires for you will follow and bless you.

GOD ORDAINED YOU!

One thing for sure is that when God ordains you for His purpose, it's a done deal. No one can change it. He makes all things for His glory and they will come to pass. When He ordains His men of God for the ministry, He sets them apart for His use. Make yourself available each and every day. God sets the course of ministry for each one to perfectly compliment the body of Christ and to glorify Him. He has predestined all things for His glory. I am always reminded that it was God who ordained the stars, and planets, and life itself. There are several things that God wants you to do and more that are ordained by God. You may not finish everything, but set goals in Christ Jesus. Jesus can help you make it through all of your goals. He made you and me before time. He already had us in mind before the world was formed. Not only did He already know us, He sanctified you. He ordained the person He wanted to ordain for His purpose. That means that God has a mission for His people. He set apart specific people for pinpointed assignments.

Do you know your assignment? Do you know where God wants you? Remember, before He formed you and me, He already knew about us. He knew everything about us. He knew our comprehension levels, He knew our intellect, and He knew our futures. He even knew whom we would marry. He knew the trust level inside our heart. He knew if we would accept Him as Lord and Savior. He knew that He would wash us in His blood for the remission of sin. He knew who would birth out baby boys, baby girls, twins, triplets, or quadruplets. God knew the morning, and the days of the year, and times of thunder, and lighting, and the floods of life. He knew how much trouble you would be faced with.

MEDITATE ON THE LORD ALMIGHTY

Philippians 4:8: "Finally, brethren, whatever things are true, whatever things are noble, whatever things are just, whatever things are pure and whatever things are lovely, whatever things are of good report, if there is any virtue and if there is anything praiseworthy—meditate on these things."

People clearly know what it means to think about pure and positive things. They will experience the impact of Godly thinking. Godly thinking does not get off course. Godly thinking stays on course. Godly thoughts of love enter your mind. Godly pictures enter your mind. Godly decisions enter your mind. There is a God of peace that enters your mind. God has a way of working those thoughts in us throughout the day.

A NEW MINDSET

ROMANS 12:1-2: "And so, dear brothers and sisters, I plead with you to give your bodies to God because of all he has done for you. Let them be a living and holy sacrifice—the kind he will find acceptable. This is truly the way to worship him. Don't copy the behavior and customs of this world, but let God transform you into a new person by changing the way you think. Then you will learn to know God's will for you, which is good and pleasing and perfect."

Our soldiers fight day in and day out. But one of the tragic perceptions in the military, and even with those retired, is the feeling of stigma. Stigma hurts each soldier because it causes each soldier to limit their means of assistance in all areas of help including mental treatment, PTSD, anxiety, psychological stress, and a host of other medical concerns. Stigma means an identity is placed on you, in your mind, and even by others. But the point of this writing is to let you know that you are free from stigma. You are free to release any concern. Your life is yours, and you should put it in God's hands.

God is the one that made professionals who they are. So He can use them for His purpose and glory. Today, I am writing so that every soldier, civilian, and all people let your stigma mentality go aside and seek the help you need. People are standing by to help soldiers in whatever area is needed.

The biggest misconception in the armed forces with soldiers, sailors, and marines is that they believe that admitting to a sickness makes them less of a person and soldier. That is totally incorrect. In fact, to admit it means that you are stronger and have courage. Do not allow anything to discourage you. It doesn't matter what it is, do not let it push you backwards, avoiding and turning down help. Soldiers are hard, and strong, and they are the very best that the military has to support.

One of the things that keep soldiers is the hardcore attitude, headstrong belief, and perhaps sense of pride that holds them back from seeking the help they need. So when they need the help necessary, a sense of feeling ashamed and weak may interfere. Today, we need all soldiers to not allow any of those traits and distracters to interfere in receiving the best treatment available. Our soldiers are heroes and they deserve the best support in all areas possible. Our soldiers serve this nation and they must be treated as heroes and receive the highest honor, respect and admiration for protecting the nation and the world. We owe it to them to help them get the new mindset by helping them to adjust back into society.

GOD, THE GIVER OF GIFTS

EPHESIANS 4:11-15: "And He Himself gave some to be apostles, some prophets, some evangelists, and some pastors and teachers, for the equipping of the saints for the work of ministry, for the edifying of the body of Christ, till we all come to the unity of the faith and of the knowledge of the Son of God, to a perfect man, to the measure of the stature of the fullness of Christ; that we should no longer be children, tossed to and fro and carried about with every wind of doctrine, by the trickery of men, in the cunning craftiness of deceitful plotting, but, speaking the truth in love, may grow up in all things into Him who is the head, even Christ."

You do not have to deny your calling because of challenges of other people and the enemy attacking. God is the one who calls and gives gifts to fulfill His purpose. The core or central move behind your calling is God. The next thing is the gift, and you believing in that gift from God. You either listen or respond to God or you just disobey Him. Which do you prefer? Obey Him! Disobeying God is not an acceptable answer. People do not know your calling. People may not know your gifts as well. You know it, so activate it today.

God knows your calling and your gift. God called you and me by name and the ministry that He wants us in. He wants us to answer Him daily. Be encouraged to accept your calling. Don't brush God off another day. There are blessings laid up for you brother and sister. God has blessings laid up for the family. He touched you and gave you the power to serve, so serve today and the rest of your life. He entrusted His power in you. He knew that you would open up to Him and allow Him to guide you in service.

There are some who do not feel the same way. Just because someone else has their opinion, or even calling in the Lord, it does not mean that they have their hands on the pulse of your calling. It is personal and they cannot accurately measure your calling. They do not have spiritual ability to tell you that God did not call you. God calls all of His children to do the ministry in some form to glorify Him.

God blesses us at different levels to witness. We just need to be equipped in the word of God and be led by God as we witness to others. We must be under the influence of God. Ask God to lead and guide you today in witnessing to the world, family, friends, and loved ones. Take a strong stand in Christ because He gifted you. You can count on God to help you take a stand in your anointing.

He is still God with all power and is ready to help you and me. Stop chasing behind someone who does not love the Lord and does not want anything to do with your spiritual gifts. God will make room for them. In fact just take a look outside and see for yourself that there is already room for it. Just preach and witness of His grace and mercy. You have a calling to tend to! Stop concentrating on other distractions. God is looking to bless you for your obedience. Stay focused. The enemy will try playing tricks on your mind but you just need to denounce and rebuke it. Start giving God all the praise and glory to reflect the victory you have in Him.

KNOW WHOSE YOU ARE

God has an army bigger than our imagination. It has more room open and available for anybody. Who wants to join God's army? All Christians are part of God's army since we are the body of Christ. Our attitude should be to help another soldier out when in need, or in trouble. The first time, in 1995 when He had me to stand before men in a circle at church to witness, I was supposed to give a testimony to about 100-200 men of different backgrounds. Instead, I ended up giving a brief sermon as the Holy Spirit moved me. I was shy in the beginning because I did not know what to say. I was not a speaker by any means. But suddenly I was over taken by the Holy Spirit and He took me *to Hebrews 4:16: "Let us therefore come boldly unto the throne of grace, that we may obtain mercy, and find grace to help in time of need."*

I discovered the word of God is sharper than a two-edged sword. The word of God moves you in a manner that God desires for His glory.

The word of God demonstrates God's power in the lives of believers and will deliver anyone in the path of the word. He transforms people through His word. I may not be sure about many things in life, but when it comes to the living word of God, I know the word can make a difference in anybody's life. The word of God changed my life. The word carries a message so divine and holy that it cannot return void. If you ever feel empty at any time in life, the word of God can touch you and you will be made whole.

When you have a calling in your life you never know how God is going to use you. Those men that day saw that the Lord was with me. I was proclaiming my calling that day in the front of men. Whenever any man proclaims his calling, God is going to answer in spite of others not responding. You see about two years later, I became an ordained deacon, and three years later I became a minister on fire for the Son of God, Jesus Christ, my Lord.

It has been almost twenty years since the Lord first put preaching on my heart. He allowed me to become one of His servants. Please understand that it was not man who called me. Paul said it himself that man did not call him. It was the Lord's calling to glorify Him. We read that of Paul in Act 9. It was the call on my life, and it was something like a Jeremiah experience. As you may recall Jeremiah said, "It's like fire shut up in my bones." He knew that the Spirit of God was inside his heart, turning things around, shaping and molding a minister for His divine plan and desire.

Do not lose the fire because of what anyone says or does or even thinks. Block it out so you can get your blessings. For me, I could not help myself. When He moves on the inside of you, He changes the heart of the matter. One brother stated, "Who licensed you preacher?" I did not say anything. I just looked at him and thought, God's got it. He knows all about it and knows that His perfect power lives within. All praise to His holy and righteous name.

1 CORINTHIANS 12:4-11: "There are different kinds of gifts, but the same Spirit. There are different kinds of service, but the same Lord. There are different kinds of working, but the same God works all of them in all men. Now to each one the manifestation of the Spirit is given for the common good. To one there is given through the Spirit the message of wisdom, to another the message of knowledge by means of the same Spirit, to another faith by the same Spirit, to another gifts of healing by that one Spirit, to another miraculous powers, to another prophecy, to another distinguishing between spirits, to another speaking in different kinds of tongues, and to still another the interpretation of tongues. All these are the work of one and the same Spirit, and he gives them to each one, just as he determines. The body is a unit, though it is made up of many parts; and though all its parts are many, they form one body. So it is with Christ. For we were all baptized by one Spirit into one body—whether Jews or Greeks, slave or free—and we were all given the one Spirit to drink."

Today is your day to know your gift and start using it for the glory of God. What is your gift from God? You possess at least one of those gifts God teaches in Corinthians 12. Otherwise why would God mention it through the Apostle Paul? If you had the gift of being a quarterback in the NFL, you would perform at the college level with maximum zeal to impress the scouts that may be looking at you or someone else. The point is that you are fully aware of your gift and who can use it.

The NFL team that selects you from college, or whatever sport or gift you might have, will use you with intensity to win games, or win different kinds of scholarly contest. It reminds me of so many young children who have the gift of spelling and enter spelling bee contests. They practice and study to know those words and to beat the next person out. I am also reminded of the gift of singing. When I think of the talent of people who sing gospel and secular songs, it simply reminds me of the awesome power of God who gives the voice to sing.

We must start living life witnessing the gifts that God put on the inside that we may glorify Him.

God shows us that there are different gifts that He alone gives. Are you using your gifts? The Holy Spirit helps me to use my gift of preaching and teaching the gospel. Although I use my gifts, please understand that Jesus is our ultimate gift given to us by God.

KNOW YOUR DESTINY

Jesus has a specific destiny for your life, which He wants you to start walking in that direction today. Do not allow the enemy to trick you out of God's plan for your life, which is to bless you and prosper you in Jesus Christ. The Lord has already set it up for you. All you need to do at this point is start moving in that direction and believe God for the outcome. The timing has been established along with the purpose. Some people will have you to think that God has nothing for you. It is absolutely false and the wrong assumption by any measure from God.

God's kingdom is open for whosoever is willing. God is no respecter of persons. He is able to strengthen His people under His anointed power for as long as He wills it. It is time for all individual believers to pinpoint their specific destiny. It is important so you can start the journey today. You can step out of the old way of life and begin anew.

God distributes the abundance and outpouring of blessings for His people. His destiny for you is filled with blessings. As long as you walk with faith, God has approved your destiny and filled it with blessings. So when you get to the other side of that destiny, watch what the Almighty God does in your life. He will rain His blessings down on us for a long period of time. He wants to get our attention. He does it by giving blessings that are free.

What was brought to my attention as blessing is that God showers us with rain because God is in the business of replenishing the earth and the substance that man is in need of for survivability and sustainability. Just like God pours the water on your house and washes your house, He also pours the water to feed the cattle on a thousand hills. He also pours the water that nourishes the crop for the farmer who has experienced a drought and needs to be successful in that trade. God always has a way of blessing us when we see things the opposite of how He has planned for us.

I want to remind us of what God said in His word. There is a latter rain that blesses us each and every day. Our blessings are pouring down on us by God. God wants us to experience that rain of prosperity, the rain of His grace and mercy, and the rain of His blessings just showering us. Let the rain blanket me too, Father.

PRAISE BREAKS PRISONS

ACTS 16:25-26: "But at midnight Paul and Silas were praying and singing hymns to God, and the prisoners were listening to them. Suddenly there was a great earthquake, so that the foundations of the prison were shaken, and immediately all the doors were opened and everyone's chains were loosed."

Praise shakes prison foundations in all aspects of life. Paul and Silas were locked up in prison and found themselves waiting for a move of God inside the prison. They were being persecuted because of their witness. They knew exactly what it took to get a breakthrough from God. The two men prayed and praised Jesus Christ in the prison. Read Psalm 146 and 147. Get this! No one told them to do it. It was already built inside them to praise the King of Kings and Lord of Lords. They knew that they had a relationship with Jesus Christ. When you have a relationship, God smiles on you and shows up. He breaks every prison foundation that keeps you locked up in the spirit. Anybody who has been there should be saying prison was not made for me!

When I visited the prison, I could feel the desire to come up out of that place. Yet at the same time, I could tell that evil spirits were at work in that place. Everyone did not attend service because their own personal reason or limitation of justice. But everyone needed to because it was deliverance time—the moment when those who believe step up, and change comes over them as the Holy Spirit moves.

He will be at your side and in your heart. God wants families to seek Him for answers. The pleasure of visiting to preach the gospel was to do the mission set at hand that it might be pleasing in His sight. But also to completely purposely set out to give Him complete worship and praise. The scripture says, "God inhabits the praises of His people."

Paul and Silas found themselves in a prison because of their witness and persecution. The enemy could not steal the gospel from their heart as long as Jesus was with them. The enemy could not steal the praise from them because it was on the inside and out. God was with them through that tough situation. He will be with you in your tough situations. When people come up against your witness, you do not have to worry; God chose the place where His word would go forth. The fact is that the word will go out and not return void and no devil in hell can stop His praise and blessings. Jesus is Lord, make no mistake about it, there is no other Lord. Anything else is false advertisement and enticement, so rebuke it.

When the preaching went out in the prison, we could tell that strongholds were being broken and people were being converted. The anointing was moving in that place behind bars. The anointing of the Lord came into the gymnasium that night and touched the hearts of men that had felt bound and low as dirt. Several came forth with a heavy desire to be transformed right then and there. That is the right attitude—when you get into praising God in His presence, expect a breakthrough. God is in the business of breaking the chains of depression, guilt, loneliness, and all those things that try to keep your mind locked up. Trust in the Lord, Jesus Christ.

It is time for you to change your mind and attitude about our Lord, Jesus Christ. You and I must trust Jesus to deliver us out of our prison mentality that keeps us bound. Ask God to break the chains that keep us down. Ask Him for deliverance from the chains of weariness, hate, wrong influence, wrong worship and praise, wrong attitude, evil-bounded things, a reprobate mind, and a hardened heart. God can do anything. In all those situations and more, start believing in God and start praising Him for the blessings and the good that He has shown you everyday of your life. When you think about, you will probably be like me; just start crying in praise because no one can do you like Jesus has done and is still blessing us.

Whatever your prison is in your life, you can praise your way out. Once you get to Jesus, nothing else is more powerful and meaningful. You will start living again. You want a right mind; praise Him because no one else deserves the praise. When you get the attitude that Paul and Silas had in the prison, watch the foundation around you get shaken and release you from strongholds and oppression, and bondage. Praise affects our lives in ways we do not even understand because we get God's attention. Yes you are correct! When you allow true praise to go forth before God, He will show up and turn things around in your life and those in your life can be and will be affected as well.

Come to Jesus today with praise on your heart. He will shake up foundations that try to keep you in bondage. Your praise can help you move further in your destiny for Christ Jesus. Let us exalt Him with all of our heart, mind, and soul. Bless the name of the Lord.

BREAKING THROUGH ALL BARRIERS

EXODUS 5:1-13: "Afterward Moses and Aaron went in and told Pharaoh, "Thus says the LORD God of Israel: 'Let My people go, that they may hold a feast to me in the wilderness.' And Pharaoh said, 'Who is the LORD, that I should obey His voice to let Israel go? I do not know the LORD, nor will I let Israel go.' So they said, 'The God of the Hebrews has met with us. Please, let us go three days' journey into the desert and sacrifice to the LORD our God, lest He fall upon us with pestilence or with the sword.' Then the king of Egypt said to them, 'Moses and Aaron, why do you take the people from their work? Get back to your labor.' And Pharaoh said, 'Look, the people of the land are many now, and you make them rest from their labor!' So the same day Pharaoh commanded the taskmasters of the people and their officers, saying, 'You shall no longer give the people straw to make brick as before. Let them go and gather straw for themselves. And you shall lay on them the quota of bricks, which they made before. You shall not reduce it. For they are idle; therefore they cry out, saying, 'Let us go and sacrifice to our God.' Let more work be laid on the men, that they may labor in it, and let them not regard false words." And the taskmasters of the people and their officers went out and spoke to the people, saying, "Thus says Pharaoh: 'I will not give you straw. Go, get yourselves straw where you can find it; yet none of your work will be reduced.'" So the people were scattered abroad throughout all the land of Egypt to gather stubble instead of straw. And the taskmasters forced them to hurry, saying, 'Fulfill your work, your daily quota, as when there was straw.'"

God is the God of breakthrough. He never accepted what Egypt was doing to His people. The primary reason God sent Moses was to deliver His people from bondage. God never accepts bondage. He specializes in destroying bondage. Once you read the entire account of what happen in Egypt, then you will understand the absolute power and love of God for His people and all people today. God does not hold back and allow bondage to destroy us. In His mysterious ways and yet blunt ways, He always has a way of getting the attention of those who harbor bondage and those who have accepted and live in it. Our God is the God that makes a way out of no way. He specializes in possibilities out of the impossible in mans eyes.

Our God breaks enslavement and things that bind men. He is a God that sets men free. The scripture says, "Where the Spirit of the Lord is there is liberty." You were made to break through all traffic, I believe God holds men accountable for their actions. The same God anoints and appoints people and gives them the task to deliver people from crimes such as this. Moses was appointed by God to announce to free people out of bondage and hatred. I believe that God sees all bondage related issues in people's lives. God sees if someone is suffering in captivity. He promises to set captives free in Isaiah 64.

When you live in a rich country and have been afforded the opportunity make contributions, you must capitalize on it because it makes sense and it is the right thing to do. People's lives will be changed for the good in so many ways. We never know who the next congressman or congresswoman might be. We never know who might be the next CEO of a business that could be life changing. So many variables could potentially be that critical link to something that is missing in society. Christians today need to make a difference like God used Moses to deliver His people from Pharoah's taskmasters that tortured people day in and day out.

THE LORD PRAYED FOR ME

John 17:6-7: "I have manifested your name to the men whom you have given me out of the world. They were yours. You gave them to me, and they have kept your word. Now they have known that all things which you have given me and from you."

One of the best things that can happen to any of us is to have faith in God. However, also remember that the Holy Spirit keeps on going to the Lord on our behalf in prayer. God hears all of his prayers. We have an advocate for prayer at all times. The Holy Spirit is our helper in so many ways. Nevertheless, in this scripture, Jesus prayed for his disciples. In verse 20, he prayed for all who will believe in Him. In this prayer, he was speaking directly to His Father in Heaven. Jesus wanted His disciples to be blessed by the Father. He knows all about who we are and our desires. If you are a follower of Christ, you might as well count on his prayer for you. The Lord prayed for me. He prayed for me because He cares. This is a prayer of the High Priest. The Lord prayed for God to keep His disciples strong in difficult times.

Jesus gave his disciples the name of His Father so they could remain in Him. Jesus set the example that we all need. He constantly spoke with His father to recognize these Holy men before His Father in heaven. Jesus' prayer gets answers directly from heaven. It is vitally important that we see how much Jesus thinks of those who love Him and serve Him. I thank God that the Holy Spirit prays for us now. I believe that when the Holy Spirit prays for us, blessings come down like rain. We need to take this personally with God as His holy men today. Ask the Lord to rain down blessings as you go out on missions.

The Lord's name is manifested throughout the world. So then as the Bible says in *Philippians 2:10: "That at the name of Jesus every knee should bow, of things in heaven, and things in the earth, and things under the earth; And that every tongue should confess that Jesus*

Christ is Lord, to the glory of God the Father." Our Father is known to be the God of glory and the God who reigns. He is omnipotent and omnipresent. He is the God who knows all things. He is the God over the universe and has all authority in His hand.

HE JUSTIFIED ME

ROMANS 5:8-10: "But God demonstrates His own love toward us, in that while we were still sinners, Christ died for us. Much more then, having now been justified by His blood, we shall be saved from wrath through Him. For if when we were enemies we were reconciled to God through the death of His Son much more, having been reconciled we are saved by His life."

Jesus took our place on the cross by dying for us. We have life today because He laid His down. He saved us by the power of His blood. He loved us then and still does today and justified us with His blood. Justification means not guilty of any wrong doing in the past or ever. We are no longer guilty of the penalty charged against us. It is just like the judge and jury in a courtroom has stated your verdict not guilty! Keep in mind, sin is sin, but grace is grace, and we abound in His grace. Nothing is stronger than His blood, love, grace, and tender mercies.

Romans 3:23 tells us that *"all have sinned and fall short of the glory of God."* No one is exempt from sin except Jesus, the Righteous one, the Son of God, our Redeemer of spirit and soul. Thanks to the Father, the Son, and the Holy Ghost, we are saved by the power of His precious blood. His blood justified us once and for all. He does not have to do anything else ever again. It was done on Calvary and all you have to do is accept the fact that it is finished as He stated on the cross. Jesus paying the price for us saved us from the wrath of the Father.

Most of us have seen different types of advertising and different shows on television, different ministries, different enticing events in the world around you that reveal things that might appear to save your life, change you, or justify why you dress or look the way you do, or even make things appear to be just fine.

We are reconciled to the Father by the blood of Jesus. Adam separated us with sin. He allowed the serpent to convince his wife in the garden to eat of the tree. You do not have to accept any more lies and deception. Your life is new in Jesus Christ because He has reconciled you. You have a light that shines before men that will see your good works in Christ Jesus. What might look down to them just means that the Holy Spirit is up to something in your life. When the enemy hears about the blood, you better believe it wants to get busy. You see the power was and is in the blood of the Lord Jesus Christ.

Today if you never accepted Jesus as your Savior, come to Him now. You may have been embarrassed.

RUN THE RACE

HEBREWS 12:1-2: "Therefore we also, since we are surrounded by so great a cloud of witnesses, let us lay aside every weight, and the sin which so easily ensnares us, and let us run with endurance the race that is set before us, looking unto Jesus, the author and finisher of our faith, who for the joy that was set before Him endured the cross, despising the shame, and has sat down at the right hand of the throne of God."

You just have to take the blinders off and run the best race of your life. It has to be a difficult task to run with weight on you. Imagine it, you are weighed down and trying to make it to the end zone and the goal line is not too far away, but you get more weight added to you. No one did it but you. Running the race will mean more than you and I can imagine. This is not an ordinary race where Olympians pass the stick and keep running and first place gets a gold medal. Those runners do not have obstacles in front of them unless it is an injury that might occur.

They are competing against one another side by side. But even Olympic runners have to have endurance to make it through the track season. Endurance counts a great deal. Hang in there brother and sister, with Christ in your heart. What also makes it so special is that there are so many witnesses to see the race. Some are influenced and some are spectators. Nevertheless, most of them are impressed.

The Apostle Paul set an example for thousands and perhaps millions in his service and witness for Christ Jesus. He went on four missionary journeys. He did not even think of blinders once those scales had fallen from His eyes. The only thing he could think of was running the race for Christ Jesus for a lifetime. His sight was not set on the problems ahead; instead, he maintained his focus on the mission for Christ Jesus. Sure there will be turmoil, interruptions, rough times, and huge challenges, but with the strength of the Lord, you can make it. You might have some struggles along the way but the Lord is there to see you through all of the tough times. If you trust in the Lord, He will see you through. God has a plan for you. *Jeremiah 29:11 says, "'I know the plan that I have for you,' says the Lord. They are plans for good and not for disaster, to give you a future and a hope."*

CROWN OF LIFE

JAMES 1:12: "Blessed is the one who perseveres under trial because, having stood the test, that person will receive the crown of life that the Lord has promised to those who love him."

Blessed signifies the joy in verse 2. He also reminds us that we are fortunate because we overcame tough tests and times. The crown really points to a blessed life with unspeakable joy. Therefore we are reminded to endure over all of our obstacles in the strength of the Lord. James tells us that Jesus promises a crown of life for those who persevere and maintain faithfulness through the tough times of life. You may have those kinds of tough times, especially trying to pass the test in your calling and ministry. Keep your head up and keep holding on to God's unchanging hand. Push yourself in Jesus Christ, especially during the rainy days. Persevere means to keep on going when things get difficult and it seems like there is no end to those difficult times in life.

Perseverance and endurance are so much alike that both remind us that we need certain strength in our lives. We need the hand of God on our life to move forward. 1 John 4:4 reminds me that, *"Greater is He who is in me than He who is in the world."* We need that attitude of hope and confidence that God will see us through. We can go the distance faithfully in Jesus Christ as long as He helps us to persevere. Tell your family and friends that a crown of life awaits us from God. Whatever your circumstance is today, God is looking and observing if you will past the test. We are reminded in this passage that man has no authority to stop you from serving God.

CHAPTER 2

GOD CAPTURES THE HEART

ACTS 10:9: "The next day, as they went on their journey and drew near the city, Peter went up on the housetop to pray, about the sixth hour. Then he became very hungry and wanted to eat; but while they made ready, he fell into a trance and saw heaven opened and an object like a great sheet bound at the four corners, descending to him and let down to the earth. In it were all kinds of four-footed animals of the earth, wild beasts, creeping things, and birds of the air. And a voice came to him, 'Rise, Peter; kill and eat.' But Peter said, 'Not so, Lord! For I have never eaten anything common or unclean.' And a voice spoke to him again the second time, 'What God has cleansed you must not call common.'"

"Rise, Peter; kill and eat!" God is telling Peter that what God had made is good. God is telling Peter that all things He made were good. You might be one to question things but when God speaks, you must understand that all authority has spoken. When God speaks, power comes forth and things are established as God desires. God blesses things so all we have to do is be satisfied. Can you imagine God speaking to Peter telling him that? "What God has cleansed you must not call common." God already cleansed what He wanted Peter to eat. God was the one who said, "Rise, Peter; kill and eat." All Peter really needed to do was to thank God. After all, the Creator of the universe is waking you up to eat what He has presented. We all need to partake in what God provides with thanksgiving. Thank God. This is a unique picture of God speaking to Peter. God will speak to all of his saints and remind us that He cleansed and what He cleanses is not common. I believe another message is in this. We as saints should not be uncommon and unclean. We walk as renewed children of God. We are not average thinkers. Our minds and hearts are cleaned. We have the mind of Christ. We walk in the Spirit and think in the spirit of Jesus Christ daily. We thank God for cleaning us up.

THE LORD SEES HIS WAY

1 Samuel 16:7-8: *"But the LORD said to Samuel, 'Do not look at his appearance or at his physical stature, because I have refused him. For the LORD does not see as man sees; for man looks at the outward appearance, but the LORD looks at the heart.' So Jesse called Abinadab, and made him pass before Samuel. And he said, 'Neither has the LORD chosen this one.'"*

God has already chosen the right man for the job. The Bible reminds us that God can search us. The Lord does not have to examine us because He already knows us. Remember, God formed us in the womb before the foundations of the world. God does not look at men the way we look at one another. He sees us with the power of love from His heart. He knows exactly who we are before we can know ourselves. He knows our destiny before we can even think of growing up into a mature life. He knows exactly who each individual will be in life. When it is all said and done, God knows who will reign in His Kingdom in heaven. When David was being sought after by the Prophet Samuel, God already knew that none of David's brothers fit the description and had the same heart that David had demonstrated before God. God had already chosen David as King and blessed him.

WALK IN OBEDIENCE

ROMAN 5:19-21: *"For as by one man's disobedience many were made sinners, so also by one man's obedience many will be made righteous. Moreover the law entered that the offense might abound. But where sin abounds, grace abounds much more, so that as sin reigned in death, even so grace might reign through righteousness to eternal life through Jesus Christ our Lord."*

Grace is always the solution from God. It can never fail because his power of love is within His Grace. In our best state of mind and physical condition of the flesh, we still need the one who reconciled us, Jesus Christ. We need more than ever before. We need Him daily in our lives, because the flesh will fail. The body has hang ups with different areas of function.

We need Him in all of our ways; we must seek Him and trust that He will show up in and through any circumstance. Keep the faith no matter what happens in life because you will be tested and tried from every angle. If you do not believe it, just get on the highway and drive a little while, watch someone provoke you with wild driving in your lane, or bumper to bumper, or just about to run you over. Keep the love in your heart even during road rage. That is just how busy sin tries to run rampant in the lives of people.

Watch out on the job where people talk about you and plot against you there and anywhere. It is called the devil's attack. All you have to do is maintain humility and the love of Christ in your heart, someone will notice and be changed by the power of Christ. Keep reflecting the good life in Christ no matter what comes your way.

The good news is that Jesus broke those spirits on the cross. If you run into road rage and ugliness on the job, pray for that person as well as yourself, because they will need it to overcome the enemy so they can be transformed to walk in obedience. Roads can be like a war zone sometimes. We need to pray for people to become obedient citizens in traffic laws to reduce fatalities and permanent injuries. You see, it is important that you keep walking in the power of obedience because you can help one person or thousands that are lost. Our actions matter more than we think! When believers walk in obedience regardless of where you are, lives will be changed. One man's disobedience caused everyone to become sinners.

We know the effects of disobedience. In the very beginning after God created man and woman, sin had knocked at the door and raised its ugly head and caused all kinds of disruption. Disobedience is what caused sin to enter the earth, the heart of man, the heart of woman. The first family had a weakness that penalized everyone and that was disobedience. *Romans 5:14: "Nevertheless death reigned from Adam to Moses, even over those who had not sinned According to the likeness of the transgression of Adam, who is a type of Him who was to come."* Adam was God's first man, made to walk in obedience and turn to disobedience. He failed God. But God had a plan and it was to send His Son who was obedient.

Even though Adam failed God, the Lord still expressed His love in Adam's family. It's just that sin tries to reign and the only way to defeat its temptation daily is to call on the name of Jesus in prayer. Adam could have prayed to the Father. Adam could have taken his family to a prayer meeting; Adam could have fasted for his family. Adam had a responsibility to guard his family. Every man has that responsibility because of the Lord's order of creation for man.

Today all of us have an advocate available in our lives each and every day. He can help us walk in obedience. You see it took Jesus to come through time and heaven to get to us and redeem us from this curse of sin. Because of His death for us, we can walk in obedience. For any offense, grace abounds much more. Through any sin, grace abounds much more. Through trials and captivity by the enemy, grace abounds much more. Grace abounds for eternity through Christ Jesus.

FAITH LIKE ABRAHAM

HEBREWS 11:8: "By Faith Abraham obeyed when he was called to go out to the place in which he would receive as an inheritance. And he went out, not knowing where he was going."

Moving on, God's request requires strong faith and commitment. You have to be able to make up your mind on who you will follow today. The only choice should be God. Abraham had been with his family for years on the same ground. When you find yourself staying on the same ground for over five years, or even longer, and no progress has been made, it is time for a change. God was looking at a man who had ambition and faith in his heart. Start looking at moving from that place that hinders you and blocks your blessing. Start looking for a place that God may have spoken to you about.

It is time to look over what everybody else said about you and look to the hills from whence cometh your help, your help is in the Lord. You might not know exactly where you are going and that is exactly what he told Abraham.

Many people believe that Dr. Martin Luther King Jr. was given an assignment from heaven to preach the Gospel under the power of the Holy Spirit. Many people were so fascinated and moved because he did not waiver nor doubt the power of God in his mission. He answered the call because he had faith in God to lead his life through this dark period of wickedness, injustice, and bondage. Faith in God would be the central power that made the difference in the lives of millions. Think about the fact that one man dared to dream and believe in that dream that God would make life right for all people regardless of color and culture and background. The love of God shapes things for the glory of God.

Dr. King gathered thousands of people together for a march on Washington, he did not waiver because the life of every human being was on the line for freedom. He marched because it was a movement to make a change in this world. When God told Abraham to move to a different land, he did not waiver because his blessing was in the hands of God and yet passed down to Abraham. He was called the Father of many nations. He moved to where God wanted him to go. Abraham was a reflection of blessings to come and the inheritance laid up for all of God's people through both Abraham and Jesus.

Sometimes you have to take a chance in life. You may have to take certain risks to make it to the promised land. You may have to lose some friends to make it to the promised land.

There could also be some cloudy and gloomy days ahead that try to trip you up. But be encouraged and strong in the power of His might. Be ready to block those fiery darts of the enemy. Keep on the armor of God. Wear your armor and go get your blessing Saints. God is for you!

ABRAHAM WALKED IN HIS BLESSINGS

When you take risks, there are abundant blessings on the other side. Why not try God and see what He will reward you with. Giving up something to the God of the universe is an honor and a blessing, since He is the one who blesses. Take a risk to step out on God's word. Take a risk and get into a ministry to serve Him with all of your heart. Take a risk by telling all of those people you pass by in the shopping mall, at the job, at the football games, basketball games, soccer games, the Olympics, and those in the media. Take a risk to lead one or a thousand to the salvation that is free for all people. Just say, "Lord forgive me of my sin, please come into my heart. I believe that you are the Son of God. I believe that you died on the cross for my sin and the Father raised you from the dead on the third day that I might live eternally."

YOU NEED A SAFETY NET

ROMANS 10:9-10: "That if you confess with your mouth the Lord Jesus and believe in your heart that God has raised Him from the dead, you will be saved. For with the heart one believes unto righteousness, and with the mouth confession is made unto salvation."

Across the tight rope, he went without any form of safety to support him. He does it as frequently as you and I work our jobs daily. It's a circus act that you and I may not comprehend his necessity and desire to do such an event. Sometimes it is a bicycle he uses to cross the tight rope and sometimes it is without. I know I cannot follow it.

It's during show time that this skillful person entertains large masses of crowds that are fascinated with his ability to walk a tight rope. Quite often even the media gets a part of recording and reporting these events. Some even reveal on national television for the entire world to see.

It is important to grasp the fact that sudden things do happen, and it can change the course of life. What would happen if the man fell from such a distance in the air—perhaps seventy or one hundred feet? One thing for sure is that life comes at you fast when you least expect it. He could either die or be critically wounded. You do want to be ready so read Romans 10:9-10. God will save you.

I have never met a person that did not require a safety net when conducting such an event. Everyone needs a safety net. Everyone needs support in one way or another. We profess and confess positive support not corrupted or evil. We confess the Spirit of the Lord being our ultimate support and strength. The Lord is our safety net. He will catch us when we fall. He will reach out His hand when we need to be lifted up.

A SPIRITUAL SAFETY NET

In every house, someone acts as the safety net, smoothing things over, comforting, and reassuring family members of the blessings and the power of God. There is always someone to display that hedge of protection in the home as well. All families feel secure when they know that the man of the house is there and will protect and love his family. Someone has to be the backbone of the family in your home. I thought about the amount of pressure that men and women experience daily at work. Then they come home and there are issues that sometimes can spark all kinds of explosives in the house and bring about a strain in relationships between man and wife and family members.

I've found out that each spouse needs to have Jesus as their personal safety net to make it through all kinds of storms. Know this for sure: you can make it. I thought about my daughter and how she needed her father in her life to demonstrate to her what kind of man she should be looking for. I believe young ladies look and desire a man they can trust like their father. They need that image of a good man to help them plot their lives out, which will help them stay on the right course of life. Life is a road map that for some reason God changes up your path although He alone can direct it. You and I need a safety net to help on the path of life. We need Jesus to be our individual safety net. Sons and daughters need their parents as safety nets to keep them. Ultimately, they both need the Lord to redeem them from the curse.

There are other times when people need a safety net. Everyone needs a person to be the fire marshal and the insurance agent in the house to keep him or her from losing everything in a fire. They require insurance that will cover the home if anything is destroyed. They are the safety net that will rebuild if needed. Jesus is there for any and all needs. He will catch you in any circumstance you find yourself engaged in. Do not allow the enemy to force you to cross a tight rope without hope and without a safety net. There are times when you do not need to even attempt to tight rope it.

Remember what Jesus did when the enemy tried to trick Him and take Him off course. He prayed to His Father in Heaven as he was in the Garden of Gethsemane. He was there, sweating great drops of blood. The enemy wanted Jesus to fall from His mission of the death, burial, and the resurrection. The devil wanted it bad just like he wants every believer to fall to the wayside, to destruction. The enemy wants you and me to fall off of our tight ropes. He knows that we get on them often. Jesus' safety net was calling on the Father. He relied on the obedience that the Father put in Him. Obedience is a safety net for mankind.

If Adam would have maintained it, things could have been different. Jesus Christ reminds us that He is the Son of God. Jesus reminds us that our safety net is in Him. He said the most amazing love statement ever. Jesus said, "Father, forgive them for they know not what they do." He said, "It is finished," and then He gave up the Ghost. He was buried in a tomb and on the third day, He rose with all power in His hand.

A SAFETY NET

JOHN 6:37-38: "All that the Father gives me will come to me, and the one who comes to me I will by no means cast out. For I have come down from heaven, not to do my own will, but the will of Him who sent me."

Have you ever heard the word willpower? For many people, it simply means the strength to overcome and push forward. A football player, specifically a running back, may be at the one yard line when he receives the handoff from the quarterback, but the defense is like a steel curtain resisting the runner. But for some reason, this running back pushes himself with about three heavy linemen and a linebacker over the goal line to score the winning touchdown. It was the willpower that God gave him that helped him to push himself and score.

Not only does God allow personal willpower, He allows us to depend on him for safety as we move in life's challenges. He alone is our safety net for life itself. It is the Lord who wills what He desires for every person and all of life and creation. God could have planned it so that the running back could not score and that the running back would have felt miserable for a long time. God could have allowed it where the running back could have come short of the end zone and possibly received injuries. Yet, in this case the running back and the entire team rejoiced and gave God thanks for what He had done.

They were blessed under the mighty will of the Lord, our God. They also rejoiced because they knew that their running back could have been injured like the college team last week's player who was paralyzed from head to toe running a similar play. God is still our safety net no matter what happens in life.

There is no higher authority and order that exists than God. His will is the reason we live. His will is His power and authority, period. Everything ordered in life, God already knows about. Everything that we think He does not know, He already knows. He does not need help with His will. He already has life predestined and in order for our lives. His will has an effect that is lifelong for His people. In the area of healing for example, it is God's will that you be made whole again from that deadly illness or disease. During the Apostle Paul's missionary journey, he mentioned that a snake had bitten him and he shook it off. It was God's will that a poisonous snake did not kill him and take him away from being a witness for our Lord Jesus Christ.

There is no higher order than His will because His love is in it. Peace and joy is in His will. His death, burial, and resurrection were in His will. His life as the scripture says, "He lives because I live." Jesus made it clear, "Father, if it is your will." Jesus made it very clear that it was not His will, but His Father's will. I think about the power and authority that God gives to man to rule over his own house. In God's will, he blesses men to bless others regardless of what it looks like. We are blessed under His will to be a blessing, not a curse. We are like that because Jesus made it possible with His love on the cross and the power of the resurrection.

Luke 22:42 says, *"Father, if it is your will, take this cup away from me; nevertheless not my will, but yours, be done."* It was God's will that Jesus continue to the mission of salvation. *John 1:12-13* says, *"But as many as received Him, to them He gave the right to become children of God, to those who believe in His name: who were born, not of blood, nor of the will of the flesh, nor of the will of man, but of God. Because of the salvation Jesus paid for with His life, we have access to salvation and the Father through Jesus Christ, even those who once rejected Him."*

The love of Jesus Christ makes it possible today for all to come to Him and be saved under the power of His grace and love. Allow Jesus Christ to be your safety net for life. No longer do you have to live an insecure and unsecured life, turn your life over to the God who keeps you safe each and every day with the power of His love.

BE BLESSED AND REJOICE IN HIM

LUKE 10:18-23: "And He said to them, 'I saw Satan fall like lightning from heaven. Behold, I give you the authority to trample on serpents and scorpions, and over all the power of the enemy, and nothing shall by any means hurt you. Nevertheless do not rejoice in this, that the spirits are subject to you, but rather rejoice because your names are written in Heaven.' In that hour Jesus rejoiced in the Spirit and said, 'I thank you, Father, Lord of heaven and earth, that you have hidden these things from the wise and prudent and revealed them to babes. Even so, Father, for so it seemed good in your sight. All things have been delivered to me by my Father, and no one knows who the Son is except the Father, and who the Father is except the Son, and the one to whom the Son wills to reveal Him.' Then He turned to His disciples and said privately, 'Blessed are the eyes which see the things you see.'"

Whenever a storm is likely to occur in your community, or near your home, your sense of expectancy heightens that lightning will strike and you will hear loud thundering. Lightning can strike some places and leave marks that are etched in our minds as well as objects. We usually have vivid memories of those storms that impact our lives. They last for a while and the only way to remove the scars resulting from storms is through the everlasting power, mercy and grace of our Lord and redeemer, Jesus Christ.

Lightning has been proven to strike a human being. Experts might say that it is a probability type of occurrence when it comes to lightning hitting something. My mother used to say to her children, be still and turn off all of those televisions, sit down somewhere. It's thundering and lightening, boy! After a while of growing up, she never had to tell us again. Some things were just understood from our mothers. Sometimes the lightning and thundering would get so bad that you would sit down before mother would say anything because of fear.

Lightning became an image inside my head that I could never get rid of. It is probably because of the way it looks and because of the loud sound. The other reason is simple—no one wants to be hit by lightning.

The sighting of a lightning strike is not rare. In fact some of the electrical waves flash across the sky and we can never really know when they will appear. Since we belong to Christ Jesus, believers of the faith; we do not have to fear anything. God has the power to control even lightning strikes.

When Satan tried to take over heaven—steal God's worship, glory, praise, and authority—God kicked the devil out of heaven as fast as lightning strikes. I imagine that was too fast to see with the naked eye. I thank God that He knew exactly what to do with the enemy attempting to invade His glory. We need to do what God did, kick the devil out of our lives. Speak a word to strike that adversary out of our lives. You do not have to get mad or grow worried, pray and call on

Jesus. Keep your prayer life fine-tuned. Do not get discouraged about anything.

SPELL BREAKING POWER

ACTS 19:11-20: "Now God worked unusual miracles by the hands of Paul, so that even handkerchiefs or aprons were brought from his body to the sick, and the diseases left them and the evil spirits went out of them. Then some of the itinerant Jewish exorcists took it upon themselves to call the name of the Lord Jesus over those who had evil spirits, saying, 'We exorcise you by the Jesus whom Paul preaches.' Also there were seven sons of Sceva, a Jewish chief priest, who did so. And the evil spirit answered and said, 'Jesus I know, and Paul I know; but who are you?' Then the man, in whom the evil spirit was leaped on them, over powered them, and prevailed against them, so that they fled out of that house naked and wounded. This became known both to all Jews and Greeks dwelling in Ephesus; and fear fell on them all, and the name of the Lord Jesus was magnified. And many who had believed came confessing and telling their deeds. Also, many of those who had practiced magic brought their books together and burned them in the sight of all. And they counted up the value of them, and it totaled fifty thousand pieces of silver. So the word of the Lord grew mightily and prevailed."

Too many households are allowing the enemy to come into their homes and leap onto family members, causing havoc, destruction, serious disturbances, division, and most of all, destroying families. God wants you to know today that Jesus' name has all power and all demons recognize His authority over all powers and principalities. Most people are not aware that their home is the first place they should be ministering. However, make sure you get ministered to first by Jesus Christ.

The objective should be to get each person in your household born again. They need a new birth experience. As long as that unsaved person in the house remains unsaved, you leave the enemy an opening to put evil strongholds on you. The very first family, Adam and Eve, experienced the worst thing that could have happened to us which is sin. They experienced the sting of sin and its full injection into humanity. They experienced sin because the house was out of obedience and order. This reality of sin was a brief encounter of disobedience displayed by Adam and Eve to God. Then there was the disobedient incident with Cain and Able, a brother slaying his own blood brother.

The key to breaking the power of the enemy's spell is obedience to Jesus Christ according to His will and purpose. When we learn to commit ourselves to glorifying Him, other things will fall in alignment with God.

Obedience starts with obeying and glorifying God. We must completely obey Him. God must be glorified over all people and things. He must be over all manner of evil and all that exist in this world, creation, and worlds to come. Glorifying God lets God know where your heart really is. He is holy in every way and must be identified so you can magnify Him. His name holds holiness, truth and righteousness. Keep His name in your heart because you will need Him daily. You will need His name in your every day walk.

I thought about some states that observe and really believe in rituals of evil practices: witchcraft, voodoo, and all other evil practices that are constantly trying to keep us from heaven. But the reality is that if you have accepted Jesus Christ as Lord and Savior, demons can't take you out of God's hands. You just need to submit to God only and never surrender to evil that tries to get you.

They want your soul for the devil's kingdom. It will not win over Jesus Christ, the Son of the living God. His blood covers us. In fact, the only place for witchcraft is hell. Jesus has a place reserved for all evil called the lake of fire, but those that believe and trust in the living God will reveal His power over all other powers and principalities. We have prevailed over all manners of darkness. We live in a world where so many teenagers and adults believe that witchcraft and evil practice is the way to live and worship. They have been blinded by the influence of others. They have no facts on the matter of becoming evil. They just think that they are correct. What people should recognize is the power within Jesus Christ. Jesus Christ is the spell breaker in all circumstances and situations. Call on Him and He will work it out.

I will never forget that man who called himself a preacher and who ended up giving poison to hundreds of people, which took their precious lives. It only takes one evil act to be disconnected from God. Everyone must be careful regardless of his or her age. I tell you that the enemy comes to kill, steal, and destroy. Jesus said He came to give life and give it more abundantly.

Paul had an experience with a woman in the Bible who practiced the art of witchcraft. He quickly rebuked it in the name of Jesus. We should do the same. Don't give the devil an inch. When we see friends in dire need of prayer, we should pray immediately because the enemy is trying to flood their lives with demonic forces. But we know Jesus who has all power to break the spells and bondage of the enemy. Praise and Glory to the only wise God, Jesus Christ, who delivers even those who practice witchcraft and any evil thing. God is able to deliver and restore your righteous mind.

The sons of sceva thought that they had the power to remove evil spirits. The biggest mistake any Christian or anyone could ever make is to believe that they have power alone to deal with evil forces. God has all power in His hands to make all evil spirits flee. He is our source of help in times of evil attacks. Although He is there when we need Him, we just need to be patient and acknowledge that He comes to our rescue. He can also manifest His power through those that He trusts that walk in obedience to His will and purpose. God must be the focus and not our own power and pride. One of the most common mistakes is believing that miracles of healing and deliverance will come by you alone.

The Apostle had to have the Holy Spirit working in his life to please God. It was the Holy Spirit who helped him on all of his journeys to witness in the name of Jesus Christ. No wonder the enemy said that he knew Jesus and Paul. Jesus had all power and authority. He rose from the dead. The same Jesus stopped the Apostle Paul, alias Saul, and made him a chosen vessel unto the Lord. The enemy knew that God had anointed the Apostle Paul after his conversion. He learned to quickly trust God. We need to trust the Lord in all things because nothing is impossible for Him. He is the one who can break all spells, deceptions and evil. He can break the spell of adultery and bondage. He can break the chains that the enemy puts on people's lives because they leave themselves open to enemy attacks and devices. Know Jesus for yourself and call on His holy name. Every day give Him thanks and glorify Him.

GRACE GRIP

Luke 16:19-30: "There was a certain rich man who was clothed in purple and fine linen and fared sumptuously every day. But there was a certain beggar named Lazarus, full of sores, who was laid at his gate, desiring to be fed with the crumbs which fell from the rich man's table. Moreover the dogs came and licked his sores. So it was that the beggar died, and was carried by the angels to Abraham's bosom. The rich man also died and was buried. And being in torments in Hades, he lifted up his eyes and saw Abraham afar off, and Lazarus in his bosom.

"Then he cried and said, 'Father Abraham, have mercy on me, and send Lazarus that he may dip the tip of his finger in water and cool my

tongue; for I am tormented in this flame.' But Abraham said, 'Son, remember that in your lifetime you received your good things, and likewise Lazarus evil things; but now he is comforted and you are tormented. And besides all this, between us and you there is a great gulf fixed, so that those who want to pass from here to you cannot, nor can those from there pass to us.'

"Then he said, 'I beg you therefore, father, that you would send him to my father's house, for I have five brothers, that he may testify to them, lest they also come to this place of torment.' Abraham said to him, 'They have Moses and the prophets; let them hear them.' And he said, 'No, father Abraham; but if one goes to them from the dead, they will repent.'"

There was a man who was discovered stretched out on the ground with no movement and appeared to not be breathing as well. A neighbor called 911 as soon as the man who was attending to him shouted out, "Help!" There were suddenly sirens approaching from different directions with the most annoying and extreme noise that one could hear. These ambulances were coming to the rescue of this man who had gunshot wounds to the back. When the ambulance arrived it appeared that this man was almost dead. When the rescue team exited their vehicle with the proper equipment, they went directly to work on restoring him.

Their efforts revived the man as they hustled to stop the bleeding and put him in the ambulance. They immediately hooked breathing machines and IVs to keep oxygen flowing and providing hydration to the man. All the effort by the rescue team and the man who found him paid off. The man who was once wounded lives the best life now. He has come back to life. One of the things that no one knew about this man was that he was a billionaire. He was rich in every sense of the word except born again. This man looked for all the rescuers and all the people involved in helping save his life. He wanted to reward them with millions of dollars. After having his life saved and giving out millions, he learned that he needed more in life.

The experience changed him from being a money hungry, self-centered man to a man who had compassion and wanted God in his life. His near death experience cause him to walk into a chapel one Sunday morning and gave his life to Jesus Christ. He accepted Jesus as his Lord and Savior. He confessed that this is the new life that he wanted more than anything. Live rich in Jesus Christ. The rich man in the story ignored Lazarus as he begged for food. God saw it and remembered. God also wants us to see that we are capable of being people that can help through the power of the Holy Spirit to save others.

I do not know how many stories we have heard of people coming back to life and accepting Jesus Christ. Nevertheless, it is a good thing when it happens, because lives are renewed and changed forever for the purpose of Jesus Christ and his Kingdom. It is good to know that there is someone who cares for you regardless of who you are.

PENTECOSTAL SAINT

ACTS 2:1- 13: "When the Day of Pentecost had fully come, they were all with one accord in one place. And suddenly there came a sound from heaven, as of a rushing mighty wind, and it filled the whole house where they were sitting. Then there appeared to them divided tongues, as of fire, and one sat upon each of them. And they were all filled with the Holy Spirit and began to speak with other tongues, as the Spirit gave them utterance. And there were dwelling in Jerusalem Jews, devout men, from every nation under heaven. And when this sound occurred, the multitude came together, and was confused, because everyone heard them speak in his own language. Then they were all amazed and marveled, saying to one another, 'Look, are not all these who speak Galileans?'

" 'And how is it that we hear, each in our own language in which we were born? Parthians and Medes and Elamites, those dwelling in Mesopotamia, Judea and Cappadocia, Pontus and Asia, 10 Phrygia and Pamphylia, Egypt and the parts of Libya adjoining Cyrene, visitors from Rome, both Jews and proselytes, Cretans and Arabs—we hear them speaking in our own tongues the wonderful works of God.' So they were all amazed and perplexed, saying to one another, 'Whatever could this mean?' Others mocking said, 'They are full of new wine.' "

You can identify bonafide believers because they are up to something in Jesus Christ. Usually saints are in the business of getting someone delivered, presenting the word of God, praying for a breakthrough, and telling people about Jesus Christ—how he died for our sins and rose on the third day with all power. The word "bonafide" means "genuine," "faith in good standing." It means real. The word bonafide counters the word fraud or fake. It helps us to depend on God knowing that He is real and glorious. He requires believers to be real followers.

Most often they are busy announcing that Jesus is the Son of God to anybody that will listen. A bonafide believer will not back down on professing their faith in Jesus Christ. You might scandalize their name, you might do all manners of evil but it will not work, they still continue in their faith.

A bonafide believer knows where to put their eyes. They know to focus their eyes and lives in Jesus Christ. I am convinced that you have to be fully converted to be a believer that pleases God. You have to accept Jesus in your life all the way as Lord and Savior and there is no turning back. In Acts, the Apostle speaks of those who waited in the upper room. It is not often that people wait in an upper for the return of the Lord from the dead. You see what sealed this is the fact that Jesus showed up, appearing before the disciples who had faith, although it was kind of dim they waited. When I think about the bonafide believer, I began to think of ways a bonafide believer expresses himself. But I definitely look at the fact the believer must have a changed life. The bonafide believer must be under sanctification.

HIS LOVE IS THE GREATEST

UNFAILING LOVE

1 Corinthians 13:1-13: "Though I speak with the tongues of men and of angels, but have not love, I have become sounding brass or a clanging cymbal. And though I have the gift of prophecy, and understand all mysteries and all knowledge, and though I have all faith, so that I could remove mountains, but have not love, I am nothing. And though I bestow all my goods to feed the poor, and though I give my body to be burned, but have not love, it profits me nothing. Love suffers long and is kind; love does not envy; love does not parade itself, is not puffed up; does not behave rudely, does not seek its own, is not provoked, thinks no evil; does not rejoice in iniquity, but rejoices in the truth; bears all things, believes all things, hopes all things, endures all things. Love never fails.

But whether there are prophecies, they will fail; whether there are tongues, they will cease; whether there is knowledge, it will vanish away. For we know in part and we prophesy in part. But when that which is perfect has come, then that which is in part will be done away. When I was a child, I spoke as a child, I understood as a child, I thought as a child; but when I became a man, I put away childish things. For now we see in a mirror, dimly, but then face to face. Now I know in part, but then I shall know just as I also am known. And now abide faith, hope, love, these three; but the greatest of these is love."

God reminds us in 1 Corinthians 13 that there is nothing more powerful than love. I never could understand why my father and my mother loved me so much. It took a few years for me to understand that there is a debt of love that they both had before resting.

God reminds us of love in this passage. The scripture reminds us that there is nothing more important than God's love for all people. We possess His great love. 1 Corinthians 13 tells us that nothing else can take lead over love. It is clear in this passage that there is no debt of love greater than the love of Christ. We can do all the different things in life, but if we do not have love, it amounts to nothing. We can preach and sing, but it amounts to nothing if you do not have the love of Christ.

KNOW HIM AND GET IN HIS PRESENCE

EXODUS 34:5-9: "Now the LORD descended in the cloud and stood with him there, and proclaimed the name of the LORD. And the LORD passed before him and proclaimed, 'The LORD, the LORD God, merciful and gracious, long suffering, and abounding in goodness and truth, keeping mercy for thousands, forgiving iniquity and transgression and sin, by no means clearing the guilty, visiting the iniquity of the fathers upon the children and the children's children to the third and the fourth generation.' So Moses made haste and bowed his head toward the earth, and worshiped. Then he said, 'If now I have found grace in your sight, O Lord, let my Lord, I pray, go among us, even though we are a stiff-necked people; and pardon our iniquity and our sin, and take us as your inheritance.'"

Moses found himself after making a heart request saying, Lord show me your glory. Can you phantom the magnitude of God's presence that day in Moses' sight? It was something because Moses was not allowed to see His face, yet Moses had seen part and was blessed beyond measure.

God will reveal Himself to who He will. We say phrases like, let me see His face. But in reality, no one deserves to see His face and if they saw His face, they would not live according to the scripture. The book of Daniel describes several portraits of God. Please do not be confused. There is only one God who is truly God. He is God alone.

There is none other. There are many names that reveal His power in those various areas, but He is God.

You might say why are you talking about His presence? It is in His presence we exist. God sees all things at all times and nothing can be hidden from Him. He is omnipresent and omnipotent and He reigns throughout eternity. There is no beginning for God and there is no end to God.

He is God by Himself and no one made Him. That is why so many want to be in His presence, because of who He is. He is the one who will bless you and restore you, guide you in victory in any area of your life. Moses had the prime time of his life discovering the power of God because he was chosen to lead the children out of Egypt. God knew that this slavery under these taskmasters and the bondage that Pharaoh kept them in had taken toll on his people. God was doing something about it.

Moses stepped into the very presence of God who was revealed in the form of a burning bush and received power that very day. Moses was changed in the very presence of God. His life changed.

His purpose changed. His heart changed because he stepped in the presence of God. It is good to be in the presence of God. When you get there, watch your life change before your own eyes. Watch how people notice the change in you. Many people will appreciate the fact that you allowed the Lord to change your life. You have to understand that there is power in the very presence of God.

The Ark of the Covenant was one form of evidence of His presence. Men fought battles to get the Ark of the Covenant into their possession. In one instance, one of King David's men died for touching the Ark of Covenant as he tried to keep it from falling. The Ark represents God's presence and no one can handle God and God cannot fall.

In the book of Hebrews, there is evidence that a Priest had to go in the Holy of Holies to make sacrifice for the people. In the Holy of Holies, you had to be pure and Holy to approach God. If you were not, then you would have to feel the wrath of God. It is said that Priest had to tie a rope around them because if they did not come back, someone would have to pull them out. God is the Lord and He must be worshipped at all times. We must be prepared to present ourselves to Him as living sacrifice, holy and acceptable to God. May every man repent before you come into the presence of God. Come with thanksgiving, praise, worship, blessing, honor, and glory.

Come with the attitude of humility and exaltation to the Most High God in Jesus' name. Lord, by your Holy Spirit, help me to present myself pleasingly to you. Hallelujah.

SUFFICIENT GRACE OVER A PARADISE EXPERIENCE

2 Corinthians 12:1-10: "It is doubtless not profitable for me to boast. I will come to visions and revelations of the Lord: I know a man in Christ who fourteen years ago whether in the body I do not know, or whether out of the body I do not know, God knows such a one was caught up to the third heaven. And I know such a man whether in the body or out of the body I do not know, God knows how he was caught up into Paradise and heard inexpressible words, which it is not lawful for a man to utter. Of such a one I will boast; yet of myself I will not boast, except in my infirmities. For though I might desire to boast, I will not be a fool; for I will speak the truth. But I refrain, lest anyone should think of me above what he sees me to be or hears from me.

"And lest I should be exalted above measure by the abundance of the revelations, a thorn in the flesh was given to me, a messenger of Satan to buffet me, lest I be exalted above measure. Concerning this thing I pleaded with the Lord three times that it might depart from me. And

He said to me, 'My grace is sufficient for you, for My strength is made perfect in weakness.' Therefore most gladly I will rather boast in my infirmities, that the power of Christ may rest upon me. Therefore I take pleasure in infirmities, in reproaches, in needs, in persecutions, in distresses, for Christ's sake. For when I am weak, then I am strong."

Dreams or visions that we have in our minds either come true or they are just a picture of something that might be important and make a huge impact in our hearts and minds. A vision is something that you see in the spiritual or natural form in your state of mind. Whatever the vision is, you see it and it's real in your conscience, and in your heart, and in your very sight. You witnessed what you saw and no one can take it away. Visions are part of a leader study. That is how real it was and how sure you were about it. If a person has experienced revelation and words and paradise, and blessings that are so real they ought to praise God because He does reveal things to us.

What is your paradise? Paul is calling paradise the third heaven, a place higher than the stars. He believes that his spirit has been exposed to the glorious presence of God through this visitation experience. He also cannot understand the extent to which he was transported and exposed. When we think of Paradise, we think of heaven and the holy existence of what is there surrounding His throne. We get a glimpse of its awesome appearance, yet we still can't really imagine it totally. We do know it's more than the mind could ever comprehend. We do know that everything must exist and revolve around Him to give Him glory. Revelation is the other point here. The Apostle Paul believed that God spoke revelation knowledge to Him and this word cannot be uttered to anyone, but by the Holy Spirit.

He was given a thorn to keep silent from boasting that he was higher than anyone else. Maybe your experience is different. God requires all the glory regardless of who you are. But beyond all other experiences and expectations, the Apostle Paul is reminded by Jesus that, "My grace is sufficient." So beyond all of his infirmities, reproach, persecutions, distress, and weakness, God is there to make him strong. The Lord wants us to know that the grace that He has is more sufficient than a paradise experience or anything else. There is power in the grace of God that blesses us each and every day. Just when the enemy thought that he had taken everything away from my life in ministry, God reminds all of us when he said, "For when I am weak, then I am strong." The Lord demonstrates Himself in our weakest moments when we trust Him.

HE HEARD MY CRY

Matthew 8:1-4: "Large crowds followed Jesus as he came down the mountainside. Suddenly, a man with leprosy approached him and knelt before him. 'Lord,' the man said, 'if you are willing, you can heal me and make me clean.' Jesus reached out and touched him. 'I am willing,' he said. 'Be healed!' And instantly the leprosy disappeared. Then Jesus said to him, 'Don't tell anyone about this. Instead, go to the priest and let him examine you. Take along the offering required in the Law of Moses for those who have been healed of leprosy. This will be a public testimony that you have been cleansed.'"

A unique picture of Jesus being approached by a man who had a disease that no one would or should be around. But Jesus was there. What is important here is that Jesus did not leave the man in his condition. He acted with compassion and healing power. It's the love of Jesus Christ that compels Him to reach out and touch this man. In doing so, Jesus healed him. As Christians, Jesus wants us to reach out and touch people under the influence of the Holy Spirit.

MATTHEW 8:5-13: "When Jesus returned to Capernaum, a Roman officer came and pleaded with him, 'Lord, my young servant lies in bed, paralyzed and in terrible pain.' Jesus said, 'I will come and heal him.' But the officer said, 'Lord, I am not worthy to have you come into my home. Just say the word from where you are, and my servant will be healed. I know this because I am under the authority of my superior officers, and I have authority over my soldiers. I only need to say, 'Go,' and they go, or 'Come,' and they come. And if I say to my slaves, 'Do this,' they do it.' When Jesus heard this, he was amazed. Turning to those who were following him, he said, 'I tell you the truth, I haven't seen faith like this in all Israel! And I tell you this that many Gentiles will come from all over the world—from east and west—and sit down with Abraham, Isaac, and Jacob at the feast in the Kingdom of Heaven. But many Israelites—those for whom the Kingdom was prepared—will be thrown into outer darkness, where there will be weeping and gnashing of teeth.' Then Jesus said to the Roman officer, 'Go back home. Because you believed, it has happened.' And the young servant was healed that same hour."

What was your cry? Babies cry all the time and it is not a surprise. In fact in many cases it is healthy. But what is unusual and heart wrenching is when you see a man cry—a broken brother in distress and no one cared to stop to lend a helping hand.

CHAPTER 3

COMPLETELY UNDER GOD'S AUTHORITY

JOHN 16:5-15: "But now I go away to Him who sent me, and none of you asks me, 'Where are you going?' But because I have said these things to you, sorrow has filled your heart. Nevertheless I tell you the truth. It is to your advantage that I go away; for if I do not go away, the Helper will not come to you; but if I depart, I will send Him to you. And when He has come, He will convict the world of sin, and of righteousness, and of judgment: of sin, because they do not believe in me; of righteousness, because I go to my Father and you see me no more; of judgment, because the ruler of this world is judged. 'I still have many things to say to you, but you cannot bear them now. However, when He, the Spirit of truth, has come, He will guide you into all truth; for He will not speak on His own authority, but whatever He hears He will speak; and He will tell you things to come. He will glorify me, for He will take of what is mine and declare it to you. All things that the Father has are mine. Therefore I said that He would take of mine and declare it to you.'"

Learning to live under the authority of God is easier than you think. You live under God's authority when you obey Him and demonstrate your love toward Him by helping other people. You can live even better under God's authority by having a humble spirit. The scripture says to humble yourself before the mighty hand of the Lord and He will lift you up. How do you become humble before God? The very first thing you have to do is to develop a relationship with Jesus Christ. You do it by repenting of your sin and asking Jesus to come in to your heart. Know that you have a new relationship with Him no matter what. God's purpose and plan is to have the righteousness of Christ to be in subjection and follow His authority. The Centurion soldier understood authority because he had men under his authority. This

Centurion soldier knew the expectation of a king's authority because he had been used to being an authority figure. In authority, there must be times to convict the world of sin, righteousness and judgment.

GRACE HOLDS ME NEAR HIM!

MATTHEW 11:25-30: "At that time Jesus answered and said, 'I thank You, Father, Lord of heaven and earth, that you have hidden these things from the wise and prudent and have revealed them to babes. Even so, Father, for so it seemed good in your sight. All things have been delivered to me by my Father, and no one knows the Son except the Father. Nor does anyone know the Father except the Son, and the one to whom the Son wills to reveal Him. Come to me, all you who labor and are heavy laden, and I will give you rest. Take my yoke upon you and learn from me, for I am gentle and lowly in heart, and you will find rest for your souls. For my yoke is easy and my burden is light.'"

The apostle Paul explains to us that all of our burdens are like heavy weights that need someone to carry them. He explains what an ox does with pulling devices and the mechanism around his head. When the enemy comes at you and you feel like the enemy has a hold on you, you need to pray and then release yourself to God. You make yourself heavy by accepting what the enemy dishes out to you. In *Matthew 11*, it says, *"Come to me, all you who labor and are heavy laden, and I will give you rest."*

You first need to come to the Lord and be humble before Him. Come with your pain. Come with whatever you have on your heart. If you have any issues take them to God. Remember when He says come, it's not a matter of how you look and feel, you just need to come. Come to release every demonic spirit and every stronghold in your life. Come to unite yourself with God and know Him and the power of His might. You first need to come to receive Him as Lord and Savior then watch Him do a work in you and through you, your life will never be the same again. God wants everything that is heavy in your life. If there is something that is holding your heart back from advancing in the Kingdom, come to Jesus and give it up. Let it go! Let it go today! Let it go right now! It's time for you to be whole again.

BREAKING THE ENEMY'S CAMP

The scripture says, "I will give you rest." God knows that you are tired of walking around stressed out, and beat up, and confused, and feeling loaded down. It is time to come out of the enemy's camp tied down and enslaved. Break out of the camp and turn your life over to God. You receive peace everlasting when you come to the Lord and obey Him. In this case, He simply says, Take my yoke upon you and learn from me, for I am gentle and lowly in heart, and you will find rest for your souls. This could be anyone who has heavy burdens and find themselves in situations where the enemy has placed you in his camp. Everything the enemy does causes burdens. It is time to come out of that situation by giving it to the Lord.

A yoke is a wooden object that goes around the neck of an ox. The wooden object is used to pull numerous loads all day and night by that ox. The loads are distributed to the yoke, which enables the ox to have leverage in pulling the load. The load is distributed to the yoke, which makes it extremely easy to carry. It does not phase the ox because the bulk of his strength is where the yoke is placed and in the yoke. His strength is used to pull and carry loads. Jesus tells us that He can and will carry our loads. He is carrying loads each and every day. He pulls heavy loads that we have and destroys them every day. Take your burdens to the Lord. He carries the world on His shoulders (Isaiah 9:6).

One of the most difficult things is living a hard life. You do not have the necessities to sustain yourself or you know someone who is suffering like that. We have to pray each time the enemy breaks a family and opens full attacks on those families. The enemy will weigh on them and cause a family to become dysfunctional. Let's cut the enemy off before he gets started. Submit to God in prayer and take your entire family with you. We need to start having desires that God will break the enemy that causes frustration and confusion in my family. Let's trust Him. My desire is to remove the weight issues off my back when they approach.

I've thought about how sin comes into the camp in different disguises. Be careful of relationships that seem to be good, but are not equally yoked. Ask the Holy Spirit to guide you because you can quickly become heavy burdened because of choices made. God wants us to remain distant from the unequally yoked issues. But if you find yourself in one, ask God to help you with the situation. People do change and all things are possible with God. You have to be guarded and put forth the effort to be in order with God. No one is supposed to cast harsh judgment on anyone. But the reality is that people are people, some are good to the core and some not so good.

We need to understand that people do grow on each other. 2 Corinthians 7 tells us of the marriage between a believer and an unbeliever. This thing called a yoke comes in different packages, and difference personalities, and different history, and different meaning. The scripture of relationships tells us in *2 Corinthians 6:14: "Do not be unequally yoked together with unbelievers. For what fellowship has righteousness with lawlessness? And what communion has light with darkness?"* God wants believers to make the right choices to be in agreement in the Spirit of the Lord.

There is a concern with natural agreement because it relies on fleshly agreements led by the power of sexual influence. You need to understand that disaster could come from such a relationship. God simply wants marriages and relationships to be equally yoked. This pleases God and the blessings will overshadow all the other things.

ABRAHAM, LOOK AT THE STARS AND NUMBER THEM

Can you imagine what God had in mind when making such a statement to Abraham? Look at the stars in the sky and see if you can number them. Look at the sand on the beach shores and see if you can count them. There is something very powerful about God testing Abraham's faith. God wanted to see what kind of relationship they had with one another. In testing Abraham's faith, God also blessed him because his faith passed the test. Abraham believed in God. Our Father in heaven wants us to act out in what we believe in for Him. You see the very act of trying to count the stars and the sand pleased God. He already knew that Abraham could not count all the sand, nor all the stars in the sky that He alone made.

The scriptures say the earth is the Lord's, and the fullness thereof, and they that dwell in it. He created all the worlds, including the galaxy, all that appear in the outer space, and in existence belongs to God. What a thought! It takes faith to go somewhere. It took faith for Abraham to leave his family and go to a place according to God's will. He had to leave family, friends, and his home to get away from complacency.

You see, friend, God wanted Abraham. And when God wants you, you cannot hide. You cannot hide behind the mountain. You cannot hide from God. Abraham did not hide. Abraham acted in obedience to please the Father. And I believe that faith and obedience is truly what pleases God. God notices things and we must be pleasing in His sight more than anything else because obedience is better than sacrifice. Remember to walk in obedience because you love Jesus Christ.

BLESSED IN OBEDIENCE

In one of Abraham's most memorable moments, God sent Abraham on the mountain to sacrifice his promised child. This was the son that God gave at one hundred years old. He may have questioned within what does this mean? The blessings of the Lord are so magnificent and He alone is worthy to be praised. A friend of mine put together a sermon which he called the four-letter word. Some of the words he put together in preparation for his series of study were wait, care, and love.

He nailed it with all three of those words and the other words he used as well. He told us that we should to wait to hear from God. We sometimes hear from the wrong source. It sounded like you thought you heard God, but you heard someone else. Abraham heard God and waited for that same promise child that God spoke to him about. If God says it is coming for you and your wife, then that will happen. Abraham waited and was blessed. He used another four-letter word—love. God expressed His love for Abraham in so much to make a covenant with him and at the same time make him father of many nations because of his faith in God. You see friend, God's love is expressed abundantly in your faith in Him.

This faith is connected to the love of God. When you have that kind of love for God, certainly you will have the faith that Abraham had for God. Faith and love are what God is looking in his people. It takes that kind of love, faith and belief to make things happen in a world so unpredictable. We also need to be reminded that Abraham was obedient to God, although in some instances he was disobedient. God was pleased with his obedience to move when he told him to move. One moment of obedience can result in a lifetime of blessings. Thank God and bless His name for all the blessings that so He freely gives.

Romans 5:19: "For as by one man's disobedience many were made sinners, so also by one Man's obedience many will be made righteous."

GRACE INSIDE MAN'S HEART

1 SAMUEL 16:7: "But the Lord said to Samuel, Do not look at his appearance or at his physical stature, because I have refused him. For the Lord does not see as man sees, for man looks at the outward appearance, but the Lord looks at the heart."

This is just like God said. Jesse had all of his sons pass by Samuel except one, David the shepherd boy. Jesse could not understand that God was not looking on the outside. Instead, He was looking at the heart of a man that loved Him. God had the authority, and still does, to send Satan from heaven to hell. He still has all authority to send Satan to the Lake of Fire in the end and He will, according to His word. God is so powerful that everything must bow before Him and everything must worship Him in the beauty of His excellence. No one is exempt from bowing down.

Noah found grace for several reasons and I believe it's important for you and I to know so we can be obedient like Noah demonstrated before God. Noah found grace because he loved the Lord. Noah also found grace because of His obedience to do what God instructed him to do. Which of course was to build the ark, no matter what people around him were saying. Noah found grace because He listened and acted on what God had spoken to him about. God has everything already planned out. He already had Noah on standby and knew that Noah would find grace because it was in God's plan.

CUT THE CORD WITH GRACE!

JOHN 17:1-5: "Jesus spoke these words, lifted up His eyes to heaven, and said: 'Father, the hour has come. Glorify your Son, that your Son also may glorify you, as you have given Him authority over all flesh, that He should give eternal life to as many as you have given Him. And this is eternal life that they may know you, the only true God, and Jesus Christ whom you have sent. I have glorified you on the earth. I have finished the work, which you have given me to do. And now, O Father, glorify me together with yourself, with the glory, which I had with You before the world was.'"

He cut. Sometimes you may have to cut the cord to gain abundant life. Jesus had to cut the cord with His disciples that He so dearly loved. The Father in heaven had to cut the cord for a moment from His Son, Jesus. He surely did. He left them to continue the work of the ministry on earth. Before He departed to heaven, He ate the last supper with His disciples to remind them of His body and the communion. He had shown them His death on the cross, He had to die and be raised from the dead. These things the disciples could not do with Him. He had taught them well. He had shown them numerous miracles. He fed five thousand people right before their eyes.

They saw Him raise a young lad from the dead. They saw Him call Lazarus from the grave. They saw Him praying on the mountain. He even delivered them from their own sinful ways and made them followers. They even saw with their own eyes Him return to life and stand right before them and speak. He had risen from the dead with all power in His hand. They had watched Him ascend to heaven. He had led captivity captive. He knew those that would go with Him someday. His disciples were not allowed because they still had a commitment.

I will never forget when I had to cut the cord at my daughter's birth. I learned that it was good for the father to cut the cord because it signifies a welcome to your child's new home. Your Father is here to receive you, guide, provide, and protect you. It was one of the happiest moments of my life. Then after she had grown up to be a young lady of age to marry, it was time to cut the cord again. You see we train up our children in the way they should go and not to depart from the Lord. You see it is time to walk in the Spirit and to live life for Christ under the shadow of His wings.

I will pray to the Father as Jesus left us the example in John 17, that He watches over you as He watched over my life. The only cord that does not get cut is the one that connects you with the Lord. You see that is the most important cord of life. Make that cord your umbilical cord that you will receive the abundance of life and eternal life with Jesus. He is your source of dependence.

A THRONE ROOM EXPERIENCE

REVELATION 4:1-20: "Then as I looked, I saw a door standing open in heaven, and the same voice I had heard before spoke to me like a trumpet blast. The voice said, 'Come up here, and I will show you what must happen after this.' And instantly I was in the Spirit, and I saw a throne in heaven and someone sitting on it. The one sitting on the throne was as brilliant as gemstones—like jasper and carnelian. And the glow of an emerald circled his throne like a rainbow. Twenty-four thrones surrounded him, and twenty-four elders sat on them. They were all clothed in white and had gold crowns on their heads. From the throne came flashes of lightning and the rumble of thunder. And in front of the throne were seven torches with burning flames. This is the sevenfold Spirit of God. In front of the throne was a shiny sea of glass, sparkling like crystal.

"In the center and around the throne were four living beings, each covered with eyes, front and back. The first of these living beings was like a lion; the second was like an ox; the third had a human face; and the fourth was like an eagle in flight. Each of these living beings had six wings, and their wings were covered all over with eyes, inside and out. Day after day and night after night they keep on saying, 'Holy, holy, holy is the Lord God, the Almighty—the one who always was, who is, and who is still to come.'

"Whenever the living beings give glory and honor and thanks to the one sitting on the throne (the one who lives forever and ever), the twenty-four elders fall down and worship the one sitting on the throne

(the one who lives forever and ever). And they lay their crowns before the throne and say, 'You are worthy, O Lord our God, to receive glory and honor and power. For you created all things, and they exist because you created what you pleased.'"

God's throne represents the place with all authority, majesty, power, honor, and glory. Take a moment to capture the picture of God seated on the throne in heaven. We worship our Lord. God sits on the throne with all His glory. John tells us that he was in the spirit on the Lord's day and was taken up into the presence of God. John was in the Spirit because God was revealing to him the things to come to past. In the midst of these prophetic and revelatory messages, God always blesses and reveals his mystery to His people.

We can truly understand that God is so good and why He calls us to the throne. God not only called us, He commissioned things according to His purpose. He called us through the Holy Spirit: God, the Father; Jesus, the Son of God; Holy Spirit—are all in agreement. The Holy Spirit was given to us for the purpose of God's glory. He was also sent to give grace, conviction, and restore us with the most powerful love imagined. The Holy Spirit presents himself and reminds us to acknowledge God as He sits on the throne in heaven. John reveals to us that heaven is real and when God calls to show you something, answer and allow him to lead you.

We are thankful that God allows us to see these great men of honor in heaven who glorified God. These men also reveal to us that even as they were appointed in heaven to recognize His glory and exalt him, they cast their crowns to the Lord as to say, "You are worthy, O Lord, our God." These men present their life achievements and blessings that came from God, back to God. Today, we need to remind everyone of the glorious rewards and blessings that God has marked out for each person.

LOOK IN THE MIRROR

2 Corinthians 3:18: "But we all, with unveiled face, beholding as in a mirror the glory of the Lord, are being transformed into the same image from glory to glory, just as by the Spirit of the Lord."

An unveiled face is uncovered. Now you can see. God removed the scales from the face. A facial expression can impact people in the most effective way, and in so many other different ways as well, especially if you allow it. We see people every day of our lives. Perhaps the most important thing to people today is their identity. There are many people that are dealing with the issues an identity crisis presents, such as low self-esteem and depression. Fashion, modeling, and TV display the images of the world's most famous people. They keep routines of beauty and makeup that set their reflection on screen in the best light to the world. It is because the face is one of the most looked at features of the anatomy. The face sends off messages communicating different messages. When you see the face, you see the eyes.

We see many forms of faces today. One in particular is the mind face. It sets aside a form of innocence. Another face is the face of man. I have seen many faces in my life. But one face stands out on screen than so many others. It is a simple story. If you have every watched the story of Forrest Gump, it would move you with tears of joy. One of my favorite scenes in that movie is Forrest's combat moment. Here Forrest was just standing in the middle of a jungle with the enemy shooting at him. In one specific action he looked toward the danger and saw his buddies being hit with multiple mortar rounds, inflicting casualty after casualty. He carried each casualty to safety. He even carried his commander to safety. The look said a lot and his action said even more.

My point is simple, we must open our eyes and face the frontal and flanking attacks that come so often against our family and friends. Then we need to take action to help one another. The film portrayed him as helping out buddies. There are other faces that the Christian community should be ready and available to help. Those are the faces of horror, hurt, and pain. They need someone right away. Jesus is the immediate answer.

In a believer, the countenance speaks volumes to your fellow believer. People you make contact with on a daily basis will be impacted by the way they see your face. If you walk with joy, they see it and they react in their way. When people see joy, it makes them see the good light of Jesus Christ in you and me. When people do not see joy in your face, they run and talk, and they wonder if you are really a Christian like you say you are.

A SET MIND

Philippians 2:5: "Let this mind be in you, which was also in Christ Jesus."

We need to always allow God to make our mind like His. In many cases, we should request to Him to refresh our minds when we get off course or need a helping hand. If we have to have a total makeover so be it. You should desire the mind of Christ if you desire to operate in His kingdom. It is important to understand that the thought pattern and thought life can block blessings in your life. Please understand that nothing can stop the move of God in your mind and your life. However, your mind needs to be open to Him always. He will reflect Himself through you to others. He will reveal things to you in order to bless you.

If your mind remains in His, you have to have a sense of awareness and aggressiveness of the mind to overcome things that try to entangle your mind and keep you in a stronghold. You have the choice to remain idle in your current condition or you can tell the enemy that you have taken on the mind of Christ because the blood of the lamb has covered you. Jesus has put His spirit inside of you and touched your mind and all of you. Today, tell a friend to take on the mind of Christ in all things. In all things keep your mind stayed on Jesus, the solid rock.

Have you ever heard of the man that had half of a mind? This man had half of a brain and used it in its maximum capability. He made movies and was a filmmaker. He was a multi-millionaire because he wrote books and they were all best sellers. One day he discovered that life was not good to him. He had faced tragedy in his family. His mind changed from the CEO mentality and the filmmaker mentality to the mind that needs something different in life. He had a void space even during the worst times in life, like family death.

This man with his half of mind called on the name of the Lord and discovered that Jesus would come into his life and transform him. This man used his half a mind that was saved during surgical procedures to build God's kingdom. What about the man that has no brain condition and has the full capabilities of his brain. If a man can accept Jesus Christ with half of a mind, surely those with a full mind can accept him and take on the mind of Christ in the lives.

FIND PEACE IN GOD

Philippians 4:7: "And the peace of God, which surpasses all understanding, will guard your hearts and minds through Christ Jesus."

Jesus wants us to know the peace of God in our lives. With peace in our lives, families, churches, and nations can be transformed and revitalized. This will be done to give all the glory to God. Now the purpose is to reveal God's love toward us so that we can release love to others. When we have that kind of love usually it signifies that we have that kind of peace that comes from God.

When we have it we can see better, hear better, taste better, and love better, as well as many other things. I always mention the scales on the Apostle Paul's eyes when he was Saul the murderer of Christians. When he received the love of Christ on the road to Damascus, he was no longer bound with the hate that was in his heart. The love of God gave him peace and he experienced great transformations like never before in his life. God wants us all to experience this great love and peace.

God has made Himself available for us to give us peace every day of our lives. Start asking God to pour out His power to convert your heart and mind today so you may experience His peace. God is not concentrating on your understanding of Him. He wants you to have the kind of faith that He gives to respond to your life and circumstances surrounding it. Faith in God gives you the fullness of peace through our Father in heaven and through the redemptive blood of Jesus Christ. We need to understand that God's peace is beyond man's comprehension. I love the expression, man did not give it to you and certainly man cannot take it away. We believe because we know that God is all-powerful and he will use his peace to guard your heart and mind.

God's peace is the kind of peace that brings you through every circumstance that comes up against you. This peace that He gives is so far beyond our ability to know how He does it time and time again, year after year, moment after moment. It is evident that we need this kind of faith. My mind is alert and I know of the power of God and I know that He can do all things but fail. In one Bible, the scripture states that the peace that God gives us transcends all understanding. The word transcend means "to rise above or go beyond the limits." The word surpass means "to go beyond excellence or achievement." Another definition says, "to be beyond the range or capacity of."

UNHIDDEN GRACE

GENESIS 6:5-8: "Then the LORD saw that the wickedness of man was great in the earth, and that every intent of the thoughts of his heart was only evil continually. And the LORD was sorry that He had made man on the earth, and He was grieved in His heart. So the LORD said, 'I will destroy man whom I have created from the face of the earth, both man and beast, creeping thing and birds of the air, for I am sorry that I have made them.' But Noah found grace in the eyes of the LORD."

Noah's story tells us that God was not pleased with the people of that time. They had allowed sin to penetrate their hearts in every imaginable way. Their minds and hearts were totally evil in God's sight. They were totally into their ungodly lifestyles. They had the worst imagination and their minds were constantly thinking evil. Through all of that, God still found a man that He could trust. God found a man called Noah. Noah found grace in the eyes of the Lord. What a thought to that God found grace in one man at the moment because of his obedience to listen to the voice of God. That is exactly what saints and believers in the world today want. We want to find grace in the Lord. Thank God that He has sent Jesus to redeem us from the curse. Thank God that He alone is so forgiving.

God still offers grace for everyone each and every day. It is His unmerited favor that is poured out on us continually. He offers Himself to men and women each day that His grace will touch all the sinful hearts that were like those in the day of Noah. You see there are people walking just like that today and need a helping hand. All the saints are continually praying for those who are walking with a heart filled with sinful imagination and thoughts. *2 Corinthians 10:5* says, *"Casting down argument and every high thing that exalts itself against the knowledge of God, bringing every thought into captivity to the obedience of Christ."* If people would honor God's word and who He is, they would begin to see a difference in their lives.

We need to trust the Lord and lean not to our own understanding, but acknowledge Him and He will direct our path. People develop wrong hearts and imaginations by their lifestyles because of the company they keep. If you want sin and keep entertaining sin, then it is sin and evil imaginations and wicked thoughts you will get. But if you want to walk upright like Job did in God's sight, change that lifestyle of lust and other sinful ways. God is looking for you to ask Him for forgiveness. That is what it takes. Repent before the Lord. The people in Noah's day had no intention to repent and that is obvious because God flooded the entire earth.

The blessing is that He who flooded the earth in an effort to cleanse it from evil people is still the same God today who loves us with an everlasting love. The same God is the one who sent Jesus, His Son, to cleanse us with His blood that we may be partakers of ministry and servants of the Most High God. We have found grace in God's eyes and His love is so great for my heart and very existence.

You should know that the same God that called the earth into existence is the same God who can transform and bless those that live in their self-righteousness. Remember Noah found grace because God desires that every man find grace and live that experience. This will change your relationship and the way you see things in the spirit and even with the naked eye. Noah found grace because God knew his heart as a man of God who desired to please God. More importantly, Noah demonstrated what God wants more in us and that is obedience. Obedience is the key in pleasing God.

KNOW HIM, HE IS COMING AGAIN

MATTHEW 24: 3-14: "Now as He sat on the Mount of Olives, the disciples came to Him privately, saying, 'Tell us, when will these things be? And what will be the sign of your coming, and of the end of the age?' And Jesus answered and said to them: 'Take heed that no one deceives you. For many will come in my name, saying, 'I am the Christ,' and will deceive many. And you will hear of wars and rumors of wars. See that you are not troubled; for all these things must come to pass, but the end is not yet. For nation will rise against nation, and kingdom against kingdom. And there will be famines, pestilences, and earthquakes in various places. All these are the beginning of sorrows. Then they will deliver you up to tribulation and kill you, and you will be hated by all nations for my name's sake. And then many will be offended, will betray one another, and will hate one another. Then many false prophets will rise up and deceive many. And because lawlessness will abound, the love of many will grow cold. But he who endures to the end shall be saved. And this gospel of the kingdom will be preached in all of the world as a witness to all the nations, and then the end will come.'"

The subject of the last days is one of those topics that too many people are afraid to talk about. One reason behind it is because of the reality that we are living in the last days. Verses 4-14 refer to false messiahs who have spanned the centuries of the church. These false messiahs have led people astray into false religious cults. They teach everything false and disguise themselves as the messiah and prophets. That is why Jesus says, "Take heed that no man deceive you." If you have seen a person grow from a baby to an adult then leave this earth, the reality is that it happens. You can't stop it, nor can I stop it. It is fixed reality! No one can change anything but the Lord. The warning and the reality are clear and that is if you are not saved, you want to be saved before things get to the point of no return or too late. Jesus stands on His word. He can never go back on it.

His words in Matthew 24:37 tell us about being watchful. Jesus says, *"When the Son of man returns, it will be like it was in Noah's day. In those days before the flood, the people were enjoying banquets, and parties and weddings right up to the time Noah entered His boat. People did not realize what was going to happen until the flood came and swept it all away."* You must be ready and watchful.

Jesus also ensures us that we will be aware of signs. In Matthew 24:30, Jesus says, *"And then at last, the sign that the Son of Man is coming will appear in the heavens, and there will be deep mourning among all the people of the earth. And they will see the Son of Man coming on the clouds of heaven with power and great glory."* Be watchful for the Son of Man. He is coming for those who believe in Jesus Christ. If you want to bypass the Great Tribulation, you better accept Jesus now. The Great Tribulation is for those who reject Jesus Christ. They will suffer during the seven years of the Great Tribulation. This is a time of the worst destruction you can think of. God will pour out his wrath on mankind and judge all creation just before the peace of the Millennium is ushered in. Be encouraged, Saints of the Most High, because you will not be here. It is for those who do not accept Jesus Christ in their hearts.

When California had an earthquake, people believed that the world was going to end. When the same state had wildfires destroying hundreds of homes, they thought the world was about to end the same day or a few days later. When Hurricane Katrina hit New Orleans, Louisiana, and left devastation and the tragic loss of love ones and friends, people still thought the world was about to end.

When most people heard of the brutal beatings, and gang violence, and rapes in Darfur, let alone the starvation of families, they were convinced that the world was ending right before their eyes. We must be reminded that Jesus said, "No man knows the day or the hour." Forget about who forecasts the return of Jesus because they are inaccurate according to the scripture. No one knows the time or the hour. When He comes it will be a lifting of the saints. One glad morning we will fly away as the songwriter puts it. What is important is that all of these things must come to pass.

When those who call themselves prophet approach and speak all manner of things to you, you need to investigate who they really are so that you will know better before you follow the wrong advice and be on the path of destruction. God made several good pastors, apostles, prophets, evangelists, and teachers. You just need to discern and ask God for guidance.

GOD IS MY SOLID FOUNDATION

2 TIMOTHY 2:19-20: "Nevertheless the solid foundation of God stands, having this seal, The Lord knows those who are His, and let everyone who names the name of Christ depart from iniquity."

Let everyone know who you are when it comes to being a Christian. God knows and sees your witness before people. You should never be ashamed of being one of God's children. You have the foundation that is needed to be a child of God. The foundation is when you accepted Him as Lord and followed up with your baptism as he commanded. Make no mistake about it; you can have a solid foundation that cannot be shaken. You can tell anyone that you have departed from iniquity. Most of them will be curious because you now call on the name of Jesus Christ everywhere you go. It is time to take a stand for who you really are in this world. Jesus always spoke of His Father as an example to all of us so that we would know that.

He is not ashamed His Father. He told all of His disciples who He was. He always mentioned that His Father was in Heaven. Jesus demonstrated that He was sealed with His Father. He said my Father and me are one. He is telling everyone who wants to listen that you and I have been sealed and no one can break the sealed relationship.

We are of God's covenant. We are in the family now. God does not allow anyone to succeed in breaking His family apart. We have a solid foundation in Christ Jesus. Climb aboard this moving train on its sound foundation. It's rolling and it's your day and your time to get on.

No one can break the seal of our Father and His Son. No one can break the seal that He has placed on us for His purpose and glory. Imagine someone trying to take away your son that God gave you. It is just like that of the Father in Heaven; He would not stand by and allow you to take His son away. It may look like it for a moment, but when you look again at God's intentions, you will find yourself blown away in mind and heart of His goodness for your life. He would not allow you or the enemy to break the seal and bond that they have already established. No wonder we always tell the enemy that he is a liar from hell and rebuke him to go back to hell.

A father's bond with his son is so unique because God has ordained it to be a blessing in His sight. God made it that way that He would be glorified. He gave Abraham a son named Isaac. He gave David a son named Solomon. He gave Jacob twelve sons. You may recall Joseph, the one he gave the coat of many colors to signifying royalty and blessings and favor. It is imperative that men stand up and teach their sons that they must be born again. Teach them that they must have a relationship with Jesus Christ, the Son of the living God. Then they will be sealed in the spirit of Jesus Christ. Then they will be sealed for life.

This seal is more powerful than the top seal that my grandmother and my mother used on preservatives, and then stored up for winters to come. Once you really trust in being sealed by God, then you will know what it really means to be in Christ Jesus.

There are all kinds of seals. Some seals that are on vehicles do not always hold. They are broken. Then a leak in your tires or your engine occurs. That is a broken seal. You have to go and pay hundreds, or thousands sometimes, to repair the broken seal. Sometimes it may not be repairable. You may just need to purchase a new car or a new engine or a new radiator system or even new tires. The point is that when they leak, you are subject to devastation. You could have a mass car pileup all because of your leak.

Today, I come to tell you that you need a seal that cannot be broken. You need a solid foundation. You need a relationship that will not leak, but instead be lasting through eternity. You need salvation. Salvation will not and cannot leak. Salvation is free and it will never fail. Salvation means you are sealed in Christ Jesus. Salvation will last forever. When you reign with Christ Jesus, it is because of salvation. Nothing can take you away from salvation—something so free, yet too many people are not accepting it. Salvation is more than all the gold and silver in existence, all the money and fame in the world, all of whatever you lust after, and whatever the enemy deceives in your heart. Salvation is more than all of it and anything else. Salvation is of the Lord. Your seal depends on your salvation.

You need to be sealed by the Holy Spirit of promise. This what Ephesians 1:13-14 says, *"In Him you also trusted, after you heard the word of truth, the gospel of your salvation; in whom also, having believed, you were sealed with the Holy Spirit of promise, who is the guarantee of our inheritance until the redemption of the purchased possession, to the praise of His glory."* The only one who seals the believer and forms a lasting relationship without strings attached is Jesus. It will not cost you anything. All you have to say is, "Yes Lord I repent of my sin. I believe that you are the Son of God and you died and rose from the dead by the glory of your Father. I believe you washed my sin away. Lord, come into my heart and save me. Then just believe and trust that He has delivered you."

I always think about those that are in different types of businesses and wonder what their status is when it comes to knowing Jesus as their personal Lord and Savior. Becoming a sealed servant in the army of the Lord makes you want to help so many others. One of the reasons I want to write a book to reach them is that they can tell all of their co-workers of the power of becoming sealed in the Holy Spirit. Tell a co-worker or family member of the power of Jesus Christ changing your life. Remember that the Lord knows who on earth are His and He will guide you and bless you.

CHAPTER 4

GOD HOLDS THE ABUNDANT LIFE

John 10:10: "I have come that they may have life, and that they may have it more abundantly."

Maybe you were thinking about becoming a millionaire or billionaire, it is not too late. Be encouraged to fulfill your dreams with the blessing that God laid for you. Those are not too far of a reach for you. You need to believe in God, knowing that His word cannot fail. Keep the millionaire and billionaire thought, and watch how God uses you to make a dream come true in the area of abundance.

It is not a question of Him wanting us to have a more abundant life. It is the fact that the Lord said that we may live our life more abundantly. This life in Christ is the abundant life we already have because in Him is the supply of every need. Our possessions are a blessing because He allows us to have them. Nevertheless, it is living with Him that makes us blessed. Today, everyone who believes in Jesus can walk in the abundant life. It is not a trick or false advertising. This abundance that our Lord makes available to us can be whatever He allows. We have favor with God because of His word and our relationship with Him.

As Christians and followers of the King of Kings, we do not have to ask anyone else because Jesus holds all the riches in His possession. No matter how you look at it, God has a hold on all the abundance that we could ever desire. Nothing is out of His reach. He owns all things. You heard it before. He owns cattle on a thousand hills. You want it, talk to God about it and see what He says. He will bless you because it is His spiritual makeup and nature to bless His children. He controls those things we need. God wants us to know that we have access to the inheritance, which is laid out for His Saints. The scripture reminds me of Psalm 34, *"I will bless the Lord at all times. His praise shall continually be in my mouth."*

COME AND HEAR ABOUT JESUS

ROMANS 10:14: "How then shall they call on Him in whom they have not believed? And how shall they believe in Him of whom they have not heard? And how shall they not hear without a preacher?"

When you visit a local church or listen to someone trying to tell you about the love of Christ, do not turn him or her away. Come and hear about Jesus. Leave that place where all the mess and confusion is and come into the house of the Lord and hear about Jesus. You need to hear the word of God and believe. You need to hear and believe and ask God to change your circumstances. You have been dealing with things that outweigh you long enough. Do not wait another day of your life. It might be too late. The bottom line is that you will be inspired to change your life and live for Him by faith. Find a preacher that preaches the Gospel of Jesus Christ. Find someone in your home who knows the Lord and does not mind praying for help. In times like these, we need someone.

Most people wait for the most turbulent days or extreme hardship in their lives in order to seek God for help. Then many of them wonder if God is listening when they call on Him. They need to remember that God is always listening. He is always available and willing to help in any circumstance according to His will for your life. God is not asleep. The Bible says, "He neither sleeps nor slumbers." God never takes a go to nap or break and stops being God. He is always on His throne listening to prayers and supplication for those who are in need. He prefers us to call on Him if we know Him and if we do not know Him. Why? It is because deliverance can happen at any time on God's time.

Today is your day to start believing in God. The scripture says how you can call on Him if you have not believed. You begin to believe when you hear the word. If a car salesman was telling you all the information about the car of your dreams as you stood in the car lot, your ears would be attentive and totally alert because it is something that you want, something that will change your life in some way. The information that the salesmen gives is critical to you because there is a cost associated with it. However, regardless of the cost, you are still listening and perhaps have already determined to purchase it based on just a little information. You will purchase because of the advantages of having your personal transportation, your brand new vehicle. Hearing the word of God has more advantages to your life than any car or any materials. Hearing the word of God is life recovery, and sustains, and it's free.

The Apostle is telling us that people need to hear and believe in the preached word of God to get the breakthrough that so desired. God does use the preacher to deliver specific messages and you just might miss your message if you do not show up to Sunday morning worship service or Wednesday night Bible study. There is a word for you today in the Bible. Non-believers need to show up to hear the word and be transformed by the power of the gospel. God's word is powerful enough to renew hearts and minds each and every day.

For many, the mentality today is that people have certain opinions of preachers. The reality is that God deals with preachers according to His word. People just need to hear the word of God and obey God by totally surrendering to Him. The word of God is power. It can deliver like lightning, only it is much more powerful. If you can imagine the thundering, lightning, and the excessive down pouring of rain, it's just a small pitcher of the power in God's word. When preachers are preaching, it's like thunder and rain coming down. Most of us need the word of God to shower us, and wash us, and make us clean. We need the word to help us to continue our walk as believers. We need the word preached to help cities, states and countries transform lives and start a new beginning.

God waters our hearts and spirits with His precious word. Today wherever you are, visit a church, open your Bible, remove the dust and read your Bible. You may want to start in Genesis, but remember Matthew 6:33, which tells us to seek first the kingdom of God and His righteousness and all other things will follow. Make Jesus your priority of life and he will bless you.

THE POWER OF HIS WORD

HEBREWS 4:12: "The word of God is living and powerful, and sharper than any two-edged sword, piercing even to the division of soul and spirit, and of joints and marrow, and is a discerner of the thoughts and intents of the heart."

When I watched a movie called King Arthur, they used the sword in the movie called Excalibur, given to King Arthur by some wizard or magician. It appeared to have some special meaning with significant power when the king used it. Even today in the armed forces, swords have specific meaning to express the will to fight. It always sends the message—live or die by the sword. It also sends the spirit to fight. It appeared to have this overwhelming power when it was time to fight against vast armies in the movies. God's word is more powerful than all the swords combined and more. It has power beyond our imagination. God's word has revelation and power. It cannot fail.

The word of God is living and more powerful than anything you can imagine, more powerful than anything that exists. Fortunately for us, the word is living for us to live by the word. It is the word that examines us and encourages us to see who we really are. It is the word that penetrates our lives. He reveals to us who we are, and what we need to do to make a change in our lives. So many people have conditions that they are not even aware of until they visit places of importance in their lives such as a hospital.

One of the most familiar problems is that of heart disease or cardiac arrest where a patient requires a heart transplant or surgery to repair their heart. In order for the surgeon to go in to replace or repair a heart, he or she needs to cut extremely important parts to remove that heart. They need an instrument called a scalpel to cut way distracters. This is a life-changing event that so many people need.

The point is that if the patient does not get the new heart or repair, the patient cannot survive. Well in this passage the same applies. If you do not allow the word of God to work on you, you will not survive. It is the word that will cut things away from snatching your soul and spirit to hell. It is the word that keeps you in God's perfect will for your life. It is the word that helps you when you have it on the inside to discern the enemy on every side of your life. You are a survivor because of the word. If you want to become better in your healing, it is the word. If you want to communicate better, it is the word. If you want to become a priestly man, it is the word. The word will work out things in your life that you have never imagined. Ask God to do surgery on you. Ask God to change your identity with His word. He can do anything but fail. He is all-powerful. He cannot fail.

This passage reminds that grace is living, powerful, and sharp as well. Grace comes from the word of God. When something is cut for God's purpose, grace fills the gap when God desires it to. Grace is all purposeful. When the word cuts us, grace is delivered. It is Jesus who came by grace and truth.

THE WORD DELIVERS

When God speaks, you will hear Him in the form of delivery that He desires. No one controls His methods of delivery. No one controls His word and the power in it. The scripture tells us that He is the word in John 1:1-2. So then what stops a man from hearing God's word? We can always blame it on the enemy, the devil. Because the Bible says he walks as a roaring lion seeking whom he may devour. However, the fact remains that there are too many people falling by the wayside because they will not hear the word of God. When you hear the word of God, your faith increases in God. When you hear the word of God, things begin to change in your life. You must also have the faith God has given and watch the word work in your life. If you trust Him, you will see the word work. Ask God to work His word in your life. When our ears are truly open to hear the word of God, you can hear God Himself speaking of the blessings He has poured in and on our lives. All around us are the blessings that God has for us.

Every person should speak the word of God in their lives, their family's lives, and the lives of saints and all people. It is high time to bless somebody else. You have what it takes. So stop holding back and encourage someone in the word and do not be complicated about it. People want realness—they can't stand fake and phony religion.

God's desire is that every one of His children maintains the word of God in their hearts. This is the primary way you can witness to others and be fruitful. God wants all people to get the word of God in their hearts. You will be delivered and start seeing change. It is the Holy Spirit who will help you understand the word. Ask the Holy Spirit to move in your life, move your tongue to speak the word of God. The word is powerful and sharper than any two-edged sword and can cut through the scales that block your hearing. Ask the Lord to help you daily.

> The word cuts through darkness because it is light that can't be stopped nor controlled. Jesus is the light of the world.

GOD IS MY STRONGHOLD

PSALMS 27:1: "The LORD is my light and my salvation— whom shall I fear? The LORD is the stronghold of my life— of whom shall I be afraid?"

Prayer can remove scars. As you pray, remember that God has a hold on you. He will not let you go. His strength and power is unfailing. When we call on Him in prayer, He answers and delivers in His time. I thought about the fact that there are so many prayers out there in books and emails that go around. Yet people still seem to doubt the power of God and what He can do in all of our lives. We can't measure the power of God. We just need to trust Him and keep on praying for others and ourselves. People are praying in church right now for others they do not know. Pray for everything in your life that Jesus Christ would be your new focus in life. It seems that one of the worst things that can happen to people is that they get scars by emotional drama, physical trauma, and instances that are just caused by human misbehavior.

The good thing is that scars can be removed. Scars can be wiped away by the precious love of Jesus Christ. Never underestimate the Lord and His power. Isaiah 53:5-6 says, *"By His stripes we are healed."* The scripture is the word of God that heals and delivers us with its power. What scars do you think have you in the corner and feeling withdrawn, sad, lacking trust, and even playing on your mind? There is more than a laundry list. So whatever it is keeping that is you in bondage and causing you to be so afraid, denounce it, rebuke it, and claim healing today in Jesus Christ. God has a place for you in His Kingdom to keep you safe and delivered.

HOLY SPIRIT FILLED

Acts 2:4: "And they were all filled with the Holy Spirit and began to speak with other tongues, as the Spirit gave them utterance."

God enables us to speak with authority because He fills us with his Holy Spirit. When we are filled in the Holy Spirit, we speak God's word with authority and power. Jesus speaks to the storm and tells it, "Peace, be still." He does it because He is filled in the Spirit to say the least; he is the Son of God and divine. When I think about the walls of Jericho, Joshua told them to go around the walls seven times and shout. Then the walls came down. The power of life and death is in the tongue. This is to inspire someone who may have a calling to serve

God. Lord, thank you for filling me with the Holy Spirit. My life has not been the same once you saved me and filled me. I pray that the power of your word is manifested throughout the earth for your purpose. Let everyone that calls on the name of Jesus be filled in the Holy Spirit and speak according to your purpose and glory. Lord, touch those that have not known you, but desire to know you. Visit those that have the enemy blocking their view and minds and hearts. Open up the reality of your blessedness in their senses and spirit. Allow them to experience the power of your touch.

Every time there is a pouring down of the rain, I get happy because I believe God poured out His spirit more than the rain we see. He poured out more than the rain combined in a lifetime—yours and mine. Why did He pour it out? He wanted then, and now, to shower us in multiple blessings. All we have to do is believe and receive in the power of faith in Christ Jesus.

THE NEED FOR FAITH IN GOD

HEBREWS 11:1-3: "Now faith is the substance of things hoped for, the evidence of things not seen. For by it the elders obtained a good testimony. By faith we understand that the worlds were framed by the word of God, so that the things, which are seen, were not made of things that are visible."

Sometimes the kid in me comes out and makes me reflect on characters that are heroes. We watch them all the time. Every year a film producer produces a new Batman or Spiderman movie. As old as I am, I still get those wonderful feelings of excitement and heroism. I've had some of the wildest thoughts about superheroes. What if they all got together—the Dark Knight, Super Man, Super Friends, Spider Man, the Incredible, the Incredible Hulk, Conan, Flash, Zeus, Hercules, the Transformers, Olympic Gold Medalists, the new Teams on sitcoms, all action heroes that play in big production movies and the remaining heroes—and tried to save the world. Could they do it?

The logical answer would be yes, but the real logical answer is no. You probably said yes, but the fact is they cannot change the world. It is God's design. We may think that they could, but the problem is the way people see each other and their audacity.

All of the heroes reminded me of the heroes of faith in the Bible, in Hebrews 11:1-32. The difference between these heroes of faith is that they dealt with God and they operate in the spiritual realm. What is so impressive about the heroes of faith is that they had a ready mind to be faithful in service for Jesus Christ, our Lord. They did not pretend nor act as cartoon characters. These men set the real example of faith and courage. He set the example of trusting in Jesus. One of the key things about these men of faith is they were active in service to please almighty God. These men were active in building the breach. These men used their faith to help restore men who were broken. God said go and heal the broken-hearted. These men went and preached the gospel to a dying world.

What set the heroes of faith apart from the heroes of our comic books and movies is the anointing on their lives. God will place an anointing on your life that will change you forever in everything you do. God can do anything. He wants to change you and me to learn and act in obedience to His will. The Holy Spirit of promise will take care of us and lead us into the righteousness of Jesus Christ.

A PERFECT LOVE LIKE NO OTHER

JOHN 3:6-17: "That which is born of the flesh is flesh, and that which is born of the Spirit is spirit. Do not marvel that I said to you, 'You must be born again. The wind blows where it wishes, and you hear the sound of it, but cannot tell where it comes from and where it goes. So is everyone who is born of the Spirit.' Nicodemus answered and said to Him, 'How can these things be?' Jesus answered and said to him, 'Are you the teacher of Israel, and do not know these things? Most assuredly, I say to you, we speak what We know and testify what We have seen, and you do not receive Our witness. If I have told you earthly things and you do not believe, how will you believe if I tell you heavenly things? No one has ascended to heaven but He who came down from heaven, that is, the Son of Man who is in heaven. And as Moses lifted up the serpent in the wilderness, even so must the Son of Man be lifted up, that whoever believes in Him should not perish but have eternal life. For God so loved the world that He gave His only begotten Son, that whoever believes in Him should not perish but have everlasting life. For God did not send His Son into the world to condemn the world, but that the world through Him might be saved.'"

Unconditional love is what saved this entire world. All of us should be extremely filled with joy. He did not have to give unconditional love to us. We were destined for wrath. We all were supposed to die, but He took it upon Himself. When He came, there was suffering, guilt, disease, extensive and explosive sin of this world and what it was capable of, destroying everyone. This kind of love is called agape love. It is unconditional and does not charge anything. This love is free. You have the power to love because of His demonstration of unconditional love.

God holds all the love in His power. His love can never be exhausted. It is endless and perfect in every way. He loves us regardless of our mess-ups, mix ups, let downs, hurts, past sins, and whatever entangled and enticed us into wrongdoing; He forgives you and me right now. There is no false pretense in His spiritual nature to forgive with the power of love.

God loves the world while still in a sin state of mind. He can change anybody whenever they request it. He will check your heart for you. He will make the alterations that you need and I need even when we think everything is okay. God loves the world because the world will not love Him like He loves them. In fact, many in the world still disobey when it comes to loving God with all their heart, and mind, and soul, and strength. That one command encompasses so much. Why does He love the world? He loves the world because the world has sin and needs to be delivered from that state. He loves the world because He made it. He loves the world because everyone has a role in society and they matter to Him.

When I was a young child, I always felt my mother's tender love and care. I knew that I needed her love no matter what. When I was burned under the neck, I needed my mother. When I was sick with bad colds and flu-like symptoms, I need my mother to rub the ointment on me to be restored.

Today, take on the love of God and allow Him to manifest that love in you and your family. He gave His only Son for everyone. Nobody gives up his or her son for people in your house to be destroyed.

THE BED IN HELL SITUATION!

PSALMS 139: 7-12: "Where can I go from Your Spirit? Or where can I flee from Your presence? If I ascend into heaven, you are there; If I make my bed in hell, behold, you are there. If I take the wings of the morning, and dwell in the uttermost parts of the sea, Even there your hand shall lead me, And your right hand shall hold me. If I say, 'Surely the darkness shall fall on me,' Even the night shall be light about me; Indeed, the darkness shall not hide from you, But the night shines as the day; The darkness and the light are both alike to you."

Do your best not to get in a bed in hell situation. Please understand the bed in hell situation can be experienced in and out of the bed. In one respect it can be a dream as you are sleeping, but you feel like those nightmares are overcoming you. When you awake, you might feel like you had been in hell. It is also a walk that you take while attacks are all around your life and you are going through a living hell on earth. You heard that expression before. You need to get Jesus to brighten up your day and your life. Life is unpredictable in so many ways that you can easily make your bed in hell. You can easily get off of the road of righteousness. Jesus wants us to follow his path of righteousness. The enemy laid out traps to get us in hell. You need to remember that Jesus has control over heaven and hell. Whatever your nightmare might be, please understand that prayer helps. Prayer helps to call on angels straight from heaven. You might as well come out of that bed in hell situation. No one anywhere in your imagination or thoughts has that power to control your life like the Holy Spirit. I would rather stay on the Lord's path where there is constant freedom, joy, deliverance, and great blessings now and on the way. I would not want to be the one for that ugly situation. No one is perfect but Him. For all of your unpredictable moments, the Holy Spirit is there to guide you. No one ever determined that you marked out your own destiny. You may have a small hand in it; God has the final say so.

The other good thing is that God knows about us before we know about ourselves. He is always looking out for your best interest. He does not want us in hell. Jesus wants us to reign with Him in heaven; it seems that there is a trust issue and a broken relationship in almost every family. Now that I can see better in my life, I clearly understand many more spiritual things. But I definitely need the power of the Holy Spirit working for me.

The thought that boggles my mind is knowing that Jesus loves me so much that if I was in hell, He would show up to deliver me out. Can you even fathom the fact that Jesus will be in hell to rescue you if you call on Him. Think about for a moment. You and I in so many ways have made our bed in hell with our sinful lifestyles. I do not know anyone else who would visit hell on my behalf. As a matter of fact, I do not know anyone who has the power to go to hell and rescue me. I do not know any person who could even act that concerned in today. Let me tell you who I do know. I know that Jesus has all power in His hand. Jesus can call on legions of angels to bring hell to its knees. In fact, He does not have to do anything. If He thinks about me, I am saved. If He thinks about casting Hell to its final destruction, it's done. God made all things and God can take away all things and God can bless those He wants to bless.

HE PULLED YOU OUT OF HELL

There are people walking around today with all kinds of bed in hell situations. Many people are living in pure hell and do not know what to do. Just because someone says, you made your own bed in hell so go and sleep in it, it does not mean you should go and do it! Others might go about their daily routine and do exactly that. It is a mistake and a trick of the enemy. Do not be lowered into the bed in hell situation. My friend, turn away from it as fast as you can. When you have any kind of situation including all of your heavy burdens, the Holy Spirit is present and available to pull you out. Call for help today.

I will never forget what I thought my worst mistake was in life. I knew that I was on my way to hell. But God had already forgiven all sin. We condemn ourselves after God has already forgiven us. Most people do it because they forget about the power in Christ. He can never fail you. It does not matter what kind of moment you are having, especially if it's a difficult moment. He specializes in getting you out of that pit of hell.

I thought about how so many people go out to some of the most troublesome places and discover that there is nothing there but evil waiting. It's time to break away from evil things that want you in hell. A man had the largest bank account that he could imagine. He was operating in the millions. It was all his money. It turned out that he got rich by robbing the local bank several times. The problem is that no one ever recognized him. He was an owner of a large business with an excellent reputation, but the problem was his record with God. Did you know that even in your worst state, God can pull you out of it? Repentance and going to God with a heart of surrender will help you. Go to God with faith with all of your issues that you face today.

There is a power called repentance. One day when this man came to the realization that what he had done had not left his heart, all he did was repent. You see repenting will bring healing and restore you. Only God can provide such deep healing that keeps you from believing you are hell-bound (Psalm 139).

LOVE BEYOND

JOHN 4:20-21: "If someone says, I love God and hates his brother, he is a liar, for he who does not love his brother whom he has seen, how can he love God whom he has not seen? And this commandment we have from Him: that he who loves God must love his brother also."

Love was given to us to show us the example that Jesus wants us to follow. The scripture also tells us that in I John 4:8 God is love. He wants us to demonstrate the love that He has shown and still shows this very day. One of the most powerful scriptures in the Bible is John 3:16 which states, *"For God so loved the world that He gave His only begotten Son, that whosoever believes in Him should not perish but have everlasting life."* There will always be a circumstance that the enemy will put in your path to try to keep you from loving God and so many other people. The best solution for anyone who experiences these attacks is to stand in the love of Jesus Christ. Stand in the love that Jesus provides daily. His love has power in it that can move mountains or anything that seems so heavy in your life. Ask God for help always.

When you look at the power of God removing scales from our love life, it puts you in a sense of awe. Let us examine a little closer what a scale does in your life. A scale suffocates you and squeezes the potential love out of you because it carries hate and evil. A scale represents blindness, which in turn gives a sense of false love. A scale blocks out the love of Jesus Christ unless you ask Him to come into your heart to remove that scale. If you feel like you are in trouble with love read Romans 5:5: "Now hope does not disappoint, because the love of God has been poured out in our hearts by the Holy Spirit who was given to us."

What is so powerful is that God already poured His love into our hearts. No one should allow scales to out demonstrate Godly love in family. God wants all of us to demonstrate the love of God to Him by allowing love to manifest in your life. Remember love is powerful and it is displayed by actions (I John 4: 7-12).

DILIGENTLY SEEK GOD

HEBREWS 12:6: "But without faith it is impossible to please Him, for he who comes to God must believe that He is, and that He is a rewarder of those who diligently seek Him."

Almost everyone wants some form of reward. People get rewards for finding a lost child, returning someone's lost wallet or car, or even some heroic act. There are hundreds of people who have saved someone's life from drowning, a house fire, from being hit by a car, and falling from a cliff of some sort. Faith in God pleases God. When you use faith to help someone come to Jesus Christ, your reward is greater. In many cases, people do not know that they need faith to please God in their lives. They need the faith that takes you beyond circumstances keeping you low and empty in heart. You need a Savior to capture your life and make you over. Often an invite to church or a mega conference or some type of spiritual enhancement tour might help. But the Bible declares that there is a remedy that will help all people in their spiritual journey.

The Hebrew writer tells us of the importance of faith in our lives. He tells us that in *Hebrews 12:1, "Now faith is the substance of things hoped for, the evidence of things not seen. For by it the elders obtained a good testimony."* The scripture gives examples of so many others that allowed God to reveal Himself. However, it took faith in

God to accept what He manifested in the lives of those with pure faith. The Bible declares that God has given everyone a measure of faith.

Romans 10:17: "So then faith comes by hearing, and hearing by the word of God." Even a mustard seed of faith as in Matthew 17 has power to move mountains. Faith is also called one of the fruit of the spirit in Galatians 5.

The Apostle Paul said without faith it is impossible to please God. That tells me that I must have faith to please him in my everyday walk. Your life is now the life of pleasing God. It is time to speak the word and say, "Please God, help me to please you in my life today."

Can faith be poured down like the rain we always experience? Yes, faith comes faster and with more power and with more substance that rain. Abraham is one the first to allow faith to be poured out of Him toward God almighty. Just mentioning Abraham, who was one of the heroes in the faith hall of fame, makes it clear that all had the desire to please God in their hearts. Hear the word of God everywhere you go. Hide the word of God in your heart. With the word you can please God. The word of God will direct your steps. The word of God will keep you company in lonely time. In times of despair, in troubled times, and in times of temptation, and when it seems like there is no way out of bondage. God's word is the way out because it puts you in direct communication with the Lord. Tell Him all about the situation at hand. He can and will according to His purpose take control. You just need to surrender and keep your trust in Him. Start living a life to please God. He will bless you.

NEVER SLAIN AGAIN

JOB 13:13-15: "Why do I take my flesh in my teeth, and put my life in my hands? Though He slay me, yet will I trust Him. Even so, I will defend my own ways before Him. He also shall be my salvation, for a hypocrite could not come before Him."

Do you feel attacked or defeated by the enemy? Do not let the enemy slay you. Trust the Lord our God and speak victory. When you are seeking results from God, speak positive outcomes. Speak healing and victory everyday of your life. The enemy's tricks and devices do not have to trample all over you as someone without power. The power you have is the power that the Lord works through you by Him. We are powerless without God by our side. You can do something about it instead of just lying down and taking the punishment. God already knows you and will bless you in a mighty way. God does not have to get back at the enemy. God is God and He does not answer to anyone. The enemy is just blowing smoke and his effort is fruitless. Surely the Lord put a dent in the adversary's plan. It is important to understand that God saw Job as a righteous man of faith in God.

The enemy would have you to believe that the blow dealt to you was so heavy that it is impossible to take, but God was there in the midst of your confusion, your lack of trust, and doubt. God is there to help reinstate your faith that you lost because of your crisis. God is there to help hold you up and keep you together. He will not leave you nor forsake you. He knows your every need—where you are wounded and even how it happened. Do not worry because His purpose is to give you a life filled with abundance. Live a blessed life in Jesus Christ. Even in the midst of you almost losing your mind over a devastating event in your life, Jesus will still stand with you.

One thing that you need to always be sure of is that God is the keeper of your mind, soul, spirit, and heart. Don't you let anyone tell you differently. You almost lost your soul because the hurt was so difficult, but God stepped in and rescued you. He gently, by His gracious power, erased the pain and suffering. Isaiah 53:5 says, *"But He was wounded for our transgressions, He was bruised for our iniquities; the chastisement for our peace was upon Him, and by His stripes we are healed."* What you did not know is that God has something in store for you. Not only is He going to bless you with more than what you had, He will bless you more than you can imagine.

Do not stop trusting God because the enemy gave you a bad day. It is all false and phony! You do not have a bad name or a bad day. You are a child of the Most High. It is all what the enemy wants to put in your head. In other words, it's an illusion—just like a mirage in a dessert. The enemy makes you see stuff you really don't see and that really isn't there.

I believe if Job was not so much of a holy man, he would probably, like me, think about applying some martial arts to the devil's weakest body points. If I could just learn some karate so I could beat that devil down for killing my children, I would feel all right. But since I do not know it, I have a force much more powerful than the martial arts. I will trust in the God that I worship. I will worship and praise Him, even when it hurts so badly. I will just trust Him no matter how hard and how far that I feel like I have fallen. "Thou He slay me yet will I trust Him."

It was pointed out to me by a relative that a close friend of the family had lost his entire family, one after the other, in one week. It was a tragedy and my prayers went out immediately for him and his family. We need to send prayers out all the time, not just when something happens. Pray for God to put a shelter of protection around us even when we know that God has a plan, a purpose, and His own time for life in our lives. I want you to understand that the enemy still patrols the earth just like he did during the life of Job.

This man lost his wife and five children in one day. Then the next day he received news that he lost both parents in a head-on collision. Sometimes when tragedy strikes, we do not know why. We are never prepared to receive such bad news. God knows all about every situation and circumstance that hurts you so deep inside. God will comfort each and every person that feels tragedy. He will fix your heart and comfort you through the hurt as long as you need Him. He will never leave you, nor forsake you.

I want to tell you today, that God wants you to lean on Him in times of trouble, and in times of rejoicing give Him praise so you will be encouraged that you have someone with you. Today, tell every circumstance and anything that presents itself to you in the form of tragedy and pain, "Thou He slay me yet will I trust Him" You see the good news is that there is a brighter day and there are blessings that are showering you right this moment. You just need to know when and how to let the walls of hurt down. Talk to Jesus, He is there in your heart. Trust Him. He will always make it all right. He loves you more than you know.

GOD'S SERVANT'S TEST

JOB 1: 6-12: "Now there was a day when the sons of God came to present themselves before the LORD, and Satan also came among them. And the LORD said to Satan, 'From where do you come?' So Satan answered the LORD and said, 'From going to and fro on the earth, and from walking back and forth on it.' Then the LORD said to Satan, 'Have you considered my servant Job, that there is none like him on the earth, a blameless and upright man, one who fears God and shuns evil?' So Satan answered the LORD and said, 'Does Job fear God for nothing? Have you not made a hedge around him, around his household, and around all that he has on every side? You have blessed the work of his hands, and his possessions have increased in the land. But now, stretch out your hand and touch all that he has, and he will surely curse you to your face!' And the LORD said to Satan, 'Behold, all that he has is in your power; only do not lay a hand on his person.' So Satan went out from the presence of the LORD."

When God asked the devil, 'Have you considered my servant Job?' He had already blessed Job because the enemy did not have the authority to take Job's life. He had already placed a hedge about Him that the enemy was not allowed to penetrate. He had already set life in motion that He alone knew exactly what would happen. God spoke and it was final. We need not worry about anything when God speaks. We just need to listen and obey Him and know that we are in His perfect will.

What I find more interesting is the fact that God looked at Him as a man perfect and upright. Although Job was considered by God to be perfect and upright, he still had to go through devastation in his family. He had to experience as a man of God one of the most horrific emotional and spiritual tragedies in life.

I want to tell you today that God has a way of handling our lives when we do not even know what makes sense. Or when we just do not understand what really happened. One thing for sure is that He is our comfort in times of need. He is always there when we need a touch of His grace and mercy. He knows how to release His grace and healing touch of comfort when we need Him most. He will never leave you, nor forsake you.

What is even more interesting is how God sees His servants throughout the world. God has priests, pastors, evangelists, teachers, prophets, and all kinds of servants in His kingdom. If He called Job His servant, surely He is calling us His servants. It is obvious to me that God can put us in the test—just as easily as He did with Job. God can allow our lives to be impacted to see if we will stand in the faith and the power of His anointing, and the blessings that He has showered us in. I believe that God wants us to press for the prized and keep on praying and serving Him until the day of His return.

PASS GOD'S TEST

We must be thankful that the challenge has not come that way just yet. You see God has the ability to allow the adversity to go from the church on one corner to the church down the street or around the corner to cause disruption and confusion. The Catholic, Baptist, Methodist, Pentecostal, Church of God in Christ and non-denominational Churches are tested with its priestly conduct, relationships, and doctrine. God has the ability to allow the enemy to touch those in the church and ministry to see if they are the elect in Christ, to see if they are faithful to the one whom they serve. You need not fret because if you believe that Jesus died and rose from the dead, you are a child of the King. If you are standing on the power of the blood, then you have the best protection. He is your shield.

Last, can you imagine the things that God asks us to consider? Take an inventory of the things that people make us consider? Has someone asked you that question? We consider our health. We consider our bank accounts. We consider our marriages. We consider if the new house we want can be afforded. We consider our own measure of faith. We consider if life is worth living. We consider if there is really a future for us. We consider if there is a person looking to get married.

We need to reevaluate our considerations of life. We need to renew our interest in life. We must take Jesus as our Lord and Savior. Let there be no mistakes about it that we have put our trust in Him. My trust is in the solid rock, Jesus Christ.

USE YOUR ANOINTED ABILITY

A great deal of talent is used in the entertainment business. Television, videos, and YouTube are some top avenues of viewing people who have certain skills and talents for entertainment. Everyone has some potential of doing something in this world. God gave all of us some talent. It's always amazing to watch people put their skills into action.

When you watch actors on the big screen at a movie theater, or even on your own 52" plus screen, you get a since of awe in their ability to memorize the script. They make it come alive with their ability to act. Most people say, "Wow! I'm impressed!" They get that "I want to be like..." syndrome and attitude. Nothing is wrong with desiring to be something good in the eyes of the Lord as long as it's something decent and pleasing in His sight.

Some people get obsessed with wanting something so badly. I think it's good as long as it's not the wrong kind of obsession. Keep it calm and be patient, for your time will come and you will be highly blessed in the Lord. Some start dreams about doing what the other person is doing. All you ever have to remember is that you can do it and you can do it even better. You just get ready to count your blessings and the money that's coming in your blessing. Keep your head up. You have the ability to do whatever God will allow you to do. Just stay away from sin city, that could be other things. So watch yourself—watch your step! Seek God about everything. Remember what we discuss all of the time, Matthew 6:33, which is one of my friends best scriptures, *"Seek ye first the Kingdom of God and all of His righteous, then everything else will follow."* It's all about Jesus first.

Today, start putting your mind to the plow. Start thinking out loud. Say to yourself, I can do all things through Christ Jesus who strengthens me. Start thinking about what you will do with your talent as a witness for Jesus Christ. Maybe you can write songs and start getting produced. Maybe you have been singing in the choir for all of those years and it is time for you to get paid while you glorify His righteous name. It is not a sin to witness for Jesus when it's the correct doctrine and you are under the anointing of God. The Bible says in Psalm 100, "Let everything that has breath praise the Lord."

Several years ago, I used to tease my daughter about trying to be like other girls in other groups. I used to tell her that if you like Destiny

Child, you can sing just like them. Be encouraged to move in your abilities and gifts that God gave you. I wanted her to know that she could do anything and be successful, if she put her mind to it. Some things you have to practice at to get. For all things we need to seek God about before we attempt them. When He gives the answers for you to move forward, start spending that time doing what God blessed you to do.

1 Corinthians 14 says much about gifts, still referring to talent in God's army. "Pursue love, and desire spiritual gifts, but especially that you may prophesy. For he who speaks in a tongue does not speak to men but to God, for no one understands him; however, in the spirit he speaks mysteries. But he who prophesies speaks edification and exhortation and comfort to men. He who speaks in a tongue edifies himself, but he who prophesies edifies the church."

The Apostle Paul said you may have different talents and abilities and gifts, but the bottom line is that God wants to use what you have. God wants you to prophesy in the lives of others. You may not prophesy in their presence, but God will use you regardless.

BE A SEED SOWER

MATTHEW 13:1-9: "On the same day Jesus went out of the house and sat by the sea. And great multitudes were gathered together to Him, so that He got into a boat and sat; and the whole multitude stood on the shore. Then He spoke many things to them in parables, saying: 'Behold, a sower went out to sow. And as he sowed, some seed fell by the wayside; and the birds came and devoured them. Some fell on stony places, where they did not have much earth; and they immediately sprang up because they had no depth of earth. But when the sun was up they were scorched, and because they had no root they withered away. And some fell among thorns, and the thorns sprang up and choked them. But others fell on good ground and yielded a crop:

some a hundredfold, some sixty, some thirty. He who has ears to hear, let him hear!'"

Jesus put the first parable in the context of agriculture. When he mentions that sower went forth, he refers to the historical and ancient seed sowers that were highly engaged and committed to planting crops. Jesus would later interpret his own words as telling them that the seed is the Word of God. Jesus tells us that the sower is the person who goes out evangelizing to the community and the world every chance they get. Evangelists go out and plant seed in the hearts of people. The seed they plant is the Word of God. Jesus wants us to be cautious about the hard-packed fields that will not accept the seed, causing it to not find root. Then the fowls, which are demons, come and snatch it away. These people have no response to the word of God being preached to them. Jesus tells us in the next category, the stony places, are stony ledges that give enough heat or warmth to at least cause the seed to sprout. But the problem is that it does not have adequate heat or moisture. Therefore, the sun scorches it, and it withers away. The third group of seed falls among thorns that are never plowed. The wild growth chokes out the seed. Then Jesus mentions the good ground, which represents well-plowed and well-prepared soil, capable of producing large crop. Whatever you do, start serving God by sowing seed to someone you care about. Give a Bible verse daily to your family members and send out hundreds through email. Invite them to come to church and publicly accept Jesus as Lord and Savior.

It is also interesting that in the book of Joel 2, he says, *"I will pour out my Spirit."* Well, He will pour out His Spirit in more intensity than the rain that flows down and runs off of your back when you're soaked and wet. Ask God to do an outpouring of the Spirit in your life and start a new walk in Christ. In the passage above, Jesus speaks about the seed and the soils. I thought about what it takes to make that seed grow. It takes water. In our case, it takes the Spirit of God to continue

His outpouring in our lives. You see we need the spirit to renew us daily to keep us fruitful.

When the Spirit of the Lord comes into us, we can yield a crop. Before we yield a crop, the seed must be planted. God will direct us to fall on good ground. He knows who will receive Him. He knows who will reject Him. The Christian witness must be directed under the Holy Spirit so that God will get the glory in the yielding process. If you are looking for soil to be planted on, ask God to plant you. Don't try to plant yourself under your own power, but be under the influence and power of the Holy Spirit, and watch God work miracles before your eyes. The yield comes from God. We glorify the name of Jesus.

THE BRIDEGROOM IS COMING

MATTHEW 25:1-13: "Then the kingdom of heaven shall be likened to ten virgins who took their lamps and went out to meet the bridegroom. Now five of them were wise, and five were foolish. Those who were foolish took their lamps and took no oil with them, but the wise took oil in their vessels with their lamps. But while the bridegroom was delayed, they all slumbered and slept. "And at midnight a cry was heard: 'Behold, the bridegroom is coming; go out to meet him!' Then all those virgins arose and trimmed their lamps. And the foolish said to the wise, 'Give us some of your oil, for our lamps are going out.' But the wise answered, saying, 'No, lest there should not be enough for us and you; but go rather to those who sell, and buy for yourselves.' And while they went to buy, the bridegroom came, and those who were ready went in with him to the wedding; and the door was shut. "Afterward the other virgins came also, saying, 'Lord, Lord, open to us!' But he answered and said, 'Assuredly, I say to you, I do not know you.' "Watch therefore, for you know neither the day nor the hour in which the Son of Man is coming."

Be prepared for the Lord to return no matter what else is going on in your life.

CHAPTER 5

COUNT ON GOD'S HOLD

LUKE 23:40-49: "*But the other, answering, rebuked him, saying, 'Do you not even fear God, seeing you are under the same condemnation? And we indeed justly, for we receive the due reward of our deeds; but this Man has done nothing wrong.' Then he said to Jesus, 'Lord, remember me when you come into your kingdom.' And Jesus said to him, 'Assuredly, I say to you, today you will be with me in Paradise.'"*

One of the worst mistakes in life is when you find yourself counting God out. When you count God out, you are saying that God is not your help and the one who rescued you all the days of your life. If you count God out, then you have counted out your true help because He is the center of life. The problem is that so many people do not fear God, nor rever the Lord, our God. He wants us to know Him and to love Him back. When Jesus was on that cross, He told a thief on the day he was being crucified that he would be with him in paradise. Can you feel His great love on the cross? You can count on Jesus anytime! He will not let you go. His grip of love is tight on you. Count on God's hold in your life.

OVERCOMER'S ATTITUDE

MATTHEW 5:10-12: "*Blessed are those who are persecuted for righteousness' sake, for theirs is the kingdom of heaven. 'Blessed are you when they revile and persecute you, and say all kinds of evil against you falsely for my sake. Rejoice and be exceedingly glad, for great is your reward in heaven, for so they persecuted the prophets who were before you.'"*

You have an enemy just like everyone else. As long as the adversary is roaming the earth like a "roaring lion seeking who he may devour," you have an enemy. The enemy tries his best to devour you each and every day. You are like a tasty meal to a hungry lion that had not eaten in day. He wants you like that lion is hunting the easy prey in the wild. He wants you just as badly. He uses people, places, and things to take up his evil operation as well to rise up against you. You just need to be aware of the enemy situation around you, let go of yourself and let God do a work on your behalf. He will stomp the enemy for you because you are one of His children.

The enemy uses people to persecute you and anyone else. We mean absolutely nothing to the enemy, except one primary thing and that is the enemy wants to use you for his demonic army. Once the enemy uses you, he completes his mission of kill, steal, and destroy with you as his assistant. Then the enemy will restart his process if you allow him with the next generation of your precious seed. You have got to get this in your spirit. The enemy does not mind destroying you and your family. You mean absolutely nothing to the enemy! Everyone who has not accepted Jesus as Lord and Savior is easy prey and recruitment to the enemy. He will use you against good people. God wants you in His army, His kingdom, to get prepared for His paradise. God wants you on His side because you are in a win-win situation by being on the Lord's side.

When I was in the military, one of the things that disturbed me more than anything else was to be in a situation where I would be trapped in a vehicle because of the enemy, or cornered and ambushed by the enemy—especially on a patrol mission. The most cautious times for me was convoying in the enemy's territory. Everything was on alert. We moved along routes as though we owned them. We definitely had the firepower to persuade the enemy to think twice and take another look at the situation at hand, but there was always that one missing link that had a wild finger ready to do something explosive. If my vehicle got hit, I never wanted to be trapped inside a burning vehicle burning up alive. I never wanted the enemy to take pleasure in seeing the devastation he caused. My intent was to always be ready and hit the enemy head-on, right where it counts. In our spiritual walk we need to hit the enemy between the eye with firepower of the word of God and with the power of prayer. We call on the name of Jesus. We understand that we are blessed in Him by His hand of protection (Psalms 91:11).

When the enemy rises up in persecution, the power of the word of God will cut through him. You no longer have to walk in fear. You walk in victory in Christ Jesus. No weapon formed against you will prosper. Keep your eyes on the Lord. Keep announcing that you are blessed and walk in it. Rejoice and be exceedingly glad, for great is your reward in heaven, for so they persecuted the prophets who were before you. Give God all the praise regardless of what it looks like to you and others all around you. If they only knew that the power of God is on your side, they would step off. Blessed be the name of the Lord.

SOMETIMES IT'S SHOWDOWN TIME!

When I was growing up it was nothing better than an old-fashioned, good old western movie where the top two characters would face off and draw. Most of us sat on the edge of our seat because we wanted the good guy to out draw the other person who was the villain. The Rifleman was one of my favorites. He could use that rifle faster than the villain with a pistol could draw. I also enjoyed watching Wyatt Earp, a cowboy who got rid of villains in the Wild West who were terrorizing and killing incident people. Now we watch movies like the Matrix, and expect the character Neo to win each time those duplicate villains approach for a showdown. Often in our lives there are multiple showdowns. A showdown in our lives is something that desires to defeat us. The name Jesus defeats the enemy every time you are challenged because there is power in His name.

Everyday someone is faced with dealing with the enemy, either face to face or indirectly. In many cases, people still get blasted by the enemy and allow their guards to go down and walk defeated. God did not give you and me the spirit of fear, but the spirit of love and power, and a sound mind. Our solution is always to profess the name of Jesus Christ and denounce fear. We are here standing under the shadow of our Lord. Sometimes it's a showdown! Remember this! All power is in His name. So it does not matter how anyone sees you. God sees you as a servant of the Most High and that is what matters. The death, burial, and resurrection are what defeated the enemy on Calvary. Because of what Jesus did on Calvary, the enemy is stomped on the spot along with all of his demons.

You need to give the enemy notice today, right now, to stop messing with you because you have the King of Kings and Lord of Lords on your side. Your confession of faith in Christ Jesus hurts the enemy every time and gives glory to the Most High. If the enemy dwells in people attacking you, speak the word that professes your faith in Jesus. Everyone knows the name above every name, Jesus Christ. Chills run down their spine. Chills run down their entire body inside out when they hear the name Jesus.

The Bible declares in Philippians 2, *"At the name of Jesus every knee will bow and every tongue will confess that Jesus is Lord."* Somehow within them they know. They know who you are talking about. The name Jesus reveals authority and power that is comprehensible yet the mind cannot absorb all of His glory. When we call on the name of Jesus, the enemy is reminded that Jesus died on that cross and there was nothing Satan could do about it but flee into everlasting darkness. Tell your enemy of persecution that they might as well go back to the pits of hell because you are a child of God and you are all about Kingdom work. You are about the witness of the resurrection and the return of Christ Jesus. Make it clear by stating the name of Jesus. Tell everything around you, "In Jesus' name, I rebuke evil and sin in Jesus' name!" Tell it, "I am protected in the blood of Christ Jesus, In Jesus' name." Speak the words, "No weapon formed against me shall prosper, in Jesus' name! I am more than a conqueror in Jesus' name." Remember in all circumstances, say Jesus' name again to remove all manner of evil and usher in a holy atmosphere.

LUKE 23:40-49: "But the other, answering, rebuked him, saying, 'Do you not even fear God, seeing you are under the same condemnation? And we indeed justly, for we receive the due reward of our deeds; but this Man has done nothing wrong.' Then he said to Jesus, 'Lord, remember me when you come into your kingdom.' And Jesus said to him, 'Assuredly, I say to you, today you will be with me in Paradise.' Now it was about the sixth hour, and there was darkness over all the earth until the ninth hour. Then the sun was darkened,] and the veil of the temple was torn in two. And when Jesus had cried out with a loud voice, He said, 'Father, into your hands I commit my spirit.'" Having said this, He breathed His last."

Because Jesus said, "into your hands I commit my spirit," he tells us that we need to commit our spirit to Him because the work He finished on Calvary means the work we start uplifts His kingdom. He finished the work of redemption upon rising from the grave to live in Heaven at the right hand of the Father. Now is our time to endure persecution and rise above the occasion of enemy attacks.

> As longs as we have Jesus, we can do anything to please Him. He breathed His last breath and said, "It is finished." He defeated everything that the enemy, Satan, had done to corrupt this world and its people. I just have to praise the Lord for His love that saved His people. My mind cannot fathom the amount of love that went into dying on Calvary. Because of His glorious love for me, I bow before Him in exaltation and adoration. We praise Him and thank Him.

WITNESS SCALES

Acts 1: 8: "But you shall receive power when the Holy Spirit come upon you; and you shall be witnesses to me in Jerusalem, and in all Judea and Samaria, and to the end of the earth."

Once you are converted, you will become a witness. You will not be forced to become a witness. You will become a witness because of the love of God inside you. To be effective in witnessing, allow the word to be in you. We are always reminded that the Apostle Paul was able to see once those spiritual scales were removed from his eyes. He became the most effective witnesses perhaps in history of course after the Triune God.

Many people believe that the Holy Spirit is present and gives power to those who serve and minister for the sake of Kingdom work. Nevertheless, we see power given to corporate leaders, political leaders, military leaders, and just about every business that has leaders within the organization. Those positions of power are nice and have advantages. However, no one has the power that God has. His position is greater and beyond great. We walk with our Lord because He is the loving and all-powerful Lord. If He says move, we move; if He says pray, we pray. If he says go out to all the earth and baptize in the name of the Father, Son and Holy Spirit, we follow.

We follow His command because we love Him and desire to obey Him. Little Marvin had five brothers and six sisters. Each one of His siblings lived in different states and some in other countries. They really did not keep in touch that much. But something happened to change that situation and division. Marvin's mother had died of lung cancer. She was a heavy smoker—for forty years she smoked. Marvin received the call last Tuesday from his aunt.

GIVE GOD YOUR BEST

JOHN 12:3: "Then Mary took a pound of very costly oil of spikenard, anointed the feet of Jesus, and wiped His feet with her hair. And the house was filled with the fragrance of the oil."

Hair is part of the body that everyone is sensitive about. You style it the way you want it. You clean it, you cut it, you baby it, and you make sure it is presentable at all cost. Well, Mary set a new standard. She used the best outer part of her to reflect humility and worship to the Son of God. Mary washed his feet with oil then wiped His feet with her hair. What was Mary doing? Mary was expressing love to the Lord.

The oil that Mary used was costly oil which had to be purchased. The oil was used to anoint the feet of Jesus. Mary was demonstrating an act of humility, obedience, and reverence. Not only did Mary use the oil as a special source of blessing and honor, she used her hair. When she used her hair, she demonstrated a more personal act toward our Lord Jesus. She basically opened herself up to the Lord in hopes that He would bless her.

When you worship the Lord in these forms of worship that Mary demonstrated, it brings about a brighter day and everything around you seems to smell so good. The scripture says that house was filled with the fragrance of the oil. When Jesus is around, there is always something good—there is always a sweet fragrance in the air. Ask Jesus to come into your home. Worship Him at home and everywhere you go. When Jesus blesses you, remember to do what the woman did, she gave her best from the start and Jesus remembered her. Our Lord remembers us when we glorify Him. Give God your best because you know He deserves it.

OVERCOME YOUR IDENTITY CRISIS

ACTS 9: 1-6: "Meanwhile, Saul was still breathing out murderous threats against the Lord's disciples. He went to the high priest and asked him for letters to the synagogues in Damascus, so that if he found any there who belonged to the way, whether men or women, he might take them as prisoners to Jerusalem. As he neared Damascus on his journey, suddenly a light from heaven flashed around him. He fell to the ground and heard a voice say to him, 'Saul, Saul, why do you persecute me?' 'Who are you, Lord?' Saul asked. 'I am Jesus, whom you are persecuting,' he replied. 'Now get up and go into the city, and you will be told what you must do.'"

People who do not know or understand their identity should seek direction and a relationship with Jesus Christ. What stems from not knowing your identity is something that is not good. Take, for example, the story of Saul. He left a huge impact in the society of that day when he did not have a relationship with Jesus. He caused more issues than one could imagine. Many people still do not know who they really are. People have many reasons why they feel lost or not sure of who they are.

Some of the reasons range from broken homes, different marriages, relationships, and the results of relationships, different mindsets, and perhaps many other things. However, the number one reason behind the identity crisis of people is sin. If you have never reached out to Jesus Christ as your Lord and Savior, sin will reign in your life. One key purpose for this book is that you come to know Jesus Christ personally. Repent and ask Jesus Christ, the Son of God, to come into your heart today.

Asking Him is the key solution in gaining your true identity back. Please understand something, God can never lose. Adam may have lost dominion in the garden, but God never lost it. Adam may have lost his original identity in the Garden of Eden, but God never lost anything. God is God and no one can change Him. He holds all power in His hand. Today ask God to get the God hold on you. What is the God hold? It is the all loving, all sovereign, omnipotent, omnipresent, powerful, infallible, perfect will of God. He is the one behind all transformations and life.

We see the struggle of identify in almost every agency, business, and institution. God desires to restore the individual person and work on the other issues in life as well. God never sleeps nor slumbers so He is always available, awake, and ready to deliver whosoever will call on the name of the Lord. As I click through channels with my remote, I am able to see so many people acting in so many different roles. Of course, it's their profession to act as specific characters. But I wonder if they know who they really are when it comes to having a relationship with Jesus Christ. I am sure someone needs to know Him for himself or herself because we knew Him each and every day. When you are on set acting for a million dollar movie, be sure to take some time out and talk to God and thank Him. He will open your eyes to see things better. The solutions to finding all the answers are in the scriptures and in the Lord, Jesus Christ.

Several models made their way for a tryout and were told that they had to appear and perform a certain way to be successful. After trying out, they did not meet the identity standard of a supermodel or even an average model. They were cut and they were sent home. These young teenagers were devastated and were on the brink of depression. Looks and appeal play vital roles in almost every facet of life. But Jesus is the center of life itself. I want to tell all of those that suffer from these types of rejections or any rejection because your performance and looks that God is always there to accept you. Jesus welcomes you no matter what the circumstance is, no matter what time it is, or who you are. He will restore you and make you feel better than ever before. Jesus' word tells us that I can do all things through Christ who strengthens me.

Confidence, faith, and a positive attitude are the keys to overcoming your identity crisis. Being transformed in the Spirit of Jesus Christ is more important. We receive more in the Spirit of Christ than from any other in this year and the time to come. We no longer have to respond to things of the world that sway us in the wrong direction. I know many people who read books might need to know the power that abides in Jesus and is transferred into the believer's heart. That is why we become His children. Jesus came to save us from wrath and the sin that was destroying the creation. He had to have the heart of His Father had blessed Him to be the one who has been given all power in His hand.

A DONKEY TELLING IT!

NUMBERS 22:21-24: "So Balaam rose in the morning, saddled his donkey, and went with the princes of Moab. Then God's anger was aroused because he went, and the Angel of the LORD took His stand in the way as an adversary against him. And he was riding on his donkey, and his two servants were with him. Now the donkey saw the Angel of the LORD standing in the way with His drawn sword in His hand, and the donkey turned aside out of the way and went into the field. So Balaam struck the donkey to turn her back onto the road. Then the Angel of the LORD stood in a narrow path between the vineyards, with a wall on this side and a wall on that side."

As we were growing up, we had certain days that we all watched television. One show constantly came on which was called Francis the Talking Mule. We must have watched the show over and over just to hear the mule talk and get people's reactions. Every time the mule spoke, he spoke around someone who did not know God can get our attention any way He wants to in the most unexpected situation, resource, and even timing. So be careful of what God just might use in your path. He will use an animal just to make you see what He wants you to see. He will make you look up to heaven and recognize who the true master and ruler is in your life. It took a donkey to tell a man that God was about to slay him for his disobedience and pride.

Who told you what was about to take place in your life for disobeying God? Who warned you about the enemy coming to attempt to kill, steal, and destroy your life. God said choose Him today over all evil devices. Are you watchful of the things that are around you daily? What is God saying to you? Listen to His voice. He speaks through His word and He sends angels to fulfill tasks at hand. He always fulfills what He set out to accomplish. I can understand some things happening in my life, but there are some obvious things that occur that we need to recognize that God is speaking, God is doing something, and then adhere to His voice.

AN ANGEL IN YOUR PATH

NUMBERS 22:25-30: *"And when the donkey saw the Angel of the LORD, she pushed herself against the wall and crushed Balaam's foot against the wall; so he struck her again. Then the Angel of the LORD went further, and stood in a narrow place where there was no way to turn either to the right hand or to the left. And when the donkey saw the Angel of the LORD, she lay down under Balaam; so Balaam's anger was aroused, and he struck the donkey with his staff. Then the LORD opened the mouth of the donkey, and she said to Balaam, 'What have I done to you, that you have struck me these three times?' And Balaam said to the donkey, 'Because you have abused me. I wish there were a sword in my hand, for now I would kill you!' So the donkey said to Balaam, 'Am I not your donkey on which you have ridden, ever since I became yours, to this day? Was I ever disposed to do this to you?' And he said, 'No.'"*

This is about God opening your eyes to see what He has for you. Have you ever had someone to rescue you? It a blessing to know that God has put things in order that you can receive help like Balaam. If it were not for the donkey being able to see the Angel, Balaam would have been dead. His donkey did everything in its power to save his master from being killed. We have to be careful when someone or something God has placed in our path is delivering a message. We need to be more discerning in our spirit.

Numbers 22:31-41: "Then the LORD opened Balaam's eyes, and he saw the Angel of the LORD standing in the way with His drawn sword in His hand; and he bowed his head and fell flat on his face. And the Angel of the LORD said to him, 'Why have you struck your donkey these three times? Behold, I have come out to stand against you, because your way is perverse before me. The donkey saw me and turned aside from me these three times. If she had not turned aside from me, surely I would also have killed you by now, and let her live.' And Balaam said to the Angel of the LORD, 'I have sinned, for I did not know you stood in the way against me. Now therefore, if it displeases you, I will turn back.' Then the angel of the LORD said to Balaam, 'Go with the men, but only the word that I speak to you, that you shall speak.'

So Balaam went with the princes of Balak. Now when Balak heard that Balaam was coming, he went out to meet him at the city of Moab, which is on the border at the Arnon, the boundary of the territory. Then Balak said to Balaam, 'Did I not earnestly send to you, calling for you? Why did you not come to me? Am I not able to honor you?' And Balaam said to Balak, 'Look, I have come to you! Now, have I any power at all to say anything? The word that God puts in my mouth, that I must speak.' So Balaam went with Balak, and they came to Kirjath Huzoth. Then Balak offered oxen and sheep, and he sent some to Balaam and to the princes who were with him. So it was, the next day, that Balak took Balaam and brought him up to the high places of Baal, that from there he might observe the extent of the people."

God wants Balaam to know that his life was spared because a donkey was responding in respect to the presence of an angel. Otherwise, the angel of the Lord would have slain Balaam for being perverse in the sight of God. So now he must speak the word of the Lord as God directed. Our God has a way of getting people's attention.

SPEAK LIFE INTO EVERYONE

EZEKIEL 37:4: "Again He said to me, 'Prophesy to these bones, say to them, O dry bones, hear the word of the Lord!'"

What would you do if God placed you in a valley with the anointing all over you? Would you use what God gave you to restore what is in your path? Would you use what God instructed you to use? In this case, the Lord specifically told Ezekiel to prophesy over dead bones. God put His anointing on Ezekiel to speak life into dead bones. Let us take a look at the power of God through Ezekiel's mission.

The Lord told Ezekiel to speak over an army of dead bones to raise them up. Can you see the picture of an entire nation of dead bones laying in front of your view and God speaking to you? One thing that can be seen is that God will bring whatever He wants back to life. If it is dead, God is able to restore it. Stand firm in the resurrection from the dead.

God does what He pleases for His eternal glory. There are plenty people that need a resurrection. Some are just those dead bones in the valley. Ezekiel had to speak in accordance with what God wanted Him to say. In Ezekiel 37: 5-10, something else jumped out at me by reading this. It seems unusual, but God is also saying that He made you to believe in Him and also to believe in yourself. He gave you enough power of decision to make up your mind to come to Him. There is a reason why these dead bones lay where they are. Likewise, you have become like those dead bones in the valley. God does not want you there just lying dead. It is because of your belief and trust. It is because you fail to step out on faith for the purpose He gave you.

I was pondering over church the other day and for a few minutes thought about how people do the same things over and over and never make progress, never make a difference in life. They just attend church to get the check mark of satisfaction. Then God reminded me that it is because they have allowed themselves to become like dead bones. So then the only possible way of changing from being dead is to preach, prophesy, and pray so that they can be resurrected from the dead state of life. God is looking for people who will become a part of His army. It is high time to become resurrected for the purpose of God's Kingdom.

It reminded that when Jesus started ministering, He begin His ministry with the word of God. He preached in *Matthew 4:17, "Repent for the kingdom of heaven is at hand."* God wants people to turn their lives around so they will not end up as dead bones with no hope. In Matthew 5:1-16, Jesus taught multitudes of people about the attitudes that get you blessed. He also identified us by saying, "You are the salt of the earth but if the salt loses its flavor, how shall it be seasoned? It is then good for nothing but to be thrown out and to be trampled under-foot by men."

We need to understand that God does the seasoning with His word. God seasons His fivefold ministry. He will not let His ministry move without His power and authority. God speaks of the prophet in His fivefold ministry and He does have prophets. They look just like you and me. But God confirms who the real prophets are. Ezekiel was one of His prophets and God instructed Him to prophesy over the dead bones. In other words, speak a word and bring them back to life.

You see there are dead conditions in the lives of so many people that God is sending His mouthpiece to the utter most parts of the earth. He wants to bring dead bones back to life. That is why Jesus said in *Matthew 5:14, "Let your light so shine before men, that they may see your good works and glorify your Father in heaven."* You see, when you use the fivefold ministry gifts and talents that God gave you, that is when people are resurrected and revived to the new life in Christ. Today, let someone know that you have the light of Jesus burning on the inside and that He saved a wretch like you. Let them know that you once walked in a dead condition that held you back from all the blessings of God. It took Jesus to preach you out of your circumstance. It took Jesus to take you by the hand and bring you out of your valley of dead bones. You are a child of God. You are to walk alive in Jesus Christ.

This story reminds me of when Peter was challenged with the question by Jesus, "Do you love me?" Peter said, "Lord you know I love you." But what Jesus told Him was striking to the heart. He told Peter to feed my sheep, feed my lamb, feed my sheep. The only way you can feed God's people is by the word of God. The only way you can feed God's lambs, those that are lost is by the word of God. You have got to let your light shine by trusting and being obedient to the Lord. Jesus knew that there would be many who would reject the gospel.

He knew that there would be those who have good days and bad days. Jesus knew that all people needed to hear the word that transforms and saves souls. Jesus wanted Peter, just like God wanted Ezekiel, to be in the soul-winning business. Both were challenged to reconnect and regenerate God's people to life. Give them a word and the word will take root and bring people back to life. The word will resurrect the dead from any circumstance and any state of mind and heart condition. Speak a word and let your light shine. Hear the word of the Lord. Prophesy saints. Call on the Most High for intervention and a breakthrough.

PREPARE A TABLE

PSALM 23:5: "You prepare a table before me in the presence of my enemies; you anoint my head with oil. My cup runs over."

My Father in heaven prepares a table for His saints in the presence of the enemy. The enemy cannot do anything about it. The enemy has to flee. When God prepares a table, He invites who He determines according to His will. Whenever the Father is in it, you're already blessed. Listen to what the writer David says: "You anoint my head with oil. My cup runs over."

It ignites a flame in my heart because I know without any reservation or doubt that only God can make my cup overflow or run over. Imagine God recognizing you as a willing vessel to move forward in the kingdom of God, preaching and evangelizing the word of God. The Father is pleased when He knows who is willing to be anointed and carry out the mission. It's God the Father who blesses us that way. Every time this scripture is recited, I can't help but to think of being anointed head to feet by God. I get excited because God is in the business of overflowing with blessings. I automatically think of the anointing all over those He called according to His purpose.

Remember the hard rain story. It pours when it pours. God symbolically shows us that He pours more than the rain, more than the shows that we use daily. Maybe you had a hard downpour today. Ask God; let His anointing take over that you will become a fruitful servant. Speak to God and say, "Lord don't stop the rain on me. Keep it coming. I need your power so you can send me. Send me to tell those in the back woods about your amazing grace. Send me to tell those that are still living deep in sin and religion that you can change things and that the word of God is truth."

OVERFLOWING CUP

When He knows you, you might as well get ready for an overflowing cup. He will fill you up with the anointing power to do the purpose set out for you. Then get all the glory because it is His. Usually we think of getting soaked and wet to the max, and end up changing out of wet clothing because of that feeling of soaked and being unbalanced. We are so used to being dry. It rained so hard that it seemed as though the sky had burst open and released billions of tons and tons of water to revive this planet.

That probably was an understatement because God does send so much down. God waters this planet with more than I realize. You would be surprised at what He can do in your life with a downpour. That right, God is in heaven doing some things we can even see. He pours down from heaven and blesses us. He rains on the just and the unjust. He is no respect of person when He rains down. He can pour out anything He wants at any given time. In Malachi, He says as referring to tithing, He will pour out blessings that you will not have room to receive it.

Believers know that God has the power to control everything from heaven and any place that He wants to control. He owns an operation center everywhere, in every country, in every nation, in every city, in every state, in every house, and in ever temple, every Church, and on every mission. No one can stop Him from controlling all things. That right, He controls the waters, the skies, the valleys, the rivers, the oceans, man, woman, children, spiritual things, life on earth, death, everlasting life, and anything the imagination can think of.

CHAPTER 6

THE GOD HOLD ON PRIEST

HEBREW 8:1-6: "Now this is the main point of the things we are saying: We have a High Priest, who is seated at the right hand of the throne of the Majesty in the heavens, a Minister of the sanctuary and of the true tabernacle which the Lord erected, and not man. For every high priest is appointed to offer both gifts and sacrifices. Therefore it is necessary that this One also have something to offer. For if He were on earth, He would not be a priest, since there are priests who offer the gifts according to the law; who serve the copy and shadow of the heavenly things, as Moses was divinely instructed when he was about to make the tabernacle. For He said, "See that you make all things according to the pattern shown you on the mountain." But now He has obtained a more excellent ministry, inasmuch as He is also Mediator of a better covenant, which was established on better promises.

Once you become a priest, God recognizes you as His priest. You are under His authority and holiness. No one can set you apart to become a priest except Jesus Christ, who has the power to choose you. The only thing that hinders you is your belief and relationship with God. You do not have to allow the enemy to come between you and your family. Do not give the enemy any authority over your family. Everything he's involved in is negative and sinful. Get away from it and stay away from it. As the man of God in your house, you are obligated to see the enemy when he intrudes, then rebuke it out of your house. You see you are set apart to be the priest in your house. God made you to continue nurturing your children and your wife. You do not have time to play around with the enemy. Get him out of your house now! Use the word on anything opposing your family. Anoint your walls with oil and pray without ceasing. Take authority, as a priest should. The man of God of the church is also a priest, or under shepherd, under God's authority only. Neither one of them can be their own priest. Every priest, preacher, evangelist, teacher, and prophet must be under the authority of the High Priest, Jesus Christ.

We as priests and saints of God must identify with Jesus as the mediator of the new covenant. Jesus fulfilled all that was necessary in the old covenant. All people, regardless of Jewish or Gentile, must recognize Jesus as the supreme ruler who has all authority over everything that exists (Colossians 1). Thank God that He has all dominion and rule over everything because if he did not, then the enemy would be loosed to reap havoc and turmoil on the world and we would not be protected. God has made a promise using His Son Jesus as the sacrifice once and for all time. Nothing else is needed. Jesus has done everything we need done.

THE PRIEST RULES HIS HOME

The priest at home must demonstrate compassion far beyond the imagination. He does not even know what level of compassion God will put inside of his heart, mind and spirit. His compassion must exceed anybody else's in the house. His role exceeds everybody in the house. He is the priest, which God placed over the house. Take your position priest. Wives, start helping him today. Don't wait for some special insight or magical visitation.

Do it now! Become a team in Jesus Christ's ministry as husband and wife. You are one in Jesus Christ. Please do not misunderstand the other part to this. The other is it is not only about the priest in the house. It is about those that hurt, and need prayer and supplication. It is about God using this couple to restore the home and all of the siblings, but do not forsake yourselves. God will not make a mistake so we need to stop acting like He will. God is holy and all-powerful. He is perfect. You are in the right location today. You are seeking the right God today. God wants to bless you.

One of the key things that the priest must know in his house is that the wife wants love and compassion, period. She wants to be recognized as your wife, not someone just hanging with you as a sidekick. She wants to support you in the ministry. Help her support you as God leads her. When at home, also recognize what she does day in and day out. If she works, once she comes home from work, or if she has been home all day taking care of the house, bless her and show her love and appreciation. Comfort her because she could have had a long day. Likewise, wives, comfort the priest and treat him like a man. Completely honor and respect him. This will also save your marriage. Leave the outside sources such as other men or other women out completely. The marriage is composed of two people with God leading and blessing them. There is no third party in the flesh. The priest has the power of Christ to comfort her.

His role is to continue to take care of his family no matter what the circumstance is. You see the enemy wants your house. The question to ask is will you give in to him. Children need compassion in so many ways. They need it when life seems like it has taken a toll. They need this compassion for their daughters before they give their hand in marriage. Compassion at the church must exemplify Christ Himself. Be the priest at home and the priest of the local church.

JESUS IS THE WORD

JOHN 1:1-12: "In the beginning was the Word, and the Word was with God, and the Word was God. He was in the beginning with God. All things were made through Him, and without Him nothing was made that was made. In Him was life, and the life was the light of men. And the light shines in the darkness, and the darkness did not comprehend it. There was a man sent from God, whose name was John. This man came for a witness, to bear witness of the Light, that all through him might believe. He was not that Light, but was sent to bear witness of that Light. That was the true Light, which gives light to every man coming into the world. He was in the world, and the world was made through Him, and the world did not know Him. He came to His own, and His own did not receive Him. But as many as received Him, to them He gave the right to become children of God, to those who believe in His name."

I wrote myself a note and left it in my desk drawer at home. It had been there for at least fourteen months. I just recently ran across it and looked closer at it. The note I wrote to myself stated, "Don't sleep with it in your grave." One point is that those were powerful words that reminded me to be a witness by using God's word. I intentionally left that note there to remind me of something so simple. It was to remind me to tell of the God that I know, Jesus Christ. Romans 1:16 tells us not to be ashamed of the gospel of Jesus Christ because it is the power of God. I do not want to imagine missing the opportunity to tell people or the entire world in some form or fashion that Jesus died for my sin. Then that He offers salvation, which is free for those who believe in Him.

I thought about how crucial it is to tell people about him because it's a matter of life and death. It is a matter of your spirit going to heaven versus going to hell. No wants to spend their life in hell. They definitely don't want to be with Satan, the most ugly thing ever. Because Jesus died for me, that means He wants me to be with Him eternally. He wants my life in His hand now and forever. I believe most people want to live with Jesus. The notion to tell everything about Jesus as a witness to His grace, mercy, salvation and everlasting love is what touches me in itself. I feel a sense of self-worth in knowing that he can use me.

The reason I wrote the note is because I know Jesus is in my heart and I do not want to fail in this life after knowing He blessed me with multiple blessings of love and kindness. The other reason I wrote the note is because I have to proclaim of His goodness and tender mercies each and every day. I am committed to tell of His awesome glory. The third reason is because of His word that lives inside of me. When the word is in you, it is like fire burning on the inside, you cannot keep it to yourself. Then the other, and most important reason, is that I believe that He died and rose from the grave and lives, seated at the right hand of the Father in heaven.

I recently read a book that a great pastor wrote. His book was powerful because He had some extremely eye-opening and factual passages in it. It is good when you know you can relate to someone like him, someone who knows the power of the living God

CHILDREN OF GOD IN THE WORD

John the Baptist was the forerunner for Jesus. He knew what His purpose was in life. When John was faced with the difficulty of confronting Herod and his family, he did not hesitate on speaking about sin. Above all, John the Baptist never stopped speaking of the one who would come to save us from sin even until death. He was the one who would help those in that time to believe in Jesus. Romans 10:9-10 says that *if you confess with your mouth to the Lord Jesus and believe in your heart that God has raised Him from the dead, you will be saved. For with the heart one believes unto righteousness, and with the mouth confession is made unto salvation.*

John's greatest example was that he demonstrated being a light for Jesus. He was the kind of witness for Jesus who would give it all no matter what the cost. I believe John the Baptist is one of those in heaven giving God all the glory and worship. John was truly a witness that did not allow his circumstance with high authority keep him from being a witness for Jesus. He is a light for the Lord. Jesus is the light that saved us from our wretched lives.

Jesus loves us so much that we that believe in Him have to the right to become children of God. The Lord loves when people receive Him. He looks upon those that receive with honor and He knows each by name. So whatever you do in life, remember that the Lord knows it already and He sees all things. Nothing can be hidden from Him. When Herod allowed the young lady to dance for his pleasure and to fulfill her hated request, God knew all about it.

FAITH OVER SILVER AND GOLD

1 Peter 1:6-7: "You have been grieved by various trials, that the genuineness of your faith, being much more precious than gold may be found to praise, honor, and glory."

In early western civilization, the settlers wanted to strike it rich. There was constantly a search for silver and gold. When anyone would find a gold nugget, life changed for that person as he or she dictated it. As I recall growing up, most people that came into contact with a great deal of money changed instantly. Their personalities, demeanor, outlook, mindset, heart, and ways changed a great deal. Please understand it may not happen to everyone, but there is a large percentage—around 90 percent or more—that will or have been affected. Becoming rich is not the problem. All of us who believe in Jesus, having accepted Him as Lord and Savior are already rich.

The problem with being rich with money, silver, and gold is the heart begins to worship it, guard it, bow before it, treasure it, and so forth. It becomes a god. People disregard the God who is above until the money is all gone. This is being written so that faith will be ignited and remain in the Lord. You see your faith has more power than the substance, possession, valuables, and any money, silver, or gold. God is looking for people of faith. You can have your riches, but God is looking for your faith in Him.

In those western days of civilization, those who discovered silver and gold took it to be examined to determine if it is really was silver or gold. Then, if so, the value would be determined through careful examination. God wants us to closely examine our faith just as we get other things that mean so much to us examined. Faith is the power that will get you a breakthrough. You just need to keep the confidence that God placed in you. You need to have an expectant spirit. Don't back down from what you desire God to do for you. *"He supplies all of our needs according to His riches in glory,"* says Philippians 4: 19. God is our provider.

God's people must learn to put faith over silver and gold. Today, gold is processed with high technological machines and placed and monitored by brokers of the stock market and banks. If the bank and the stock market decline or lose shares in the abundance, there is a chance you may lose some of your stock. But with faith, all things are possible. If your faith is stronger than possessions, your blessings will be greater than the silver and gold and what appears to be a loss to you. See your faith has to be at level to reach God. The scripture tells us that it must be to the praise and glory of God. But first it must be genuine faith. God knows the genuineness of our faith.

If your faith has been shaken and is no longer genuine, seek God in prayer to get your faith life back. Get that faith that keeps you in the presence of God. Get that faith that keeps you rich in the Lord. Get the faith that moves mountains and people see it happening through you. Faith over silver and gold is more powerful than possessions.

A NEW RELATIONSHIP

ROMANS 6:1-8: "What shall we say, then? Shall we go on sinning so that grace may increase? By no means! We died to sin; how can we live in it any longer? Or don't you know that all of us who were baptized into Christ Jesus were baptized into his death? We were therefore buried with him through baptism into death in order that, just as Christ was raised from the dead through the glory of the Father, we too may live a new life. If we have been united with him like this in his death, we will certainly also be united with him in his resurrection. For we know that our old self was crucified with him so that the body of sin might be done away with, that we should no longer be slaves to sin—because anyone who has died has been freed from sin. Now if we died with Christ, we believe that we will also live with him."

When I was given the assignment to draw a set of blueprints in college, I was shocked at the level of obedience and discipline required to complete such an assignment. There were some things that I was unfamiliar with that were extremely necessary to accomplish each project. I was not an experienced drawer by any means. My skills were not developed, so I had to learn quickly if I wanted to survive in that particular course. For most assignments you need to take it home to complete it with a fast turnaround. I did not understand the power of design from the inner core of my mind. Now that I think about it, God has so much amazing power in every facet of life—every measurement of life, every imaginable way of life. Truly His design of life is in us as His creation. God, our Father, has the blueprint of creation in His hand and all that is made by Him.

I did not realize that at least four to six scales had to be utilized in the drawing of blueprints. I was tasked to draw blueprints of residential homes and commercial buildings and they were expected to be flawless at the completion of turn in. They were to be utilized for a real construction project. In doing so, the correct scale had to be used with the accurate measurement. There are seven key elements of a blueprint that goes into establishing a blueprint relationship. When formulating a blueprint relationship, there are many things to consider. There are also seven are helps in the process of what goes into the process of becoming God's people and remaining one of His in relationship.

These seven consist of obedience, faith, sacrifice, baptism, unity, worship, resurrection, and teaching. He is my designer no matter what my mind thinks at any given time. I must remember that it was He who made me and not myself. See *Matthew 28:16-22: "Then the eleven disciples went to Galilee, to the mountain where Jesus had told them to go. When they saw him, they worshiped him; but some doubted. Then Jesus came to them and said, 'All authority in heaven and on earth has been given to me. Therefore go and make disciples of all nations, baptizing them in the name of the Father and of the Son and of the Holy Spirit, and teaching them to obey everything I have commanded you. And surely I am with you always, to the very end of the age.'"*

A NEW MAN, MAKE ME OVER

1 CORINTHIANS 2:14-17: "But the natural man does not receive the things of the Spirit of God, for they are foolishness to him; nor can he know them, because they are spiritually discerned. But he who is spiritual judges all things, yet he himself is rightly judged by no one. For 'who has known the mind of the LORD that he may instruct Him?' But we have the mind of Christ.

The natural man is a man who has not received salvation in Christ Jesus. He has no relationship whatsoever with the King of Glory. The natural man has no understanding of the word of God. He fights against the word of God. He has severe hang-ups in his life that keeps him from honoring God. A natural man is not spirit-filled by the Holy Spirit. He does have the potential to have dry places inside that the enemy may enter. He depends on his flesh desires and opinions of others in the flesh. He relies on false wisdom, and those that tell fortunes, and deal with witchcraft and false gods. He is stuck on Himself and has no intentions on getting to know anything about God.

In one respect, the natural man has already been defeated as long as he remains a friend of the enemy. He lives for and thrives on the lies of Satan and does not know it. However, some do know it, but the blindness blocks the reality of deliverance. When the wisdom of God is presented before the natural man, he does not believe because everything that is of wisdom is foolish in his site. He cannot comprehend the mind of Christ, nor the blessings from within the mind of Christ because he is extremely engaged in the secular world.

I am reminded of a young man who plays football. Every day he goes to practice and he believes in the playbook that coach uses to run plays in practice. He never sees the book but believes in the diagram painted by the coach. He runs the plays effectively in practice. However, he gets hit even harder in practice.

A judge may have all the power in his district courtroom or wherever his courtroom may be. But when it comes to judgment of the saints, his rule of judgment has no authority over those who truly love God and are called according to His purpose.

This might be a good time to talk about DNA. God made DNA. Man did not create it. God made the imprint of man. DNA captures each human's inner identity given by God. It identifies a person involved in a crime on many movies. It identifies a person who is responsible for a baby's birth. It knows exactly how to read blood tests and blood cells.

SECRET PLACE OF THE MOST HIGH

PSALM 91:1-8: "He who dwells in the secret place of the Most High shall abide under the shadow of the Almighty. I will say of the LORD, 'He is my refuge and my fortress; my God, in Him I will trust.' Surely He shall deliver you from the snare of the fowler and from the perilous pestilence. He shall cover you with His feathers, and under His wings you shall take refuge; his truth shall be your shield and buckler. You shall not be afraid of the terror by night, nor of the arrow that flies by day, nor of the pestilence that walks in darkness, nor of the destruction that lays waste at noonday. A thousand may fall at your side, and ten thousand at your right hand; but it shall not come near you. Only with your eyes shall you look, and see the reward of the wicked."

Our Father always has us in the palm of His hands. He has a secret place for each of us as well. He already knows what we want in Him. Our God is loving and kind and desires to fill your and my requests. Whatever we need, the Father is there. When we get discouraged we do not have to accept anything. We have a God who looks at us from all types of angles. But more importantly, He is the God of a secret place.

ENTER INTO GOD'S REST

HEBREWS 4:9-11: "There remains therefore a rest for the people of God. For he who has entered His rest has himself also ceased from his works as God did from His. Let us therefore be diligent to enter that rest, lest anyone fail according to the same example of disobedience."

Everyone wants to enter into God's rest. When we think of God's rest, we believe that we will be in a place of peace, serenity, and holiness. We like to think of getting in a place where all of the stress and intense labor is not present. That is correct but it is much more than that. God made it a place of blessings for His people.

The Lord gave us the example of the children of Israel. They were supposed to enter into the Promised Land. In the Promised Land all they could ever want was there. All they had to do was to possess it. The Promised Land was a place to have total freedom in the Lord. They didn't have to worry about all the outsiders who wanted to fight and war. They would have rest. Everything they needed was in the Promised Land. The main problem for not entering in is disobedience and lack of faith.

All believers have the opportunity to enter in the Promised Land that God has made for you. You just have to seek Him and believe what He is speaking to you. God has provided a peace that surpasses all understanding for you in Christ Jesus. He has made available the abundance for you to take it and prosper. You can find it where God is telling you to get it from. You just have to walk in faith and know that God is speaking to you. We need to obey God and have a trusting heart to enter into His rest.

God wants us to enter in. He wants a personal relationship with you and me. You certainly will have rest with a personal relationship. It is time to remove the scales from your eyes and thoughts so you will know Him for yourself. When you spend time in His word, you are in His rest. When you spend time in prayer, you are in His rest. When you commune with the Lord, you have entered in His rest.

I believe that when you get into the word of God, you have entered into that rest with God. The word has everything you need. The word has God's wisdom in it. You cannot go wrong with God's word guiding you. You also have the Holy Spirit guiding you. The best thing for all of God's people is to stay in constant prayer and meditation on His word.

I mentioned once that it was God's word that brought me to Him. All it took was that one day when His word became alive to me. I see it as clearly as I can see anything else. Otherwise, I probably would have been a sideline Christian or backslider. It just took God to show me one amazing glimpse of His glory through His word.

Today, you can have that rest that you always wanted. You can get away from the gangs and violence. Just trust in Jesus, the Son of God. You can have better relationships in your family if you just trust and believe that Jesus is the Son of God and accept Him into your heart. You will have everlasting life. That is the rest you want. You want to know that you are going to heaven to live with our Lord forever. You want that for your entire family like everyone is supposed to. God made it for you and me. Salvation is free. You rest knowing that it's free. It is your day. Do not wait another day because that day could be too late. He just might break the sky and pull all of His saints up to Him. Jesus is Lord of rest.

PRODUCING MORE GOOD FRUIT

MATTHEW 7:16-20: "A good tree cannot bring forth corrupt fruit and a corrupt tree cannot bring forth good fruit."

Most people will know you by the fruit you bare. In many cases you might not even know the fruit you were responsible for producing. Your ministry reflects wherever you go and everyone that is watching you. Don't worry about the fruit looking like you, or acting like you. You may have been a model for that new person in the ministry. You just need to know that this new fruit is for God's purpose. You need to know that God placed all of the fruit in your possession for a very simple reason. It's because He must be glorified continuously. The moment we stop glorifying Him is when self-exaltation and self-glory begin to enter the heart of man. Be careful, man of God. Be careful, saints, to not exalt yourself.

God is in the business of producing more fruit. This time He is producing the unusual and those with new imagination in the Spirit. When my time passes, then it's somebody else's time to make a difference in the ministry. God is no respecter of persons. Even during my time and yours, it's somebody else's time to preach and witness of His unfolding grace and salvation.

The Lord knows our hearts. He knows when we confess in truth. He knows if we want to bear fruit. The Lord knows that your salvation will lead to more fruit. Anyone who has been born again will tell you of their excitement of knowing Jesus—of being born again. They will witness and fruit will be added to His kingdom. When you preach, you are instantly in season because you will draw fruit under the power of the Holy Spirit. You are not doing this alone. It's all about Him. He holds the future in His hands.

God produces fruit by using those who are transformed and dependable. He enables us to help those that are hurting and need deliverance. He also helps us to reach out to those who have been living in the darkness of Satan. Yes, you are correct, God changes people who were once living in darkness and makes them become witnesses of Jesus Christ. He causes them to bare fruit as well. Fruit can come from those who have been hurt, and those that look like they don't have hope in the sight of man. God is able. He will shine His marvelous light upon their hearts and remove anything unclean within. God knows how to clean up and dress up His fruit to produce more good fruit. He knows how to multiply good fruit with good fruit, and keeps on multiplying in His Kingdom.

THE SECOND DEATH

Revelations 21: 5-8: "Then He who sat on the throne said, 'Behold, I make all things new.' And He said to me, 'Write, for these words are true and faithful.' And He said to me, 'It is done! I am the Alpha and the Omega, the Beginning and the End. I will give of the fountain of the water of life freely to him who thirsts. He who overcomes shall inherit all things, and I will be his God and he shall be my son. But the cowardly, unbelieving, abominable, murderers, sexually immoral, sorcerers, idolaters, and all liars shall have their part in the lake which burns with fire and brimstone, which is the second death.'"

Surgery means a lot to those that need some kind of operation on the human anatomy. As I sat and watched a show about a team of surgeons conducting surgery on a woman who had a hidden aneurism. She said many doctors would not conduct the surgery because it was in a place off-limits, meaning that there was no chance of survival with such a brain aneurism. This aneurism was hidden deep in the brain's nervous system. There was only one doctor alive that would attempt this surgery and this lady had to undergo anesthesia. She was in such a deep comatose state that she was not supposed to know anything that happen during the surgery. She was infused with medication. Her brain was shut off from all sources of life biologically. This lady had an out of body experience. She was characterized as having a near death experience. This means that she was in a state of death. Some call death a big sleep. This lady was able to see her surgery take place. Life is precious and people want to live forever, but when you're able to see what happens to you on the death bed, life will take on a new meaning if you have a second chance at life. To all the professional doctors, and surgeons, and those in the field of medicine, it was a chilling experience to hear this lady speak of everything that happened to her. The Bible talks about a second death. It is much more powerful than a near death experience. The second death is a spiritual death that involves permanent torment. This kind of torment will last forever due to the decisions and choices people have made.

They either chose God to serve or the devil and his demons to serve. God wants you to serve Him and allow Him to be your master. No one wants to live in torment at any time. In Revelations 20:14-15, John describes, *"And death and hell were cast into the lake of fire. This is the second death. And whosoever was not found in the book of life was cast into the lake of fire."* God is saying to His people to get their lives in order and make the right choices. It was disobedience and bad choices that allowed sin in the beginning with Adam and Eve. John is saying that at a set time death and hell will be cast into the fire.

Revelations 21:8 reminds us that souls will be cast in there as well if they have not accepted Jesus Christ in their heart. It will be pleasing to God to see lives transformed and added to the kingdom of God and avoid that second death. This is the day that you want your name to be written in the book of life. You must be born again in order for your name to be in the book of life. You must accept Jesus as Lord and

Savior in this lifetime. All you have to do is to say the words in Romans 10:9. This will give you salvation that you will live with God eternally. Repent before asking for forgiveness. No one needs to go to the lake of fire. But all have the opportunity to be with God forever. See 1 Thessalonians 4:16. You want to be one of the saints caught with Jesus when He returns. If you trust in Jesus, you will have the best out of body experience ever because you will be born again and then in the Kingdom of God.

NEW LEVELS AND

A WISE MASTER BUILDER

1 Corinthians 3:5-17: "Who then is Paul, and who is Apollos, but ministers through whom you believed, as the Lord gave to each one? I planted, Apollos watered, but God gave the increase. So then neither he who plants is anything, nor he who waters, but God who gives the increase. Now he who plants and he who waters are one, and each one will receive his own reward according to his own labor. For we are God's fellow workers; you are God's field, you are God's building. According to the grace of God which was given to me, as a wise master builder I have laid the foundation, and another builds on it. But let each one take heed how he builds on it. For no other foundation can anyone lay than that which is laid, which is Jesus Christ. Now if anyone builds on this foundation with gold, silver, precious stones, wood, hay, straw, each one's work will become clear; for the Day will declare it, because it will be revealed by fire; and the fire will test each one's work, of what sort it is. If anyone's work which he has built on it endures, he will receive a reward. If anyone's work is burned, he will suffer loss; but he himself will be saved, yet so as through fire. Do you not know that you are the temple of God and that the Spirit of God dwells in you? If anyone defiles the temple of God, God will destroy him. For the temple of God is holy, which temple you are."

Moving to a new level in life could be a challenge for you, for so many others, and for me. Every time someone moves to a new level, something is required. Before you move to a new level you have to have demonstrated that you have the potential to operate at that next level. It could easily be in a business, moving from assistant manager to general manager. It could be moving from vice–president to senior business partner. You can be a co-radio announcer and move to be the owner of a radio station.

Do you remember starting out as second string player then ending up being the star guard, forward, or center? It could easily be one of those examples. You learned what you had to learn to move to a higher position. You could have been motivated by money or the actual position itself. Nevertheless, you made it to a new level and everyone gave you more respect and you were confident in what you did. Christians want to move to new levels. God is the one who determines that move.

The Apostle Paul wanted to ensure that the church in Corinthians knew that God is the source of all growth and increase. They argued over whom they wanted to follow and who was most effective in the ministry. They missed the entire fact that regardless of how good your preaching, teaching, prophesying, evangelizing, or any function appears, God gets the glory because God is the actual minister of all true ministering.

It was a blessing that the Apostle Paul told these Corinthians, that he planted the seed and Apollos watered the seed. They both had their own season and the ministry they had was by God and not of themselves. The Apostle Paul was a missionary man. He believed in getting the gospel out. Apollos as well and his ministering was to build the faith in the word. In other words, God gives the increase. It you convert because of the preaching of the word, it is because God is at work. Man cannot convert you, but he can demonstrate the faith in his witness for Jesus. The Lord does the converting once you let Him into your heart. God is always at work doing new things.

The Apostle Paul also reminds us that the foundation of the church is Jesus Christ. He is our wise, master builder. He is the foundation of our lives. Any other building and any foundation will not stand long—it will soon be destroyed. We have to have a foundation in Christ Jesus who will never fall and who can't perish. God will be with us forever. God wants us to know that Jesus is the foundation. He also wants us to know that this is about ministry for your brothers and your sisters. This ministering is about building brothers and sisters in Christ Jesus. You see them falling. You help pick them up. There is all kind of spiritual warfare out there. But we have an advocate for us Jesus, the Son of the living God.

The apostle also points out to us that we are the temple of God. Do you not know that you are the temple of God and that the Spirit of God dwells in you? If anyone defiles the temple of God, God will destroy him or her. For the temple of God is holy, which temple you are.

God is looking for those who will stand the test of time. He wants those who will stand the attacks of the enemy. We need to remember that the same God who gave the increase is the same God who will save us.

ROLL BACK THE STONE

MATTHEW 28: 1-8: "Now after the Sabbath, as the first day of the week began to dawn, Mary Magdalene and the other Mary came to see the tomb. And behold, there was a great earthquake, for an angel of the Lord descended from heaven, and came and rolled back the stone from the door, and sat on it. His countenance was like lightning, and his clothing as white as snow. And the guards shook for fear of him, and became like dead men. But the angel answered and said to the women, 'Do not be afraid, for I know that you seek Jesus who was crucified. He is not here; for He is risen, as He said. Come, see the place where the Lord lay. And go quickly and tell His disciples that He is risen from the dead, and indeed He is going before you into Galilee; there you will see Him. Behold, I have told you.' So they went out quickly from the tomb with fear and great joy, and ran to bring His disciples word."

TBN has the world connected to satellites and is witnessing all over the world. They call it the satellite station. Hundreds of preachers come to host and preach the gospel. Singing artists are there, lifting the name of Jesus in song. What is amazing about this is the opportunity to do what God told the disciples to do in Matthew 28—in the great commission—is demonstrated today in so many broadcasting stations. Do you really know the impact of this television show that witnesses around the world? Not only does it send out the message of hope and salvation, it spreads the word of God that lifts people out of many circumstances. I believe more importantly than anything else with the cross is the resurrection of Jesus. People are reminded over and over that Jesus has risen.

Everyone needs to understand the importance of believing that He is risen to be set free in heart, mind, and in spirit. When people are convinced that Jesus has risen from the dead to save all people from their sin is when they believe in deliverance.

Many people have issues in their lives that are like heavy stones. They are heavy stones like the one that was used to close and open the tomb. Thank God that the angel of the Lord descended from heaven and rolled back the stone from the entrance of the tomb.

I want to tell you today that only God could have orchestrated moving such a heavy stone. You have stones in your life that need to be moved by the power of Jesus. He already removed the sin that was entangling you and I each and every day. But for some reason, we need to have Jesus in our lives to remove stones that keep rolling back in place. We need Jesus to remove the stones of hatred, jealousy, disobedience, pride, and lack of love. We need it to have a free spirit to worship Him in the beauty of His Holiness. Jesus desires that we be set free. There is nothing too hard for God to roll back from your life. He rolled back death and Jesus rose from the dead. He lives in heaven and his eyes are on everyone full of love, joy, and power.

CHAPTER 7

GRACE WATCHING OVER YOU

MATTHEW 8:5-13: "*Now when Jesus had entered Capernaum, a centurion came to Him, pleading with Him, saying, 'Lord, my servant is lying at home paralyzed, dreadfully tormented.' And Jesus said to him, 'I will come and heal him.' The centurion answered and said, 'Lord, I am not worthy that you should come under my roof. But only speak a word, and my servant will be healed. For I also am a man under authority, having soldiers under me. And I say to this one, 'Go,' and he goes; and to another, 'Come,' and he comes; and to my servant, 'Do this,' and he does it.' When Jesus heard it, He marveled, and said to those who followed, 'Assuredly, I say to you, I have not found such great faith, not even in Israel! And I say to you that many will come from east and west, and sit down with Abraham, Isaac, and Jacob in the kingdom of heaven. But the sons of the kingdom will be cast out into outer darkness. There will be weeping and gnashing of teeth.' Then Jesus said to the centurion, 'Go your way; and as you have believed, so let it be done for you.' And his servant was healed that same hour.*"

Anytime you find yourself in a position of authority, you are charged to be a watchful servant. Just like any good soldier, you never want the worst-case scenario to happen under your watch. You always want to take the extra effort that will secure the situation at hand. If you are standing guard over an entire city, you will serve with a watchful eye. It means that much to you and the people depending on you. You are so confident that no enemy will penetrate or impede your position to get to the people on your watch. If you are a pastor or bishop, someone in the ministry for the Lord, you are on watch for the Lord and His people.

Just like any strategic general, you want the best outcome for your soldiers. When the devil and his legions of demons attack a saint, every saint should be lifting up holy hands and their voice of prayer and supplication should be going up to the heavens to God. Then it is the Almighty that calls the enemy off. All of us need to know that He is able to stop the enemy in his tracks. We need to know that God is always protecting us. God is always in a watchful position to see His saints. When He returns He is looking for His own people.

Watch for He shall return with the sound of the trumpet and the dead in Christ shall rise. We are waiting for that day when He returns to bring us to Him. It will be fast.

Today is the day to declare that God is the one who watches over us like the good soldier who stands guard. He knows our deepest secrets and our heartfelt pain. He knows who we are by name and who we are in our lifestyles. God knows that the enemy wants to steal your heart and rob you of your right to stand with Him. That is why the Lord is always dispatching angel after angel, even by thousands or more, to protect His people from the dark side of life.

God is able to keep us from falling into the traps and entanglements of the enemy. If you speak to the Lord in prayer, He will acknowledge you. Start placing your trust in the person who loves you more than anyone else. The same God who said that He would never leave you, nor forsake you, is the same God who watches over you day and night. He loves you with an everlasting love. Help your brother and sister to avoid becoming paralyzed. The enemy will do everything possible to paralyze each person he can. I need to tell you that it takes faith to fight it off.

ABUNDANCE IN MANNA

EXODUS 16:35: "The Israelites ate manna forty years, until they came to a land that was settled; they ate manna until they reached the border of Canaan."

Manna was given to the children of Israel In the wilderness that is exactly what happened. God provided fresh manna from heaven to the Israelites. It is typical of God providing blessings in the life of people. Manna poured down from heaven to satisfy the need of the people's hunger. God is always our provider. No matter how bad things look, God always comes through. Our Lord demonstrated to the children of Israel that He was their provider, even when people complained. God demonstrated his power to pour out food from heaven to feed people who felt like God had abandoned them.

Have you ever met anyone that would take the time out to feed you for forty years? The only person is really that personal in a situation like being in the desert is God. God was with them until they came to a land that would suffice the Lord and they could settle there and serve and worship God. What is so significant also in this passage is that God fed them to the borders of Canaan. They were blessed up to this point. God wants us to see that the land of Canaan is also a blessed land hand-picked by God for the children of Israel. God wanted his people to see that this land called Canaan is a land of milk and honey. It is a land that has everything that each person could possibly need or desire.

The land of Canaan was a land that God used for a blessing to His children. All that God requires is obedience and believing in God. The Lord, our God, is pleased with all the murmuring and complaining spirits because God spends his time blessing people—regardless of who you are. I came by today to tell you that God has been feeding you and I all of our lives, and he never fells. God started feeding us when we were in our mother's wombs. He was taking the mother's body and feeding us through her with the best of nourishment. Today, God is still feeding us through his word so that we can make it to his kingdom. He is pouring fresh manna out of heaven at this very moment. It may come by the form of revelation. It may come by the form of his word. He is looking to recruit those who need Him. He will feed them manna that are already in his service. He also feeds those who need to join God's army. God's kingdom is big enough for all to get in and worship Him in spirit and in truth. No matter what things look like in those forty years, remember that God is working it out. He is always on time.

DANIEL KNOWS THE LORD

DANIEL 1:8-16: "But Daniel purposed in his heart that he would not defile himself with the portion of the king's delicacies, nor with the wine which he drank; therefore he requested of the chief of the eunuchs that he might not defile himself. Now God had brought Daniel into the favor and goodwill of the chief of the eunuchs. And the chief of the eunuchs said to Daniel, 'I fear my lord the king, who has appointed your food and drink. For why should he see your faces looking worse than the young men who are your age? Then you would endanger my head before the king.' So Daniel said to the steward whom the chief of the eunuchs had set over Daniel, Hananiah, Mishael, and Azariah, 'Please test your servants for ten days, and let them give us vegetables to eat and water to drink. Then let our appearance be examined before you, and the appearance of the young men who eat the portion of the king's delicacies; and as you see fit, so deal with your servants.' So he consented with them in this matter, and tested them ten days. And at the end of ten days their features appeared better and fatter in flesh than all the young men who ate the portion of the king's delicacies. Thus the steward took away their portion of delicacies and the wine that they were to drink, and gave them vegetables."

Daniel was a stand up man of God with the kind of character that pleased God. He was filled with the Spirit of the Lord and committed to God. He placed all of his trust in the Lord, His God. Daniel made it his priority and focus to be obedient to God. It is important to know that Daniel had favor with God because of these things mentioned. He was not about to turn his back on the only person who had blessed him by watching over him and answering his prayers. What was so significant with Daniel was that he listened to God and moved regardless of what other people would say or think. God has a way of allowing us to know that the rain is symbolic of blessings flowing in our lives. Rain signifies that there will be some fruit that will get watered. There is some fruit that has been stable, stagnant, and burdened because it has not be nourished by essential nutrients.

CHOOSE GOD

DANIEL 3:10-18: *"'You, O king, have made a decree that everyone who hears the sound of the horn, flute, harp, lyre, and psaltery, in symphony with all kinds of music, shall fall down and worship the gold image; and whoever does not fall down and worship shall be cast into the midst of a burning fiery furnace. There are certain Jews whom you have set over the affairs of the province of Babylon: Shadrach, Meshach, and Abed-Nego; these men, O king, have not paid due regard to you. They do not serve your gods or worship the gold image which you have set up.' Then Nebuchadnezzar, in rage and fury, gave the command to bring Shadrach, Meshach, and Abed-Nego. So they brought these men before the king. Nebuchadnezzar spoke, saying to them, 'Is it true, Shadrach, Meshach, and Abed-Nego, that you do not serve my gods or worship the gold image which I have set up? Now if you are ready at the time you hear the sound of the horn, flute, harp, lyre, and psaltery, in symphony with all kinds of music, and you fall down and worship the image which I have made, good! But if you do not worship, you shall be cast immediately into the midst of a burning fiery furnace. And who is the god who will deliver you from my hands?' Shadrach, Meshach, and Abed-Nego answered and said to the king, 'O Nebuchadnezzar, we have no need to answer you in this matter. If that is the case, our God whom we serve is able to deliver us from the burning fiery furnace, and He will deliver us from your hand, O king. But if not, let it be known to you, O king, that we do not serve your gods, nor will we worship the gold image which you have set up.'"*

These three men had a reverent kind of attitude for God. They had a committed passion to stand for God. You might have a fiery furnace situation in your life. But God is on your side. No matter how hard things get with you, believe in right over wrong and continue to stand in Jesus' name. You will come out with the blessings of the Lord. Always remember to bow down and worship only God almighty, the Creator of the universe and all creation. Don't think too much about it. Just follow the example of the Hebrew boys and choose God first in your life.

DANIEL IN PRAYER

Daniel 10:1-9: "In the third year of Cyrus king of Persia a message was revealed to Daniel, whose name was called Belteshazzar. The message was true, but the appointed time was long; and he understood the message, and had understanding of the vision. In those days I, Daniel, was mourning three full weeks. I ate no pleasant food, no meat or wine came into my mouth, nor did I anoint myself at all, till three whole weeks were fulfilled.

"Now on the twenty-fourth day of the first month, as I was by the side of the great river, that is, the Tigris, I lifted my eyes and looked, and behold, a certain man clothed in linen, whose waist was girded with gold of Uphaz! His body was like beryl, his face like the appearance of lightning, his eyes like torches of fire, his arms and feet like burnished bronze in color, and the sound of his words like the voice of a multitude.

"And I, Daniel, alone saw the vision, for the men who were with me did not see the vision; but a great terror fell upon them, so that they fled to hide themselves. Therefore I was left alone when I saw this great vision, and no strength remained in me; for my vigor was turned to frailty in me, and I retained no strength. Yet I heard the sound of his words; and while I heard the sound of his words I was in a deep sleep on my face, with my face to the ground."

A SET HEART AND MADE UP MIND

DANIEL 10:10-20: *"Suddenly, a hand touched me, which made me tremble on my knees and on the palms of my hands. And he said to me, 'O Daniel, man greatly beloved, understand the words that I speak to you, and stand upright, for I have now been sent to you.' While he was speaking this word to me, I stood trembling. Then he said to me, 'Do not fear, Daniel, for from the first day that you set your heart to understand, and to humble yourself before your God, your words were heard; and I have come because of your words. But the prince of the kingdom of Persia withstood me twenty-one days; and behold, Michael, one of the chief princes, came to help me, for I had been left alone there with the kings of Persia. Now I have come to make you understand what will happen to your people in the latter days, for the vision refers to many days yet to come.' When he had spoken such words to me, I turned my face toward the ground and became speechless. And suddenly, one having the likeness of the sons of men touched my lips; then I opened my mouth and spoke, saying to him who stood before me, 'My lord, because of the vision my sorrows have overwhelmed me, and I have retained no strength. For how can this servant of my lord talk with you, my lord? As for me, no strength remains in me now, nor is any breath left in me.' Then again, the one having the likeness of a man touched me and strengthened me. And he said, 'O man greatly beloved, fear not! Peace be to you; be strong, yes, be strong!' So when he spoke to me I was strengthened, and said, 'Let my lord speak, for you have strengthened me.' Then he said, 'Do you know why I have come to you? And now I must return to fight with the prince of Persia; and when I have gone forth, indeed the prince of Greece will come.'"*

Daniel saw a vision and it caused fear inside of his heart. He was not sure of what was actually happening at the moment. Daniel was in such a panicked surprise that he lost his speech, and he felt weak and helpless at that moment. Daniel saw a vision as a result of his prayers unto God. His prayers were answered and the presence of God's angel appeared to him. Your prayers are engaged in good and evil because the battle is constant and we need an advocate every moment of life. No one but God can measure the degree of evil that lurks, but instead of measuring evil, God takes full command and control to denounce and destroy the enemy and its kingdom. We rejoice because of God's kingdom coming on earth as it is in heaven. We have the victory just like Daniel. We just need a relationship and prayer, which changes things.

Daniel's prayer is the key to getting God's attention. It appears that the Lord answers fast to the prayers of the righteous and the hearts of those who are sincere. In the previous verses, Daniel had refused to eat the king's meat and certain foods. Daniel was an honorable man. He made sure that he would stick to God's plan for his life no matter what the circumstance was and who was in a position of authority. Daniel believed in fasting and prayer.

One of the things about prayer and fasting is that it produces fruit, it causes God to hear from you, it amuses God, it destroys the yoke of bondage, it helps that person to let go and let God, it crucifies the flesh, and helps to move in the spirit. Fasting helps the believer to understand that he does not bow before any graven image. Daniel made it clear that he was not bowing before any other God. His God is God and has all power in His hands. Prayer and fasting is the way to get your breakthrough. What pleased God most was the worship to His own God. Nothing was about to shake the foundation of Daniel's belief in God.

Some maybe recorded, seen, and verbalized the witness. If you were lying in your bed and suddenly someone touched you and awakened you from your sleep, what would you do? Certainly a moment of fear would exist.

BREAKING PHARAOH'S EMPIRE

EXODUS 12:12-16: "For I will pass through the land of Egypt on that night, and will strike all the firstborn in the land of Egypt, both man and beast; and against all the gods of Egypt I will execute judgment: I am the LORD. Now the blood shall be a sign for you on the houses where you are. And when I see the blood, I will pass over you; and the plague shall not be on you to destroy you when I strike the land of Egypt. So this day shall be to you a memorial; and you shall keep it as a feast to the LORD throughout your generations. You shall keep it as a feast by an everlasting ordinance. Seven days you shall eat unleavened bread. On the first day you shall remove leaven from your houses. For whoever eats leavened bread from the first day until the seventh day, that person shall be cut off from Israel. On the first day there shall be a holy convocation, and on the seventh day there shall be a holy convocation for you. No manner of work shall be done on them; but that which everyone must eat—that only may be prepared by you."

When God speaks, He speaks clear, loud, precise, but more importantly, He speaks His commands strictly in holiness, in spirit and in truth. He is God and whatever He says will come to pass. He has no respect of persons. His voice is irreplaceable and it will not be mistaken. When God sent Moses to set His people free, He set in motion the freedom from captivity and bondage that the evil one had established in Egypt. Nevertheless, the Lord God would change the course of Pharaoh's empire.

Pharaoh was the full representation of evil on earth during that time period of Israel in bondage. Thousands were under the influence of Pharaoh's slave empire and his armies.

He used his best taskmasters to drive the people in building the temple by stepping on straw and dirt to make mortar. He used his taskmasters to drive them with whips and barely any water. When you have lived in a slave mentality, a captive mentality, conditioned with a slave mind, and robbed of your rights to live, stripped of your humanity, left with no dignity and individual significance, looked upon as a nobody, worth nothing by a force that believes that you are less than dogs and labeled as heathens, it may be then when you understand that you need the one and only true God's intervention. Yes, He is able to do abundantly and above and beyond all that we can imagine.

You must know that there is a God who lives and reigns in the heavens and shows himself on earth to express His will. Throughout all those conditions in Pharaoh's kingdom and Satan's kingdom, you are not beyond repair. In fact, in some cases, the worse it gets sometimes only means that you are just getting set up for blessings that will overflow in your life. You just need to keep the hope of Jesus in your heart. You are not beyond redemption. There is hope that you can move into the direction of blessings flowing in your life.

How do you break Pharaoh's and Satan's empires? You and I cannot do anything without the Lord during battle. The battle is not yours or mine. The battle is the Lord's. He has might, power, and the will to do anything He wants. I believe God was speaking and saying that Satan's spirit was interrupting His holy convocation through Pharaoh. What is convocation? It is time to assemble His people in His presence. It is defined as "one of the two provincial synods of assemblies of the clergy." It also declares the area of assembly. It is a time to give God all worship and praise and recognize individually who He is in your life and as a body. God expresses unity in Israel. It is a time of fellowship with God, set aside by God. It is a specific time for God's people to recognize his covenant. No man is allowed to break it or intervene in it. Surely Pharaoh would have to be broken to realize who God is and who He is to His people kept in bondage under Pharaoh's authority.

God desires to be with His people daily. We all are God's people, those who have accepted Him and He will also accept those outside of His word once they accept Him. God sent Moses to set His people free. Moses went with a simple message, "Let my people go." That is what expressed through Moses, a man of God. So then that was what God expected to happen. However, the Lord God had to allow for Pharaoh's heart to be hardened. This would allow the Lord to work miracles in the sight of His people in Egypt. But nothing could have been plainer than the three acts of God, although God gave more than three acts to reveal Himself.

Moses appeared with a staff and his staff swallowed Pharaoh's serpents. That should have been enough to break Pharaoh. God allowed the water in Pharaoh's empire to be turn into blood, there was no water for days. Pharaoh should have been convinced. God allowed several plagues to happen in the empire of Pharaoh. Pharaoh's heart was still hardened, believing in his false god. God allowed the destroyer to come through the Pharaoh's kingdom. That night was the night to break everything about Pharaoh's hardened heart. The scripture declares that all first borns would be killed that night. "For I will pass through the land of Egypt on that night, and will strike all the firstborn in the land of Egypt, both man and beast; and against all the gods of Egypt I will execute judgment: I am the LORD."

The blood would protect anyone who was covered by the blood. Lamb's blood had to be on the doorpost of the house so that the destroyer would pass those who obeyed God. When God expressed His judgment, then and only then, would the breaking point be revealed in Pharaoh. So then God dealt Pharaoh one last chance. Pharaoh had such a hardened heart, so hard that even after God took his first-born, he still didn't want to be in the will of God. Pharaoh sent his army to chase God's people in the desert. God revealed two more miracles to Pharaoh. He made a whirlwind of fire to block the army from God's people and the Red Sea. Moses held the rod up and the sea open and the people went the other side. Pharaoh's army went into the red sea and God closed the sea on his army. It was finally then when Pharaoh was convinced that God is God. Moses' God is God and there is no other like Him.

Today, after all that you have read and heard, there are people who struggle to shake the enemy off of their hearts. They have hard hearts that are so similar to Pharaoh's. Today is your day to allow the blood of Jesus to cover you. But first accept Him as Lord and Savior, know Him for yourself. You may have gone through all manners of evil in your life and persuaded with the most appealing and elegant speaking. You may have had the most charismatic person in you life to persuade you in the wrong religion, you may have people persuading with a look of the eyes and prideful speaking, but do not be fooled. You stick with the word of God. You start speaking by faith and speak the covering of the blood over life and away from a hardened heart.

"WHEN I SEE THE BLOOD I WILL PASS OVER YOU"

EXODUS 12:17-24: "So you shall observe the feast of unleavened bread, for on this same day I will have brought your armies out of the land of Egypt. Therefore you shall observe this day throughout your generations as an everlasting ordinance. In the first month, on the fourteenth day of the month at evening, you shall eat unleavened bread, until the twenty-first day of the month at evening. For seven days no leaven shall be found in your houses, since whoever eats what is leavened, that same person shall be cut off from the congregation of Israel, whether he is a stranger or a native of the land. You shall eat nothing leavened; in all your dwellings you shall eat unleavened bread. Then Moses called for all the elders of Israel and said to them, 'Pick out and take lambs for yourselves according to your families, and kill the Passover lamb. And you shall take a bunch of hyssop, dip it in the blood that is in the basin, and strike the lintel and the two doorposts with the blood that is in the basin. And none of you shall go out of the door of his house until morning. For the LORD will pass through to strike the Egyptians; and when He sees the blood on the lintel and on the two doorposts, the LORD will pass over the door and not allow the destroyer to come into your houses to strike you. And you shall observe this thing as an ordinance for you and your sons forever.'"

Can you imagine what things would have been like if the death angel would not have passed over? Egypt may have continued to be the same as far as people remaining in slavery and a broken mentality. They would have had scars all over. People could have remained content for many reasons. The blood was absolutely necessary. The instructions were to put the blood on the lintel and two doorposts. God already knew who was going to protect. The Spirit was visiting the iniquity of Egyptians to ensure that Pharaoh understood the clear instruction to let God's people go. Let God's people go!

He was showing his mercy and power to those who believed and those who did not believe. God protected his people that loved him. He was clearly sending a message to make people understand that His blood covers us against all enemies. Every man, woman and child, you want the blood on your life. You want your doorpost anointed by the power of God. When he devil comes by your host, he will have to flee. There is power in the blood of Jesus. His blood washed me whiter than snow. There is nothing but the blood of Jesus.

LIFE FIXED IN JESUS CHRIST

LUKE 16: 19-31: "There was a certain rich man who was clothed in purple and fine linen and fared sumptuously every day. But there was a certain beggar named Lazarus, full of sores, who was laid at his gate, desiring to be fed with the crumbs, which fell from the rich man's table. Moreover the dogs came and licked his sores. So it was that the beggar died, and was carried by the angels to Abraham's bosom. The rich man also died and was buried. And being in torments in Hades, he lifted up his eyes and saw Abraham afar off, and Lazarus in his bosom.

"Then he cried and said, 'Father Abraham, have mercy on me, and send Lazarus that he may dip the tip of his finger in water and cool my tongue; for I am tormented in this flame.' But Abraham said, 'Son, remember that in your lifetime you received your good things, and likewise Lazarus evil things; but now he is comforted and you are tormented. And besides all this, between us and you there is a great gulf fixed, so that those who want to pass from here to you cannot, nor can those from there pass to us.'

"Then he said, 'I beg you therefore, father, that you would send him to my father's house, for I have five brothers, that he may testify to them, lest they also come to this place of torment.' Abraham said to him, 'They have Moses and the prophets; let them hear them.' And he said, 'No, father Abraham; but if one goes to them from the dead, they will repent.' But he said to him, 'If they do not hear Moses and the prophets, neither will they be persuaded though one rise from the dead.'"

God has the power to bless those that are righteous toward His name. He has the order of things already in place. No matter how hard we try to fix things, God has everything in order. In Ephesians, He calls us predestined, meaning predetermined by God. At the same time, in His own infinite wisdom, He allows people—regardless of who they are—

to make a decision between Him and evil. He wants us to understand that by choosing Him, you gain all inheritance. You become rich with the abundance of life overflowing in you. If you choose otherwise, you have nothing but hell to look forward to.

God ensures that His glory is His and no one else's. You can live a rich life on earth and be happy as long as you have Jesus in your life. You'll be rich and honor God. We never have to worry about the resources in your possession as long as God is first in your life and not your treasures and possessions. If a person is rich, it is not sin. God strictly warrants it in His word. See Ephesians 1,2, and 3. The problem with riches is that for some people, money takes root at the heart and defiles them, read Timothy 6:10. God must be the root of our hearts. If we allow substance to take root at the heart, we will fall every time.

We need to be wise in spending and handling money and possessions. We must not allow money or any possession become the ruler of our lives. We must trust God that the Holy Spirit will lead us into His righteousness. Ask the Holy Spirit to fight off addiction's power that penetrates our hearts. If you have a need for anything, someone should be able to provide for that need. If you see a beggar, stop and fulfill the need. Who knows it just might be an angel from testing you. God knows we do not want to have the crumb experience like the rich man and do the exact same thing that he did.

As a child of God, we do not stand by and let a person suffer while we live the good life. Give until it hurts; give to others until you know you are satisfied. Don't allow hell to get you because you failed to obey God. Tell your family today and all of your friends that you will give in abundance, not in crumbs. You will make it count in Jesus' name. Our lives were not designed to be in a place of torment and everlasting hell just because we disobeyed God with a wicked heart. Remember to tell your brothers and sisters about the salvation that Jesus offers. Accept Jesus Christ as Lord.

I was on the phone with my brother when he was sick and God led me to talk about salvation to him. We were hundreds of miles away, but he still accepted the Lord as savior. Leading someone to salvation could be the crumb that God sent with you.

JOB'S LIFE BLESSING

Job: Thou He slay me, yet will I praise you.

He lost his entire family and never refused his faith and love of God. He never turned his back on God. He was a righteous man who walked upright and feared God. It is clear to me that even though Job was a righteous man in God's sight, he still was human and subject to the same or similar affects those other righteous men of God experience. "We walk by faith and not by sight." He kept on the path of righteousness because he kept his sights focused on Him.

Job blessed us by the Spirit of God with his behavior and sustaining power with God. Have you ever known anyone to adapt an attitude like Job's even after he lost his family? Job demonstrates faith that so many people struggle with, yet they can also have it. If you trust in the Lord at that degree of trust, surely God will smile on you and bless you like He blessed Job.

In Job's story, it is very clear that the enemy cannot wait to destroy entire families. It is clear that the devil is attacking God's people out in the open. The enemy acts as though he does not fear anything. That is exactly why you need the word of God. You need to speak the word over your house, your temple, your children's lives, and speak the word over yourself also. You need to be encouraged daily that Jesus is your Lord.

One of the most popular statements made in scripture and in the book of Job is, "Thou He slay me, yet will I praise Him." The meaning is to trust in Jesus no matter what happens in life. God will always be God and there is no changing Him. He is eternal and there is no one like Him in all the earth and creation. When I think of Job making such a statement, I think of how he saw things in life. Job has proven that spiritual scales do fall from your eyes. Job proved it by believing in God to deliver Him through the storm. God blessed Job with more than he had in the beginning. God gave him more children, more animals, and more possessions than he had before the enemy sought to destroy him.

It is important to understand what is exceptionally important here and that is God is in control of our lives. He has His hand upon us and can remove it at any time according to His purpose. We need our heavenly Father to send His angels to monitor our lives. We need the Holy Spirit to guide our lives into service for the Lord.

Today is the best day of your life. You get the opportunity through your rough and crazy situation to say to God, "Thou He slay me, yet will I praise Him." You and I can have blessings like God blessed Job. When things seem so difficult and it appears like you will not recover from the heartache and pain, trust Him completely. God never gives up on you and I because of His love for us.

A NEW VISION

GENESIS 45:3- 13: "Then Joseph said to his brothers, 'I am Joseph; does my father still live?' But his brothers could not answer him, for they were dismayed in his presence. And Joseph said to his brothers, 'Please come near to me.' So they came near. Then he said: 'I am Joseph your brother, whom you sold into Egypt. But now, do not therefore be grieved or angry with yourselves because you sold me here; for God sent me before you to preserve life. For these two years the famine has been in the land, and there are still five years in which there will be neither plowing nor harvesting. And God sent me before you to preserve posterity for you in the earth, and to save your lives by a great deliverance. So now it was not you who sent me here, but God;

and He has made me a father to Pharaoh, and lord of all his house, and a ruler throughout all the land of Egypt. Hurry and go up to my father, and say to him, 'Thus says your son Joseph: 'God has made me lord of all Egypt; come down to me, do not tarry. You shall dwell in the land of Goshen, and you shall be near to me, you and your children, your children's children, your flocks and your herds, and all that you have. There I will provide for you, lest you and your household, and all that you have, come to poverty; for there are still five years of famine.' And behold, your eyes and the eyes of my brother Benjamin see that it is my mouth that speaks to you. So you shall tell my father of all my glory in Egypt, and of all that you have seen; and you shall hurry and bring my father down here.'"

A vision is a picture in the mind of men that speaks out to the action and steps out in faith. A vision allows you to see the future success down the road. God reveals visions and dreams. He reveals a great deal of what He expects and already has purposed for your life. What is your vision? Today is your day to start formulating a vision. You can do it. Sit down start writing your dream, mission, desires, goals, and purpose in life. Ask God for what it is that He is revealing to you. Ask Him to help you understand it. God can give you one of these or all of these to help you to develop your vision. God is the answer for you and I to have a successful vision. Is your vision a new ministry? Is it to be a movie star? Is your dream to be an R&B music artist or country artist? Is your desire to be an athlete? You can be a doctor, lawyer, priest, judge, fireman, or any specialty you desire to be.

It is important that you start seeing yourself in the very moment of that dream. Do you remember Joseph? Joseph was the son of Jacob who had twelve sons. Joseph was betrayed by his brothers, cast into prison, and taunted by Pharaoh's wife to have a sexual relationship. Prior to having all the troubles in life, Joseph had a dream that his brothers and family members would bow before him. He had a dream that He would be in a high position. He became the second highest in command of Egypt. It was a dream and it was the favor of God.

It is time for you to get your vision and start putting it into action. We all have to get a jump-start. Look to the Lord and get your jump-start on to begin the new business operations. God has blessings waiting for you. Look to the one who created all things and will never fail. Joseph blessed his family once God set him free from bondage. We can all take a lesson from Joseph. He listened to God. He knew God and never turned his back on the Lord. Joseph walked in favor knowing that God would surely give him favor for the sake of his family. When you have a vision, you do not have to impress anyone. You do not have to prove anything to anyone. But because of the visions and favor in Joseph's life, his brother had to witness by sight that God had preserved their brother and blessed him just like he said God would. I thank God for the attitude of Joseph. What an example to his blood brothers and all that were around him. His kissed his brother to bless them and express the remarkable glory and forgiving power of the living God. Vision can take you to somewhere to bless you.

LORD, BLESS ME

Genesis 48:10-22: "Now the eyes of Israel were dim with age, so that he could not see. Then Joseph brought them near him, and he kissed them and embraced them. And Israel said to Joseph, 'I had not thought to see your face; but in fact, God has also shown me your offspring!' So Joseph brought them from beside his knees, and he bowed down with his face to the earth. And Joseph took them both, Ephraim with his right hand toward Israel's left hand, and Manasseh with his left hand toward Israel's right hand, and brought them near him. Then Israel stretched out his right hand and laid it on Ephraim's head, who was the younger, and his left hand on Manasseh's head, guiding his hands knowingly, for Manasseh was the firstborn.

"And he blessed Joseph, and said: "God, before whom my fathers Abraham and Isaac walked, the God who has fed me all my life long to this day, the Angel who has redeemed me from all evil, bless the lads; let my name be named upon them, and the name of my fathers Abraham and Isaac; and let them grow into a multitude in the midst of the earth.

"Now when Joseph saw that his father laid his right hand on the head of Ephraim, it displeased him; so he took hold of his father's hand to remove it from Ephraim's head to Manasseh's head. And Joseph said to his father, 'Not so, my father, for this one is the firstborn; put your right hand on his head.' But his father refused and said, 'I know, my son, I know. He also shall become a people, and he also shall be great; but truly his younger brother shall be greater than he, and his descendants shall become a multitude of nations.' So he blessed them that day, saying, "By you Israel will bless, saying, 'May God make you as Ephraim and as Manasseh!' And thus he set Ephraim before Manasseh. Then Israel said to Joseph, 'Behold, I am dying, but God will be with you and bring you back to the land of your fathers. Moreover I have given to you one portion above your brothers, which I took from the hand of the Amorite with my sword and my bow.'

"So then Jacob blessed Ephraim before Manasseh as he crossed his arms and hands to place the right hand on Ephraim."

Our God will bless whomever He will bless. He uses whomever He will use to carry on blessings throughout generations. At the same time, He is there to ensure the blessings are carried out in the lives of His people. Jacob loved Joseph and He had favor all in his life. Joseph proved to be the one that Jacob believed God had smiled upon. He already knew it because God revealed it to him. There are some people in your house that God has already revealed that have favor and blessings and will make an impact.

It was a tradition that the older son received the blessing. But God made it His choice when He choose the younger of boys. He seemed to have done it often. He chose David over all of his brothers. Joseph was chosen over all of his brothers. It is not that God looks over the elder brothers; it's just that His choice is the younger and He sees the heart of each person.

SOLOMON DEDICATES THE TEMPLE

2 Chronicles 7:1- 6: "When Solomon had finished praying, fire came down from heaven and consumed the burnt offering and the sacrifices; and the glory of the LORD filled the temple. And the priests could not enter the house of the LORD, because the glory of the LORD had filled the LORD'S house. When all the children of Israel saw how the fire came down, and the glory of the LORD on the temple, they bowed their faces to the ground on the pavement, and worshiped and praised the LORD, saying: 'For He is good, for His mercy endures forever.'

"When the king and all the people offered sacrifices before the LORD. King Solomon offered a sacrifice of twenty-two thousand bulls and one hundred and twenty thousand sheep. So the king and all the people dedicated the house of God. And the priests attended to their services; the Levites also with instruments of the music of the LORD, which King David had made to praise the LORD, saying, 'For His mercy endures forever,' whenever David offered praise by their ministry."

When Solomon had completed his prayer as part of the dedication, he recognized that God had the power to bless it and make this temple a holy place for Him to dwell in. This fire that God sent is symbolic of continuous fires burning under the altar of burnt offerings. God was pleased with the temple so he sent fire as a representation of his spirit to bless it. The fire represents the presence of God in the temple. Dedication means to set apart something for a particular purpose. Solomon had this temple constructed to dedicate it to God for the purpose of worship.

This dedication also reminds God's people to have a worshipping heart for God. God also wants His people to dedicate themselves to Him. It is time for God's people to experience the glory of the Lord in the temple. God's presence is available for all of those who need Him. We must come reverently with a humble spirit and an attitude of true worship if we want to experience the glory of God in your church and your life. When we experience the glory of the Lord, we need to bow our faces to the ground and exalt His name. Christians need a worship experience where God will consume them with blessings because His glory showed up in the temple. Once God's glory fills the temple get ready for a release of the anointing and His glory revealed in your life. God has a hold on everything including the temple that Solomon preached God's word in.

MY STRONG TOWER

Proverbs 18:10: "The name of the LORD is a strong tower; The righteous run to it and are safe."

Buildings that we live in and those that surround us are man-made and we appreciate them and the comfort of life. Our families are happy and glad that we have shelter in the midst of storms. One thing for sure is that we look at our homes as strong buildings with strong walls that somehow will protect us from all the ugly stuff outside. Our homes are nice and they are part of God's blessings. Our temples and church buildings that we go to for worship are temporal on earth. God made them for us to worship Him. But the truth of the matter is that God is our strong tower. We need the Father to be our strong tower. We need Jesus to guard us against multiple attacks that are on every front. Some we cannot see and some you see coming directly at you. Nothing else on earth can be our strong tower. It is Jesus alone who sits on the throne and blesses us continuously.

One of the most horrific and sad stories in the Bible was the story of Nimrod. Nimrod thought that he was the king above all the earth. He had convinced people that he was in control to an extent that the culture had brain-washed people with power and control. He thought that if he built a tower to the heavens that would make him some type of God who would be exalted. God had to reveal Himself to this man to make him aware that there is nothing he could do to outdo God. He could do nothing to take God's glory.

CHAPTER 8

JESUS' PRAYER HOLD ON ME

JOHN 17:6-10: "I have manifested your name to the men whom you have given me out of the world. They were yours, you gave them to me, and they have kept your word. Now they have known that all things, which you have given me, are from you. For I have given to them the words which you have given me; and they have received them, and have known surely that I came forth from you; and they have believed that you sent me.

"I pray for them. I do not pray for the world but for those whom you have given me, for they are yours. And all mine are yours, and yours are mine, and I am glorified in them."

One thing for sure is that when Jesus prayed for me, all things were answered and blessings came in abundance. His prayers are more than the rain pouring down. His prayers are answered immediately because He is the Son of God. At the same time, He answers prayers according to His will. Jesus prayed for me and I was healed, delivered, and came to Him with an open heart filled with worship and praise.

When Jesus identified His disciples and presented to His Father that these men were His and they believed in Him, He prayed that they would be protected and strengthened in the will of the Father. Everyone called into the fivefold ministry or any ministry of Jesus and all believers should be assured that He prays for us.

BIND AND LOOSE IT

MATTHEW 18:18: "Assuredly, I say to you, whatever you bind on earth will be bound in heaven, and whatever you loose on earth will be loosed in heaven."

People speak their way out of almost anything when it comes to being disrespected, cheated, or put down. Most people who have a high self-esteem hardly ever let anyone get away with making them feel less than a person, or less important. They speak up and usually tell someone off with a piece of their mind. It is your time to start binding those thoughts that have kept you in bondage by using your faith in God. Bind those issues that target your family and try to destroy them. It is time to move on with your life. Jesus is saying bind it now! There is a tremendous amount of binding with our personal lives. Clean up the house now by binding the enemy and kicking him out of your life. The inner man needs to be free.

What is it that needs to be bound in your life? Take the mirror and see the reflection. See yourself like Jesus wants you to be. He only wants the best for all of us. That means it is time to get rid of pride and flesh and over emotional reactions and attitudes that hinder you day in and out. God wants us to bind those addictions and sin in our lives.

DENY YOURSELF

MATTHEW 16:24-27: "Then Jesus said to His disciples, 'If anyone desires to come after Me, let him deny himself, and take up his cross, and follow me. For whoever desires to save his life will lose it, but whoever loses his life for my sake will find it. For what profit is it to a man if he gains the whole world, and loses his own soul? Or what will a man give in exchange for his soul? For the Son of Man will come in the glory of His Father with His angels, and then He will reward each according to his works.'"

Have you ever been given an invitation to do something or be somewhere, like a wedding or ball? Deny yourself and follow Jesus. What is denying yourself? It means to give up yourself—crucify the flesh. Count on God for everything. The Holy Spirit will carry you over. He will not deny you. Jesus offered his disciples perhaps the biggest invitation of their lifetime. If you desire to come after him, pick up your cross and follow him. This signifies that your desire for the Lord is a true and genuine one in so many ways. First of all, you are giving up something valuable. You are giving your time and resources back to the Lord.

Jesus teaches us not to be concerned with making a profit. Rather be concerned with giving your life up for him. Those that give their life to Christ for the mission, those are the people he is looking to save and bring home to him. Jesus tells us that we find our life in Him when we give up things for him. It might look bleak or bad to you when you are doing something for the Lord. But hold onto what you are doing to glorify Him. You will find yourself picking up your cross and following him.

Jesus reminds us of that man who has worked so diligently all of his life to gain the world, to impress the world, and be something that people approve of today and deny tomorrow. He wants us to know that if we had all the riches and the most popular and well-known names, it will not profit anything in Jesus' eyes. If it is not for God or of God, it is of Satan. We cannot compromise to appease someone. This is about winning Jesus over. It is about not losing your soul to anything or any person. Jesus wants your soul saved, not lost. We should deny ourselves daily to find a way to please God. Win a soul today by telling them what Jesus did for you. Let them know that he came to your house and changed you because you let him into your heart. Tell them that Jesus is the one behind your faith. It was my faith that helped me to be pushed to Jesus Christ. Are you willing to give yourself to Christ today? Don't ever give yourself to Satan.

Jesus is coming back to reward those who serve him. He will be looking for those who have decided to save souls. He will be looking for those who have decided to live with him forever. He will be looking for the true worshipers—those that worship Him in spirit and truth. Be one of Jesus' disciples today and follow Him. Your life will never be the same.

FIGHTING STRONG

JUDGES 7:4-8: "But the LORD said to Gideon, 'The people are still too many; bring them down to the water, and I will test them for you there. Then it will be, that of whom I say to you, 'This one shall go with you,' the same shall go with you; and of whomever I say to you, 'This one shall not go with you,' the same shall not go.' So he brought the people down to the water. And the LORD said to Gideon, 'Everyone who laps from the water with his tongue, as a dog laps, you shall set apart by himself; likewise everyone who gets down on his knees to drink.' And the number of those who lapped, putting their hand to their mouth, was three hundred men; but all the rest of the people got down on their knees to drink water. Then the LORD said to Gideon, 'By the three hundred men who lapped I will save you, and deliver the Midianites into your hand. Let all the other people go, every man to his place.'

"So the people took provisions and their trumpets in their hands. And he sent away all the rest of Israel, every man to his tent, and retained those three hundred men. Now the camp of Midian was below him in the valley."

An all too familiar statement in the morning newspaper is that Kabul, Afghanistan, or Central Iraq are both in need of more soldiers to assist in accomplishing the mission. The paper always says something like this: the top U.S. officer said that the Pentagon could send more troops by doubling the size by next summer with more than 60,000 troops. It always ends with this could be the largest estimate of potential reinforcement ever.

It is one of those things that soldiers know could happen at anytime. Soldiers train to be ready for the call of duty, but there is always a fear factor. Family members and spouses all know the very real cost of war. War cost lives and people need a saving grace, someone to hold on to in times of this troubled world of wars. So yes, the idea of deployments are more realistic and threatening to everyone now more than ever before. But there is a God who holds the future of hope. In hoping for the best, we need prayer in our lives.

What Soldiers need now more than ever before is to adapt to a prayer lifestyle. Soldiers and their families need to change their lives into being prayer warriors. Pray to the Lord in Heaven, make your request known. He will deliver according to His will and purpose for you. Soldiers and their families need to believe in the power of prayer. It is prayer that will hold things together. Prayer will save the soul. Prayer will deliver and help your spirit. Prayer will lift you up every time if you trust in Jesus. You need prayer to call on Jesus to send your guardian angels. Pray for protection like in Psalms 91:11. God said, *"I will give my angels charge over you, to keep you in all your ways."* What a blessing to know that God will do this holy thing for you and me.

Pray to protect our troops from tragedy and defeat. All of the saints should be praying to protect the 30,000 in Iraq and the 60,000 soldiers that are deployed to Afghanistan. Pray for peace and protection and the families affected by this deployment. Pray that the power of love reaches out in the midst of war. God will surprise you with the things He alone can do.

During this time of war, every soldier needs to pray for a deeper more intimate relationship with our Father in Heaven. Pray for salvation. Pray for deliverance from any troubles, bondage or addictions. Pray for what you need Jesus to answer in your life. If you want a relationship, accept Jesus as Lord and Savior in your life. Just say, Lord Jesus, forgive me of my sin, I repent of my sin! I believe that you are the Son of God. I believe that you died on the cross and were raised from the grave on the third day for the remission of my sin. You have just confessed to the Lord, read Romans 10:9. Now you are saved. You are a new creature in Christ Jesus. The old person has gone. Start reading your Holy Bible daily and trust Jesus. His Holy Spirit will guide you all the days of your life.

Remember, we need 30,000 prayers now and 60,000 prayers a day for our troops, our hero of peace in Afghanistan, Iraq, and all nations. In Matthew 6: 9-13, Jesus said in prayer as He taught the disciples, "Our Father in heaven, hallowed be your name. Your kingdom come. Your will be done on Earth as it is in Heaven. Give us this day our daily bread. And forgive us our debts, as we forgive our debtors, and lead us not into temptation, but deliver us from the evil one. For yours is the kingdom and the power and the glory forever. Amen.

Always acknowledge Him. He will acknowledge you with blessings in your life. Jesus is Lord. Start using this model prayer because it will speak directly to the Father. Then make requests to God for our troops.

REMOVE THE BEAM FROM YOUR OWN EYE

MATTHEW 7:1-5: "Judge not, that ye be not judged. For with what judgment ye judge, ye shall be judged: and with what measure ye mete, it shall be measured to you again. And why beholdest thou the mote that is in thy brother's eye, but considerest not the beam that is in thine own eye? Or how wilt thou say to thy brother, Let me pull out the mote out of thine eye; and, behold, a beam is in thine own eye? Thou hypocrite, first cast out the beam out of thine own eye; and then shalt thou see clearly to cast out the mote out of thy brother's eye."

God is the only true judge. No other judgment matters. Human judgment will not pave the way to heaven. Jesus simply wants us to examine ourselves before we can help someone else. Too often people cast their judgments on others when their own lives are not repaired or restored. We get restoration from the Lord, Jesus Christ. One point of the passage is that we all need it in some form or fashion. Nevertheless, if we stop casting judgment and concentrate on fixing our own lives by walking in the spirit, walking in faith, and exercising Godly love, we will not be overcome by this issue. Judgment is primarily God's lane of responsibility.

Yes, the Bible is clear about how we will judge angels, however, how can you judge angels while you're really missing the opportunity to correct yourself with issues that the enemy keeps putting in your life. God knows that the righteous will be able to judge because of their obedience in Jesus Christ. These are the people that really belong to God, no question about it. Nevertheless, we all need to remove the beam from our eye. It is something in life that is blocking your spirit walk and vision. Jesus wants you and I to have blessed favor and let nothing, especially demons and ourselves, hold us back. When God gets a hold on you, you will be changed. You might fight against God, but his hold is stronger than the strongest man on earth. God's hold will force you to surrender to him completely.

You see God's hold when it comes to judgment is chance after chance until you get to the final judgment. I want to solicit every man and woman, husband and wife, child and grandchild, to turn their lives over to Jesus and let go of all the judgment against God, Christianity, Christians, and the Church. God wants you to be on his soul winning team.

DON'T LOSE YOUR SOUL

MATTHEW 16:26: "For what profit is it to a man if he gains the whole world, and loses his own soul? Or what will a man give in exchange for his soul?"

We live in a world where everything revolves around profits. Financial gain is the target reason for businesses to exist. You can increase earnings in so many strategies. It can be made in every ministry, every business, and in all kinds of stores in the market place. What makes a man work so hard to get that profit of money and substance is his desire to be ahead in life and gain recognition. It does not have to be that way. Don't lose your soul to gain the whole world. Jesus' disciples made a conscious decision that they were going to follow Jesus. They did follow Him and wrote the Bible to reflect His words with power and authority.

There are many people that give up free salvation because they have fallen and now give their lives to the enemy to use them as a playground. Do not lose your soul to anything, nor anybody. Accept Jesus as Lord in your life today.

Matthew 17:1-9: "Now after six days Jesus took Peter, James, and John his brother, led them up on a high mountain by themselves; and He was transfigured before them. His face shone like the sun, and His clothes became as white as the light. And behold, Moses and Elijah appeared to them, talking with Him. Then Peter answered and said to Jesus, 'Lord, it is good for us to be here; if you wish, let us make here three tabernacles: one for you, one for Moses, and one for Elijah.' While he was still speaking, behold, a bright cloud overshadowed them; and suddenly a voice came out of the cloud, saying, 'This is my beloved Son, in whom I am well pleased. Hear Him!' And when the disciples heard it, they fell on their faces and were greatly afraid. But Jesus came and touched them and said, 'Arise, and do not be afraid.' When they had lifted up their eyes, they saw no one but Jesus only.

Now as they came down from the mountain, Jesus commanded them, saying, 'Tell the vision to no one until the Son of Man is risen from the dead.'"

Jesus allowed Peter and James to see Him in the transfigured state of being. They needed to see His glory revealed.

FULL OF EYES AROUND AND WITHIN

Revelations 4:6-8: "Also before the throne there was what looked like a sea of glass, clear as crystal. In the center, around the throne, were four living creatures, and they were eyes, in front and in back. The first living creature was like a lion, the second was like an ox, the third had a face like a man, and the fourth was like a flying eagle. Each of the four living creatures had six wings and was covered with eyes all around, even under his wings. Day and night they never stop saying: 'Holy, holy, holy is the Lord God Almighty, who was, and is, and is to come.'"

God lives in us and He sits on the throne in heaven that is designed specifically for Him alone. Glory and honor and thanksgiving be unto His Righteous name. Glory and honor is given to our Lord who reigns forever and ever. He alone perfects and purifies all things to His pleasure and glory. He alone is God and there is no other. We praise Him with alleluia to the lamb slain—he who took away the sins of the world. He is worthy of all honor, and praise, and thanksgiving. Eyes from heaven are constantly looking down at His creation.

YOU ARE WORTHY O'LORD

Revelations 4: 10-12: "The twenty-four elders fall down before Him who sits on the throne and worship Him who lives forever and ever, and cast their crowns before the throne, saying: 'You are worthy, O Lord, to receive glory and honor and power; For You created all things, and by Your will they exist and were created.'"

When people come into the reality of knowing that God is all powerful and full of blessings, that He alone grants us blessings daily and moment by moment, it is then when they come to the understanding and desire to bow down and worship Him as they worship Him in heaven. "The twenty four elders fall down before Him. They cast their crown before the throne, saying you are worthy O Lord, to receive glory and honor and power." They recognized that he had created all things, including that moment to glorify Him and cast their crowns to give complete submission, worship, reverence, and exaltation. God deserves the praise that no one can take away. You deserve the praise because you are God and the one who holds my soul in your hands. Worship to you O Lord! You are magnified forever and ever through eternity.

There was hard thundering and lighting today as I slept through the night. My wife had awakened me so that I could get up, be the man, and go and check things out in the house. I checked every corner and every room in the house to ensure that nothing was leaking and that nothing was struck by lightning. For a split second in time, I had a thought of the awesome power of God to control the thundering and lightning, and even the heavy down pour. It reminded me of the fact that nothing is impossible for Him.

Nothing controls Him, He controls all things. He is God. He stops the thundering and lightning as He sees fit. He stops the downpour as He sees fit. I thought about how I have a roof over my head and a bed to sleep in and not get wet and be hungry. He did not have to provide for me. I thought about life's lessons learned and how Jesus keeps on revealing His mercy and grace. So then as I read the scripture and thought on those things, I started seeing the clear understanding of worship to God, the Father. I started seeing in my mind and heart that God is worthy of glory, honor, power, praise, and thanksgiving.

THE INFINITE GOD OF INHERITANCE

Hebrews 1:1-4: "God, who at various times and in various ways spoke in time past to the fathers by the prophets, has in these last days spoken to us by His Son, whom He has appointed heir of all things, through whom also He made the worlds; who being the brightness of His glory and the express image of His person, and upholding all things by the word of His power, when He had by Himself purged our sins, sat down at the right hand of the Majesty on high, having become so much better than the angels, as He has by inheritance obtained a more excellent name than they."

Jesus is revealed as the agent of God's revelation. He is far greater and superior than old testament old prophets. In Jesus Christ the message is complete. In verse 3, Jesus in his personal character, position and power are expressed. Jesus is being expressed as the brightness of God's glory. Jesus was already divine and deity. He never tried to boast or brag. He was equal with the Father.

NEW COVENANT

Hebrews 8:1-13: "Now this is the main point of the things we are saying: We have such a High Priest, who is seated at the right hand of the throne of the Majesty in the heavens, a Minister of the sanctuary and of the true tabernacle which the Lord ereced, and not man.

"For every high priest is appointed to offer both gifts and sacrifices. Therefore it is necessary that this One also have something to offer. For if He were on earth, He would not be a priest, since there are priests who offer the gifts according to the law; who serve the copy and shadow of the heavenly things, as Moses was divinely instructed when he was about to make the tabernacle. For He said, 'See that you make all things according to the pattern shown you on the mountain.' But now He has obtained a more excellent ministry, inasmuch as He is

also Mediator of a better covenant, which was established on better promises."

PROGRESS IN GOD'S WILL

Hebrews 6:1-8: "Therefore, leaving the discussion of the elementary principles of Christ, let us go on to perfection, not laying again the foundation of repentance from dead works and of faith toward God, of the doctrine of baptisms, of laying on of hands, of resurrection of the dead, and of eternal judgment. And this we will[do if God permits. For it is impossible for those who were once enlightened, and have tasted the heavenly gift, and have become partakers of the Holy Spirit, and have tasted the good word of God and the powers of the age to come, if they fall away,[to renew them again to repentance, since they crucify again for themselves the Son of God, and put Him to an open shame. For the earth, which drinks in the rain that often comes upon it, and bears herbs useful for those by whom it is cultivated, receives blessing from God; but if it bears thorns and briers, it is rejected and near to being cursed, whose end is to be burned."

Your life can progress in Christ Jesus. Once you have tasted of His heavenly call and know of His loving kindness and salvation, He will always be with you. So then you have no reason to fall away. Other people are not a reason to fall away. It is the devil's excuse. He always interrupts lives to use that old excuse. You are a warrior of the living God. The word is abiding in you now. You use the word each and every day of your life. You are a walking epistle, a living testimony unto God for His people. Your life will progress in Christ Jesus for He holds the mystery of His perfect will.

CARRY ME OVER

Hebrews 8:7-13: "For if that first covenant had been faultless, then no place would have been sought for a second. Because finding fault with them, He says: 'Behold, the days are coming, says the LORD, when I will make a new covenant with the house of Israel and with the house of Judah—not according to the covenant that I made with their fathers in the day when I took them by the hand to lead them out of the land of Egypt; because they did not continue in My covenant, and I disregarded them, says the LORD. For this is the covenant that I will make with the house of Israel after those days, says the LORD: I will put My laws in their mind and write them on their hearts; and I will be their God, and they shall be My people. None of them shall teach his neighbor, and none his brother, saying, 'Know the LORD,' for all shall know me, from the least of them to the greatest of them. For I will be merciful to their unrighteousness, and their sins and their lawless deeds I will remember no more.' In that He says, 'A new covenant,' He has made the first obsolete. Now what is becoming obsolete and growing old is ready to vanish away."

When I think about who it is that will carry me in this lifetime and throughout eternity, my soul and spirit receives the answer by the power of the Holy Spirit. My friends, the answer to this process is God Himself through the precious blood of Jesus Christ.

When I think of such an experience with the Lord, I am also reminded that even through this life up to the time of my funeral procession, the glory of God will still shine in my life—even while I sleep. This, my friend, is the confidence that we all must have that God will carry us in all circumstances, even when He returns, breaking through the sky to lift us up to be with Him forevermore. I thank God for life experiences and all of His wonder of blessings now and to come.

One of the things in my life and in the military career that I will never forget are those days of carrying my rucksack on several quarterly, fifteen-mile road marches. You had to pack it just right with the proper amount of weight and the contents had to be exactly by the packing list given from the commander or your leader. It had socks, boots, clothing, and a tent inside of it along with other items. We were prepared to be survivors at any given time.

A road march meant in my mind several things. It meant carrying a big bag of stuff on my back for several hours in the dying heat. It meant learning how to discipline myself. It also meant preparation for missions to come. It meant learning how to lead someone through movements and over rough terrains and challenging paths. It meant developing endurance. One thing is for sure, it did help me mentally envision the possibility and probability of me having to have to carry someone in combat or even at home.

I thank God for discipline and strength. You never know in this life when you might have to carry someone other than yourself, a buddy, or even your household. A soldier might get wounded in the heat of battle and you might find yourself in the situation where you have to carry that soldier to safety. You might find yourself doing what the character Forrest Gump did. He carried several buddies to safety.

You might find yourself in a situation at home where you might have to carry a family member. You might have to carry the entire family. For a husband, the priest of the house, he is obligated to take care of everyone living in his house. However, there are things that are outside the immediate responsibility of the priest in that house. So then the question is, would you use the rucksack effect to help with things like drug addiction, teenage sexual issues, depression, financial support, religions development, and educational advancement, college support, and so many other areas? I remember distinctly that it was the load that was bothering me the most. It was the weight inside the rucksack that kept forcing my straps to dig into my shoulders and armpits, causing extreme, irritating pain.

I always had to readjust it time and time again to inch it over to a different area. It made the march seem longer. I also recall that it was the irritating blisters that came about during that long march. I left with clean, non-irritating feet and returned with ugly blisters on the bottom that required immediate attention.

One thing I learned is that family has to stick together through the toughest of times and maintain a relationship with Jesus to help carry each family member through. Families need to understand from the beginning of time God made it His business to make family a covenant. Your blood is tied together in that one family. Today, you need to understand that His blood is what sustains life now. His blood is what carries you over into eternity.

The only way the man in the house can carry such a load to help his family is that he must turn the load over to Jesus. There is no rucksack, duffle bag, plain bag, nor any kind of load that He cannot carry. Jesus is an expert at carrying our pains, suffering, depressions, sin, mistakes, and messy attitudes, dysfunctional lives, edgy marriages, and all things you need Him for. You see it is the perfect and righteous Holy Priest who has redeemed us from the curse.

We need Jesus because the enemy will try its best to come in like a flood and take over your life. But as long as we have Jesus as our new covenant—the promise that God gave to us—we are reminded of the victory that He has already won on our behalf. Jesus outweighs the enemy's manipulation, tricks, and deception. He is our anchor in life.

REMOVE THE MASK

MATTHEW 24:30: "*Then the sign of the Son of Man will appear in heaven, and then all the tribes of the earth will mourn, and they will see the Son of Man coming on the clouds of heaven with power and great glory.*"

You hear it all the time now by young generations and old generations of people—please take off the mask and be real. You hear and feel it with vibes from other people in the church and out. They want truth, trust, leadership, and fellowship in the absolute freedom of worship and praise. They are not looking for a false sense of strings attached and the "I owe you" mentality. Instead they want someone that they can have fellowship with and love and experience the power of the Holy Spirit. They want the mask off in and out of the church.

When I viewed the movie entitled Mask by Jim Carey, I found it to be hilarious, very funny, and entertaining. The character in that movie was able to turn himself into whatever and whoever he wanted to be to fit the occasion and the situation at hand. If he wanted to put fear into the gangsters, then he would become something to intimidate the gangsters and make them back off. If he wanted to express love, he would make himself look like he was either desperate for love and make himself appear that he could sweep a woman off her feet. Whatever the case was, he could adjust to it almost perfectly in his eyes. It's funny how he got the mask. Somehow it appeared in his apartment from being found in the bottom of the ocean.

God will make a way in our lives to remove the mask that we will bless people. Somehow He will go against the grain of what other people dare to do. We need to understand that the mask is used to cover up. It hides some things, but not all things. Sooner or a later it comes off and God intervenes. If you ever had a mask on like so many people, it has to be the greatest feeling on earth—you are set free from false imprisonment.

FILLED IN THE SPIRIT OF THE LORD

Ephesians 5:17-19: "Therefore do not be unwise, but understand what the will of the Lord is. And do not be drunk with wine, in which is dissipation; but be filled with the Spirit, speaking to one another in psalms and hymns and spiritual songs, singing and making melody in your heart to the Lord."

A stunning relationship between man and woman can be so strong that you can even drift for a moment into a hypnotized state. I thought it was kind of funny when a brother tried to shake it off or snap out of his trance after hugging and kissing his wife outside in front of everyone. That was one of the scenes played in the movie Barber Shop. The brother literally shook it off as his wife walked away. It took a moment for him to shake it off. The expression meant that he was so caught up into her beauty and kiss for that moment that he forgot completely about who he was and everything else around him. He was in a dream world and nothing else mattered until he finally shook it off and came to his senses.

It was clear to me at that moment how much that brother loved his wife and their relationship. We live in a world where there are so many things happening that when it surprises us, we seldom adapt the attitude to shake it off. I tell you today that you have to shake off all the frustration and troubles in your life to experience peace in the spirit of holiness.

I thought about how much God does for us every day. He never ceases to give of Himself to us. He is always blessing us and making the impossible come to life when it seems that there is no hope. When I think about the fact that I have a heartbeat to love someone back, I have to thank Him for giving me the heartbeat each moment of life.

The best love story, even if it was a blockbuster, could not give me more than the grace of God. The Lord satisfies my every need. He provides that grace and love each and every day. Believers know about that grace that God gives. There is not a moment that goes by when He is not there intervening, molding, and shaping our relationship with Him and with others. He fills us with perfect love.

If I had to be hypnotized, I would rather it be by the Holy Spirit every day of my life. I want that intimacy that no money can purchase, no bribing and manipulation can hinder, and that nothing can take away. I submit to be under His anointing that I may be transformed, renewed in the spirit of holiness and in his perfect image.

It is the Holy Spirit in whom we are concerned with for our lives. We believe that what matters most is the life in Christ Jesus. He promised to leave the comforter and He did. We must be bold enough to petition Him with ultimate humility, reverence, and confidence.

The Holy Spirit has the power to turn us around at any moment in life. It is the Holy Spirit who gave you the power to love and react to your mate. The Holy Spirit guides us in love. The Holy Spirit is the one who will take you through those moments of being in a trance by the evil one. The point is that you must be born again so that you can be filled in the Spirit and walk with full authority over those who oppose your walk with God.

GOD HOLDS BACK THE FLOODGATES

Romans 1:16: "For I am not ashamed of the gospel of Christ, for it is the power of God to salvation for everyone who believes, for the Jew first and also for the Greek."

God opened my mind in 1994 when I came back to Him, the word floodgate was presented to me. He was reminding me of His everlasting grace and mercy on humanity. He was also allowing me to get in touch with Him to have a better relationship. I was not sure what He was referring to until one day it hit me—His everlasting blessings on life itself. I am only living because He allows it. He spoke to me as clear as day and said that He holds life in His hands. He holds back the demons from destroying my life. It was clear to me that God said to me, "I hold the demons back from touching your life." They flee at His very thought and presence. God has done more for me than I could ever imagine.

When I look back at certain events in my life that I made it through, I can't help but think of His love. It is He who removes the demonic spirits and sends angels to guard my life. His power annihilates the enemy in an instant. I thank God for the blood because the blood destroys demons.

What was interesting to me was the picture that He showed me—a dam filled with water and Him holding back all the floodwaters. He reminded me that He sees the water as if they were demons. He held them back then, and He holds them back now at the wall of the dam. He is the gate of the dam. He holds them back from touching our lives and causing damage. The Bible clearly says that He will come in like a flood and make a standard.

Today, Jesus is the one who holds all the floodgates back that the enemy loves to unleash on us. If it had not been for the blood of Jesus, we would be over run and destroyed by demons and the wrath of God. We owe Him our worship and praise. I believe more than anything the Lord wanted me to know whom to serve—my Lord of life. Without doubt and hesitation, Jesus is my Lord. You should claim that right now no matter what is going on. Do you ever wonder what God held back in your life so that you can be successful in your job, home, child bearing, marriage, friendship, and the love you have for Him? There is a lot that we do not see that God takes care of in His own wisdom and mystery. I thank God for revealing His word. I thank Him for everything. Now I see why the Apostle said that He is not ashamed of the Gospel of Christ because His word is what saves us. His word keeps us alive and worshipping Him. His word sustains life.

A GLIMPSE OF GOD'S CREATION IN ACTION

PSLAM 8:

O LORD, our Lord,

How excellent is Your name in all the earth,

Who have set Your glory above the heavens!

Out of the mouth of babes and nursing infants

You have ordained strength,

Because of Your enemies,

That You may silence the enemy and the avenger.

When I consider Your heavens, the work of Your fingers,

The moon and the stars, which You have ordained,

What is man that You are mindful of him,

And the son of man that You visit him?

For You have made him a little lower than the angels,

And You have crowned him with glory and honor.

You have made him to have dominion over the works of Your hands;

You have put all things under his feet,

All sheep and oxen—

Even the beasts of the field,

The birds of the air,

And the fish of the sea

That pass through the paths of the seas.

O LORD, our Lord,

How excellent is your name in all the earth!

Yellowstone National Park was America's first national park. It was established in 1872. It is located in Wyoming, Montana, and Idaho, and it is home to a large variety of wildlife including grizzly bears, wolves, bison, and elk. Preserved within Yellowstone National Park are Old Faithful, a collection of the world's most extraordinary geysers and hot springs, and the Grand Canyon of the Yellowstone. When you just see the amazing sites on the History Channel or a report given from CNN or New Magazine, you get a feeling of awe.

Clearing this park displays a number of creatures that have not all been seen. In the beauty of Yellowstone National Park there is still the need to survive. If you lay down too long, you just might have an unexpected experience. The point of this passage is to reveal what so many people do not know, and that is the beauty of God's creation in this park. One fact remains so clear to me and that is that God wants to reveal His creations so that we will not doubt the fact that He made the world and the world to come. Today is your blessed day. If you have visited the Yellowstone National Park, You have been blessed to see the wonders of God's creation.

More importantly, if this does not convince you that there is a real God who sits on the throne, then you must keep praying until you get a breakthrough. God is able to give you a breakthrough. Please understand that God made all things, including all national parks. You saw with your own eyes what the Creator could do in this world. It is time for you this day to know that He will deliver you from the old lifestyle to a life filled with blessings. Since you know that He created the grizzly bear and the lions, the tigers, and all the grass, the snow, rain, and all substances and environments within environments, He can give you eternal life. You and I can live with Him forever in heaven.

PSALM 77:14-20:

You are the God who does wonders;

You have declared Your strength among the peoples.

You have with Your arm redeemed Your people,

The sons of Jacob and Joseph. Selah

The waters saw You, O God;

The waters saw You, they were afraid;

The depths also trembled.

The clouds poured out water;

The skies sent out a sound;

Your arrows also flashed about.

The voice of Your thunder was in the whirlwind;

The lightning lit up the world;

The earth trembled and shook.

Your way was in the sea,

Your path in the great waters,

And Your footsteps were not known.

You led Your people like a flock

By the hand of Moses and Aaron.

SCAN LIFE'S DREAMS

GALATIONS 5:18-24: "But if you are led by the Spirit, you are not under law. The acts of the sinful nature are obvious: sexual immorality, impurity and debauchery; idolatry and witchcraft; hatred, discord, jealousy, fits of rage, selfish ambition, dissensions, factions and envy; drunkenness, orgies, and the like. I warn you, as I did before, that those who live like this will not inherit the kingdom of God. But the fruit of the Spirit is love, joy, peace, patience, kindness, goodness, faithfulness, gentleness and self-control. Against such things there is no law. Those who belong to Christ Jesus have crucified the sinful nature with its passion and desires."

In the military, during the first initial phase of training, soldiers are taught marksmanship. In marksmanship, we were given four fundamentals to use in an effort to hit the target. There is a great deal of target practice. The four-step technique was: steady positioning, aiming, breathing control, and trigger squeeze. Of the four steps of marksmanship, aiming is perhaps the most important, however they compliment one another. Nevertheless if you can't see what the target looks like and where it is, you have not focused on the point of aim at that target or objective. Therefore, focusing of the eye is the key place to start and finish. "A proper firing position places the eye directly in line with the center of the rear sight aperture."

When the eye is focused on the front sight post, the natural ability of the eye to center objects in a circle and to seek the point of greatest light (the center of the aperture) aid in providing correct sight alignment. For the average soldier firing at combat-type targets, the natural ability of the eye can accurately align the sights.

Therefore, the firer can place the tip of the front sight post on the aiming point, but the eye must be focused on the tip of the front sight post. This causes the target to appear blurry, while the front sight post is seen clearly. There are two reasons for focusing on the front sight post.

Aiming error: only a minor aiming error should occur since the error reflects only as much as the soldier fails to determine the target center. A greater aiming error can result if the front sight post is blurry due to focusing on the target or other objects. Focusing on the tip of the front sight post aids the firer in maintaining proper sight alignment.

Sight picture: once the soldier can correctly align his sights, he can obtain a sight picture. A correct sight picture has the target, front sight post, and rear sight aligned. The sight picture includes two basic elements: sight alignment and placement of the aiming point.

Placement of the aiming point varies, depending on the engagement range.

Scanning and aiming is hard work in the life of ministry and in everyday life. We need a focus point in life. We need techniques that only God can provide. If we keep our focus on grace, mercy, loving kindness, and salvation, we would hit the target each time being lead by the Holy Spirit. We need to be empowered and lead by the Holy Spirit who helps us exercise the fruit of the Spirit. Galatians 5:18-24 gives us the fruit of the Spirit directing us from the old focus of life's sins.

Galatians 5:22-24: "But the fruit of the Spirit is love, joy, peace, patience, kindness, goodness, faithfulness, gentleness and self-control. Against such things there is no law. Those who belong to Christ Jesus have crucified the sinful nature with its passions and desires."

We use these qualifications of marksmanship to be prepared for the battlefield of life. We use and improvise by the power of the Holy Spirit to the fruit of the Spirit to win souls on the battlefield using the techniques of focus and a variation of techniques that the Lord has given us. We use the word of God against our enemy, the adversary, who is seeking to kill, steal, and destroy. In Ephesians 6, that same opponent throws fiery darts that only the Holy Spirit can block from us. We want to be able to move in our lives to be fruitful in the Lord. But we must be equipped.

CHAPTER 9

THE POWER OF SALVATION

ROMANS 1:16: "For I am not ashamed of the gospel of Christ, for it is the power of God to salvation for everyone who believes, for the Jew first and also for the Greek."

This scripture reminds us that we should never be ashamed of our Lord, Jesus Christ. Apostle Paul makes it clear in his witness that the gospel of Christ has power in it through Jesus Christ. Many Christians and unbelievers alike are ashamed of their relationship with Jesus. I can not believe the amount times that I have been around people who claim to be Christians, however never witness to other people. In fact, many people get intimidated or too afraid to tell of him because of their old lifestyle. Sometimes, people play the blame game or use excuses that others are talking about them, so they stay away from church.

Tell all of your neighbors, family, and friends to stop staying away from God's house based on what they heard or what the enemy tricked their minds into thinking. We serve a mighty and loving God for all people to approach. The power of God is what we truly need in our lives more than anything else. Make no mistake, God made us to need one another and him. We want to encourage everyone to get to know Jesus as Lord of their lives today.

Read the word of God for yourself and study with a friend or family member. Go to a local church that believes in Jesus Christ dying on the cross and rising from the dead. Today, get activated. Get off of that sofa or that chair watching those football games before church and get to church and accept Jesus Christ. When you accept Him, watch everyone praise God for you. His power is available to every believer and non-believer. This power of salvation is for the believer to help the non-believer know Jesus Christ. Anybody can't just have salvation—

they must be born again. So do not keep it to yourself, it makes no sense. You must give God all the glory.

FASTING FOR GOD'S GLORY

MATTHEW 6: 16-18 "Moreover, when you fast, do not be like the hypocrites, with a sad countenance. For they disfigure their faces that they may appear to men to be fasting. Assuredly, I say to you, they have their reward. But you, when you fast, anoint your head and wash your face, so that you do not appear to men to be fasting, but to your Father who is in the secret place; and your Father who sees in secret will reward you openly."

The best restaurants can easily capture my attention since eating is one of America's favorite pastimes. When you mention all the different types of meals and even when my wife cooks, I am instantly ready to engage in a tasty meal. My eyes don't see the calories, sometimes it does not see the fat content, and certainly—like thousands of other people—I forget and somehow neglect the labels on food content. The bottom line is that we fall in love with food and the lust of our bodies more than we love God at times. Today is a new day and a new commitment to life.

Fasting is a challenge for so many people because it requires us to put aside the things that grip our taste buds and our extreme desires. The flesh cries out for more, and more, and more—the "I want it now" desire. In some cases, it stimulates the mind and speaks to it saying that you have to have it. It is a case of mind over matter, but and it has to be put into subjection under the anointing. Fasting and prayer will be part of my new lifestyle. I will commit to God to please Him. Fasting is healthy for us. Fasting helps us get a breakthrough from God. We walk by faith and not by sight. We walk in the Spirit so we will not fulfill the lust of the flesh.

God desires that we fast and pray to get a breakthrough from Him. We fast for no other reason but to please God. God is telling us that we need His strength for breakthroughs and the only way is to put our plates down and get obedient is to let something go.

Jesus fasted for forty days and nights. The enemy approached Him and tried to tempt Him in bowing down and serving the devil (Matthew 4). Jesus did not give in to the devil's devices. He used the word. Whenever you fast, you need to use the word for your strength, deliverance, and your protection against principalities and all those in high places. You will have a challenge, but God will reward you because you fast for His purpose. God sees you fasting and knows your reason for fasting. When Jesus fasted He received His breakthrough. He made it through all the issues and attacks, the cross, the burial, then He rose from the dead. The enemy wanted to stop Him in His tracks early. God demonstrated the power of fasting and prayer. Jesus is Lord and He must be the center of your life when fasting and during your entire life.

YOUR GENEALOGY

MATTHEW 1:1-17: "The book of the genealogy of Jesus Christ, the Son of David, the Son of Abraham: Abraham begot Isaac, Isaac begot Jacob, and Jacob begot Judah and his brothers."

God saw everything before the beginning of time because He is the Creator. He saw all the generations to come and all things before we arrived here. In Matthew 1:17 it says, "So all the generations from Abraham to David are fourteen generations, from David until the captivity in Babylon are fourteen generations, and from the captivity in Babylon until the Christ are fourteen generations." God has shown us His loving son Jesus who came to redeem us from our wicked ways of life. When we were not expecting a Savior God already had it in His mind to rescue us from the powerful injection of sin. God revealed to us in Matthew a picture of the genealogy of Jesus Christ. This is important because people need to look at their own genealogy to determine what it is that God has purposed in their life. Find out where you fit in the picture for Christ's great work. You have a gift just like everyone else. You either see it now or God will reveal it to you in a telescopic view.

God saw everything before time and telescopes and any devices could be made. However, He gave us the tools to see with at a better angle and perception. The naked eye could not see what He shows us at times. So we look at the telescope view method. The telescope view allows us to see at distances beyond the naked eye. It allows us to see nearby planets and galaxies. We get the close up view at planets and what goes on in the outer space. We see explosions occurring and various objects like meteoroids, asteroids, and debris of all types floating through space.

Today God wants you to take a telescopic view of your life's situation. What is your situation? Can you see that God has placed grace on you? Can you see that God has put blessings before you instead of curses? I believe once a person asks God to remove the spiritual scales from their eyes, then and only then will they see the glory of the one God. I believe God placed people in the Bible so that we could replicate some of the ministries. He wants us to have that view so that we can be one of His followers. God wants us to see through the telescopic view you have to use the gift He gave. Stir up the gift within you (1 Corinthians 12). He wants us to exercise our gifts. In 1 Corinthians 13, He wants us to exercise love like He does each and everyday.

Several years ago, the NASA Space Center launched what is called the Hubble Telescope. The purpose was to monitor and record events occurring in space. NASA wanted to observe anticipated and spectacular events in the galaxy and beyond. The telescope is an awesome scientific instrument for new discoveries in space operations and manifestations outside of the naked eye. Surely, we know now that telescopic lens projects images that man could never see if God had not allowed the development and the intellect behind the development of such a device of scientific innovation and discovery breakthroughs.

WHAT HAPPENS ON YOUR JOURNEY

A ROAD TO JESUS

ACTS 9:1-12: "Then Saul, still breathing threats and murder against the disciples of the Lord, went to the high priest and asked letters from him to the synagogues of Damascus, so that if he found any who were of the Way, whether men or women, he might bring them bound to Jerusalem. As he journeyed he came near Damascus, and suddenly a light shone around him from heaven. Then he fell to the ground, and heard a voice saying to him, 'Saul, Saul, why are you persecuting me?' And he said, 'Who are You, Lord?' Then the Lord said, 'I am Jesus, whom you are persecuting. It is hard for you to kick against the goads.' So he, trembling and astonished, said, 'Lord, what do you want me to do?' Then the Lord said to him, 'Arise and go into the city, and you will be told what you must do.' And the men who journeyed with him stood speechless, hearing a voice but seeing no one. Then Saul arose from the ground, and when his eyes were opened he saw no one. But they led him by the hand and brought him into Damascus. And he was three days without sight, and neither ate nor drank. Now there was a certain disciple at Damascus named Ananias; and to him the Lord said in a vision, 'Ananias.' And he said, 'Here I am, Lord.' So the Lord said to him, 'Arise and go to the street called Straight, and inquire at the house of Judas for one called Saul of Tarsus, for behold, he is praying. And in a vision he has seen a man named Ananias coming in and putting his hand on him, so that he might receive his sight.'"

A new beginning with sight began in the life of Saul of Tarsus, who became the Apostle Paul, one of God's leading men to witness on earth of God's everlasting salvation, grace, and mercy. The Apostle experienced a touch of God so unique. He was needed as a servant for the Most High God, Jesus Christ. He experienced a conversion by Jesus Himself while going about attempting to do evil. All believers and ministers, those who operate in the fivefold ministry, and those that are lost must need to experience a touch of Jesus in specific areas of our lives. No one is exempt of His loving touch to fill the purpose He has set for us.

The Apostle Paul's life was converted by the touch of Jesus Himself who saw Saul on the road to destruction. Everyone in society needs a touch because of the sin that creeps and desires to reign over our lives. We need His touch everyday because we fall short of His glory. We need His touch because we all have been persecutors and violators of the faith in Christ in some form or fashion. However, He is forever forgiving and always delivers us through our weakness and sin. We do not have to act all cute, and prestigious, and high society, and set in our ways in this life. You see everyone has something broken that will require God's attention. It is because everyone has something broken in his or her life that requires Him only to restore or fix. The only one who can fix it is Jesus. Whatever it takes for God to do a new thing in your life, whether it is conversion or a blessing with wealth, healing, or even the ability to step out in faith for your life, ask God to do it and do it now.

The enemy wants to stop you in your tracks, but God wants you to prosper in His Kingdom. You have a purpose in Christ. Your purpose means more to the Lord than to the enemy because God sees you as one of His. The enemy is just a deterrent. He has a goal to make you turn you back on Jesus. But Jesus has all eternal power that is instantly manifested in your life for His Kingdom's purpose.

It is important to start this lesson out giving the essential makeup of blessings and being able to explain the necessity of sight in the spiritual realm. It is much needed and has been avoided too long.

Sometimes people cringe at the fact that there is a spiritual realm and two different spirits looking at you and both forces existing for different purposes.

God desires to bless you and curse those who curse you. The enemy simply comes to steal, kill, and destroy. The question to you today is, which one do you chose? I am sure you made the right choice today. If you have salvation in Jesus Christ, you want the spiritual realm to see what the Lord wants you to see and will reveal to you.

One of the most effective parts of Jesus' ministry was the demonstration of restoring sight. Jesus is the only one who can restore and give sight. There is no other and certainly do not be fooled by the enemy. Jesus dealt with a blind man who needed sight because he was born with a birth defect from his mother's womb. He dealt with religious leaders who were confused about the new birth. They had no vision and no concept of the new birth, being born again. Their sights were limited by their spiritual conditions. Jesus made it very clear that you must be born again. They were too blind to understand and to see that the Son of God was in the midst of healing and revealing His gracious, loving kindness. They were too caught up with the facts of the law, rather than the truth that was standing before their very eyes. They had different interpretations of the identity of Jesus.

The number one priority was to restore life in the people of God for the purpose of salvation, love, witness, grace, and His never-ending mercy. God is no respecter of persons. He reigns on the just as well as the unjust. Jesus restored people for more than one reason. His primary reason for restoring is love. He loves us more than a parent can. It was the demonstration of love in Him. Because He sees all things, and we ourselves see nothing without the blessing of spiritual sight, God has been protecting us.

Christians alike have a unique lifestyle that must be projected and demonstrated at all times. People watch to see if you are setting an example in your walk. They want to know if you act like a Christian, demonstrating the love that Jesus gives. They want to know that you are filled with the Holy Ghost. So then show them that you are filled in the spirit of Christ. Draw them to Christ under the anointing power of God. Use what you got to draw them. When the apostle was drawn in, he spent the remainder of his life drawing people to the Lord. In fact, that became his mission for Christ. He was a chosen vessel. When God removes your scales in the spirit, then you will see and become effective witnesses in Christ Jesus.

When we expect to see things, we must be patient that God will reveal the blessing in time. Count on your spiritual sight. The Apostle Paul said in 2 Corinthians 4:18, while we do not look at the things which are seen, but at the things which are not seen. For the things which are seen are temporary, but the things which are not seen are eternal.

I believe that once God changed Paul, he could adopt this passage under the anointing. We see to get the blessings and be obedient to His will and commands.

JESUS PIERCED IN THE SIDE

JOHN 19:31-37: "Therefore, because it was the Preparation Day, that the bodies should not remain on the cross on the Sabbath (for that Sabbath was a high day), the Jews asked Pilate that their legs might be broken, and that they might be taken away. Then the soldiers came and broke the legs of the first and of the other who was crucified with Him. But when they came to Jesus and saw that He was already dead, they did not break His legs. But one of the soldiers pierced His side with a spear, and immediately blood and water came out. And he who has seen has testified, and his testimony is true; and he knows that he is telling the truth, so that you may believe. For these things were done that the Scripture should be fulfilled, 'Not one of His bones shall be broken.' And again another Scripture says, 'They shall look on Him whom they pierced.'"

In history we read about the research and facts that surround blood issues and discoveries and makeup of DNA. Surely they have had a profound impact in the lives of millions of people, especially the believer. The blood has impacted every life on earth.

One of the first times of hearing about blood issues was in the case surrounding Cain and Abel. Cain slew his brother Abel. Cain killed his brother because he was jealous over the sacrifice that Abel had presented before God. He was jealous over a sacrifice that pleased God. Cain did not please God with His sacrifice of fruit. Do not misunderstand and think that fruit is not good because, on the contrary, it is good. However, it's not the sacrifice that God was looking for. The sacrifice had to have blood involved in it. Abel pleased God with the sacrifice of meat. He was the keeper of sheep. Meat is the reflection of the Lamb that would be slain someday for all of Israel and all of God's people and those lost in this world. The Lamb would be the perfect sacrifice because the lamb had to be slain so blood would have to be spilled. This would be a picture of Jesus Christ the lamb who was slain for the remission of sin. The lamb that was slain, that I would be redeemed for life and now to worship and praise Him in the beauty of Holiness.

The fruit that Cain presented to God was good, but it could not serve as a sacrifice. It did have its connection to the garden because the garden was filled with fruit and God had blessed everything. At the same time, God is looking for your best offering. The Lord notices what you give. Do not allow sin to take your best offering away from God. The enemy specializes in sinful ways.

During that particular time, sin had taken its course and reflected on the first family. Whenever a family has been blessed, you need to understand that the enemy will do everything in its power to destroy your family and anyone else involved. We are dealing with a force that has been defeated. However, this enemy still chose to raise its ugly head thinking that it has power to defeat you. Thank God that He is our refuge and strong tower. He covers us in His blood.

THE GOD HOLD ON DNA BLOOD

Scientists made a breakthrough discovery in DNA. The breakdown is in the identity of the individual blood of a person. Many law enforcement agencies use DNA to investigative and solve crimes. Upon examination in specific investigations, investigators know exactly who the person is that left the blood at the crime scene upon careful examination. They know who to track down and at what height, weight—a full description. They trace different factors and characteristics about the blood DNA in specific people. They can do it for people and all living creatures that have blood. Animals are also analyzed and put to test. They know your blood type.

When I was in the hospital at an early age, I discovered that my blood type had a common trait with other bloods. More importantly, my blood needed my father's to strengthen it because of blood lost. I knew that my blood was the source of my life—my lifeline. I knew that if my blood were in trouble with a disease or anything similar, I would be in trouble. God equips our mind to take care of our blood systems with vitamins and a proper diet. Because God supplied my need, I came out of the hospital in the best of health.

God on the other hand has the people to know, to see things from any view. He sees all things in every possible way of life spiritual and natural life. Abel's blood was on the ground and he was innocent. God could hear the blood crying from the ground. Cain was scared and did not want to tell the truth, but God already knew. He already knew the circumstances surrounding killing of his brother. He knew Cain had struck his brother over jealousy of an offering.

In all history, one thing that every citizen, every person of God's Kingdom and those who have not committed to Him must know of without a doubt is that the blood of Jesus Christ was applied to the hearts of those who believe. They must know that the blood is what saves us from being destroyed by God's wrath.

We are reminded of the many wars that were fought that blood was shed for freedom. Some people are moved about the fact that wars were fought for freedom and peace. As a result of those wars, blood was shed on the battlefield and the only help and relief you and I get is knowing that God saw our relatives through those battles and wars. He is still protecting us now and bringing us through the wars that we constantly have with principalities, demons, and all of our enemies. God is all merciful and graceful in protecting us from harm and danger.

Today we live because the blood of Jesus was applied over our lives. He covers our heart, mind, soul, and spirit, and strengthens us, which enables us to be victorious against Satan in every way. Satan was defeated by Jesus because of His love demonstrated on the cross and the power in His blood applied. When Jesus' blood was applied, He did not miss any of us. He covered then and covers all of us now; the lost and those that feel abandoned. He covers us because He loves us more than we love ourselves. His love transcends imagination and any intellectual thoughts or ideas of man. He paid our debt to the Father. Because of His love for us, He washed us whiter than snow. He removed the sin stain (Isaiah 64). He removed what the enemy wants you and I to keep in our lives which is sin. But thanks be to the living God, who has delivered us from darkness and the grips of sin.

Anybody can apply almost anything in life. But life has too many applications for one man to try to take hold of and cure them. Jesus is our cure any way you want to see it. Any application outside the will of God will be useless because it is limited and it does not have the power of Christ in it. But the application of His word will bless us throughout eternity.

NOTHING BUT THE BLOOD

Nothing else could wash the sin in the world but the blood of Jesus Christ. It is more evident today that people are missing this great salvation of Jesus Christ. The songwriter says, "Nothing but the blood of Jesus." There is no religion that can wash away your sin and mine, but the blood of the lamb which is Jesus Christ. He took on the diversity of cultures sin. Jesus broke every barrier and boundary that the enemy had put in place to keep God's Saints from prospering and receiving the blessing of the blood. No one can stop that blessing.

God specified through the work of salvation that there is no hindrance to the power of His blood. It has always been true. There is no substance on earth to compare to the power of the blood of Jesus Christ shed for the remission of sin. Everyone living today is alive because of the power of the blood of Jesus Christ. Do you recall any time in your life that you knew nothing else could satisfy you or fulfill your appetite for a certain desire? Well, I can understand your difficulty of not finding anything because there is simply no replacement.

Today is your day to tell a dying world or friends and family members who do not know Christ. Tell them that Jesus saves each and every day. He will not let you down. Accept Jesus Christ as Lord and live a new life by the washing of the blood.

NO WEAPON FORMED AGAINST ME

ISAIAH 54:17: *"'No weapon forged against you will prevail, and you will refute every tongue that accuses you. This is the heritage of the servants of the LORD, and this is their vindication from me,' declares the LORD."*

If we would search the entire world over for every highly esteemed, well-respected chemist, biochemist, biologist, and physicist or any professional that deals with such chemicals and organisms, or new scientific developments to create or formulate an agent to remove sin, they could not do it. If all the chemists and all geniuses of the world past and present combined put their minds together in an effort to develop such a cure for sin, it could not be done by any of them ever.

There is no chemical agent in existence that can wash sin away from a person made by man. There will never be one made by man. Not only are there no chemicals available, no substance is available as well but one. It is the perfect substance from God. Only the blood of Jesus has the power to wash away sin. If there had been a washing machine built specifically for human beings to be washed and dried up, it still would not work with all of its consuming power and agents. When I was growing up, the expression used with dealing with fights and other matters was, "Ajax will not be able to get it out." Whatever stain you had, Ajax could not solve it. It always goes back to the solution that God gave. The solution is simply the blood of Jesus.

It is also vital to understand that there is a supernatural power in the blood of the Lamb. There is supernatural power in the blessings that come from the shed blood of Jesus Christ. We cannot explain it, nevertheless it exists for His glory and purpose to save the souls of those who are destined for eternal life. God does not misuse His eternal power. He uses it to bless people always.

RICHES

LUKE 16:19-21: "Jesus said, 'There was a certain rich man who was splendidly clothed in purple and fine linen and who lived each day in luxury. At his gate lay a poor man named Lazarus who was covered with sores. As Lazarus lay there longing for scraps from the rich man's table, the dogs would come and lick his open sores.'"

We use money as purchasing power in our lives every day because of our desires and wants. There is nothing wrong with using money, as it is applied and necessary in this economic system to exchange for goods and services. It is good to have an economy that works well with the flow of money being applied appropriately throughout society. Money is an essential part of the life of this earth.

Nevertheless, the most essential aspect of this life on earth is knowing that you live for Jesus Christ. Never let substance outweigh your position with Jesus Christ, the one whom your relation is valued with much more. We need to start understanding that there is nothing more powerful than the blood of the Lamb applied to our lives. There is nothing that can be compared to the precious blood of the Lamb.

Money and power will not do the fix in your spiritual life. Winning the lottery will not fix your soul's salvation. There is nothing wrong with having money, but we need to understand that Jesus died for us to give us life and give it more abundantly. He has made all things possible for us. So it really does not matter whatever else you apply in your life outside of the precious blood because the blood is the only thing that can save you. Today is your day to accept Jesus Christ as the Lord of your life.

Rich people apply millions of dollars to Wall Street and banks, millions of dollars to renew investments every day. Some would debate that these millions do not mean anything nor do they have impact. I want to say to you that God has a blessing for you. Do not get discouraged. Just remember, do not let Jesus pass you by with all of your investment each and every day. Instead, grab hold of Him and get your blessings. Make Jesus the investment in your life from now on. He made you His! He washed you in His precious blood to atoned you and I from the wrath and the grips of the enemy. Remember, you are covered in His blood and you are rich in His kingdom. You can't help but to be highly blessed.

Governments apply billions of dollars each month for war, and foreign relations, and foreign policy. They invest to maintain relationships and peace. They invest top dollar to bring war to a close and find peaceful solutions. Why not invest in Him who loves to bring peace to our hearts and minds? Invest in His kingdom by first accepting Him in your life. It is then when you will know that the blood was applied.

Jesus defeated Satan on Calvary for the world to come back to Him as He took away the sin. His blood was our atonement. He identifies with His blood and us. Someone made a joke one day of who had made him clean through and through. He wanted to see the evidence of who cleaned him. He wanted to know how the blood was applied. God is able to do all of these things. Somehow in His own infinite wisdom, He broke us out of the prison of Satan and allowed us to sup with Him. You can be transformed by the renewing of your mind.

The blood applied is your way to get to heaven and bow before His throne. He knows each of us by name. He knows the impact of His blood. We know that He is the God that blessed through the power of His blood.

We take communion to recognize His broken body and His blood that cleansed us (Corinthians 11:23-34). We identify with His death burial, resurrection, and return.

It appears that in order to get something new to happen and something to be victorious in, there always had to be blood involved. I am so glad that Jesus was made the perfect sacrifice for my sin. He became sin on a cross for all my transgressions, all of my mistakes, all of my failure in loving other people. He became the one and only perfect sacrifice. His bloodshed was and is the perfect purpose and means of new life. Jesus is the one who made life possible to live and worth living for in this world. Father, thank you, for your Son, Jesus, who carried the cross and was crucified on the cross. Your love on the cross saved me from the Father's wrath by your tender mercies. Let us follow Jesus' example of rich love. He never hesitates nor turns us down. His love contained more than any riches could ever mean.

THE CROSS

JOHN 19:31-35: "Therefore, because it was the Preparation Day, that the bodies should not remain on the cross on the Sabbath (for that Sabbath was a high day), the Jews asked Pilate that their legs might be broken, and that they might be taken away. Then the soldiers came and broke the legs of the first and of the other who was crucified with Him. But when they came to Jesus and saw that He was already dead, they did not break His legs. But one of the soldiers pierced His side with a spear, and immediately blood and water came out. And he who has seen has testified, and his testimony is true; and he knows that he is telling the truth, so that you may believe."

That day was the day that every man, woman, and child should never forget. This was the day that love was demonstrated beyond measure. No other event in history and in our minds could compare. This is the most critical event that could have taken place on earth. Jesus was put to death for you and me. People cry when they think of the fact that one man, fully divine, innocent of every charge that was placed against Him, took a beating that no one could ever have made it through.

People cry when they think of the fact that He loved us so that He was willing to hang on a cross for others that He never met in the flesh. Jesus never met us and He still hung on the cross for the remission of my sin. He was also raised from death to prove His love for me.

To this day my heart still tries to imagine how He could love me so that He had to carry His own cross while being beaten and disrespected. He allowed mean and cruel men to degrade Him by every means of the word, and then be nailed to a cross by evil men. There is a deep mystery in His love that man is still trying to figure out. Most of us continue trying to imagine the fullness of His love. Imagine it, the Creator placed His Son here on earth to take on my sin. The God that we worship created everything, including time, and never met me in the flesh, however He still saved me with His love. In

Isaiah 53, it is written, "by His stripes we are healed." We were on our way to death by the wrath of God possibly being poured out on us. He already recognized us as a wretched people yet precious in His eyes. But Jesus stepped in and saved us. The cross is precious to all people because Jesus carried it and died for our sins. In those times, they hung criminals on the cross and waited for them to suffocate. This particular time they nailed Him to the cross and pierced Him in the side and blood came out with water.

We know that Jesus is precious in our hearts for what He has done. We also want people to know that there is nothing similar to the cross.

IT IS FINISHED!

JOHN 19:29-30: "Now a vessel full of sour wine was sitting there; and they filled a sponge with sour wine, put it on hyssop, and put it to His mouth. So when Jesus had received the sour wine, He said, 'It is finished!' And bowing His head, He gave up His spirit."

When we see the cross, we see the most precious commitment to love that has ever existed in this world and in time itself because of the blood of the lamb. He died for you and me. It is when people truly receive that truth in spirit in the heart is when change in worship and heartfelt thanksgiving is activated on the inside. Some people may wear a cross as a symbol, but it is a reminder of what Jesus did for a world entrenched in sin. It is a reminder that people have been redeemed. It is the evidence that sin was destroyed on the cross by the power of God invested in His precious Son, Jesus. God destroyed sin in His Son's body on the cross. No one or any other sacrifice could take the place of Jesus. He was and is the only way out of sin. He is the only way to everlasting life. Jesus is the way, the truth, and the life, and He is the only way to the Father.

WORSHIP HIM

REVELATIONS 7:13: "Then one of the elders asked me, these in the white robes who are they, and where did they come? I answered, Sir, you know. And he said, these are they who have come out of the great tribulation; they have washed their robes and made them white in the blood of the Lamb."

John had a vision that allowed him to see in the heavenly realm. In fact he was taken to heaven in the Spirit to see what God wanted to reveal to Him. In that event, John was moved in the spirit, like in a time portal. He was allowed to see those dressed in white robes. He was allowed to see several things that would come to pass. Jesus even showed John Himself. He revealed the throne to John. He revealed the fountain of blood that never runs dry to John. He revealed what would take place in the future to John. In one scene, one of the elders in heaven saw John and responded to him. The elder had identified the thousands and thousands of worshipers as those that came out of the great tribulation.

God blessed all worshipers in that He allowed their robes to be washed in the blood of the Lamb. These are those that believe and have accepted Christ Jesus as Lord and Savior. They made it through the roughest test of faith. There is no one else that can make robes white by the washing of the blood. Our Father in Heaven can do things beyond our comprehension and our wildest imaginations. He washed us in the blood of the Lamb.

God wants His people to see where they will spend eternity when they become one of His believers and followers. God wants His children to see the blessing of eternal life. It is the will of God that we spend eternity with Him. His will is for you to join Him in Heaven when the time comes. So believe in Him and worship Him and be watchful for when He breaks the sky wide open. Life will no longer be as you know it. He is Lord!

Our white robes are not ordinary robes. We wear robes for so many reasons. Some are for walking around in the comfort of your home. Some robes represent those that fight in the boxing arenas. There are robes that are specifically designed for priests. We have been designated to wear the robe to represent priesthood. Jesus wore His robe and it was designed perfectly to fit our High Priest. You can worship in any clothing attire, but the white robe that Jesus will place on us is to recognize and set apart those that made it through the tribulation. They are anchored in praise for the Most High God. Today is your day to know for sure that you will wear a white robe that was washed in the blood of the Lamb. Get God today and worship Him in the beauty of His holiness.

Please understand that the Lord washed those that followed Him and gave them a new identity in heaven. When the Lord gives you a new identity, it's time to act on it and use what you have from the Lord. Ask God to anoint you for His purpose.

Most people have an identity crisis that plagues their lives. Some have an identity crisis that takes over their lives, and their families as well. Today is a new day and the old day has passed away. It is high time for you to get your blessings. Look for your blessing that will get you to heaven.

When all the Christians get to heaven, they will have joyous time in worship and in praising His righteous name. There will be a continuous party in heaven. It will last forever because there is everlasting rejoicing in worshipping God. There is joy to be in His presence. So, can you imagine those that have and those that are destined to come out of the great tribulation? When you come out of the tribulation, this is an indication that you are a conqueror in Christ Jesus. He said, in Romans, that we are more than conquerors in Christ Jesus.

I believe it to be absolutely true because His word in Revelations 7:17 says, *"For the Lamb on the throne will be their shepherd. He will lead them to springs of life-giving water. And God will wipe every tear from their eye."* These believers came out of the tribulation. You see when you worship and serve the Lord in faithfulness; He will bless you to the point of bringing you out of the tribulation. Then you will reign with Him forever. Praise to His Holy name.

Father, thank you for delivering your people through the great tribulation. Thank you for the white robe that you have prepared for I pray to have on a robe and enter into your kingdom of righteousness. You made my life better. Thank you for making me over into a child of God and a priest to serve you. Lead me to witness on this earth that I might be pleasing to you.

WISE LEADERS

PROVERBS 9:10: "The fear of the Lord is the beginning of wisdom, and the knowledge of the Holy One is understanding. For by me your days will be multiplied, and years of life will be added to you."

Wise leaders must be in place everywhere you go especially for key decisions pertaining to life, death, and everyday important business transactions. Wisdom is important for those whose job requires leadership and supervision. Wisdom comes from the fear of the Lord. In other words, you must revere the Lord with all your might and with all of your heart, soul, and mind. You should have an understanding of who He really is in your life. Wisdom is a requirement to have an effective family life. You cannot lead your home if you do not have some wisdom. You might be making it by your coattail, but sooner or later, you will see the need for wisdom.

Some of the most amazing questions asked are by children. They love to ask questions such as, "Where did God come from?", "Where is God right now?" They like to ask questions like, "Daddy, why do you not go to church?", "Momma, who do I look like the most you or Daddy?", "Momma, where is Jesus and why He loves me?", "Daddy what is the planet made out of?", "When will the earth come to an end?", "Who is my real daddy?" Yes, they put all of them together at one time and ask a dozen questions and expect intelligent and accurate answers. Children do not want any answer. They want reasoning behind the answer. They want to understand what is really going on.

A man without wisdom cannot truly answer those questions because He has no word in Him. He has no insight to who God really is. That's why it's so important that every man takes that step of salvation and commits himself to the word of God. Get anchored in the wisdom of the Lord. You can learn more than you ever imagine in the word of God and be set free at the same time. There is nothing wrong with college degrees. You can have as many as you desire, but if you have no word, you have degrees and you are flapping in the wind with zero wisdom. Wisdom will give you vision and boldness. You may gain worldly wisdom, but not godly wisdom. The other mistake is that he has not accepted Jesus Christ as his personal Savior and Lord. Know that He is your Lord and Savior.

This is a dangerous thing for his life and his family. You mean to tell me that there are men who are not training their children up in the way that they should go and not depart. It is a hurtful thing to know that I am not equipping them to have faith in the Most High, God Himself. They need that nourishment more than they need the food they eat each day.

I will never forget the day my daughter looked at me and asked me those questions. I became so dedicated in the Lord that I wanted her to memorize verses and tell them to me. I wanted ministering to happen all around my house. You see, I know where the word is, the Lord is working on something in my life and my family. When you have the word truly rooted in your heart is when you know nothing else will separate from the love of God. You know He becomes your source of strength and you know it without a shadow of a doubt.

I learned early as a young boy growing up with my mother to fear God. When I began to understand that one day I would leave this earth and go to sleep and be put in the ground, I dreamed about living a long life. It became much clearer to me the value of living a good life and just having life inside me.

You see, if a child is able to comprehend that God is needed in his life, surely adults can grasp the necessity of having God in their lives. The scripture says when I was a child, I thought as a child, but when I became a man, I put away foolish things. God is saying sometime in life, we have to grow up and be responsible for our lives and those you have a responsibility for as well. Wisdom tells me that God controls it all no matter what. Wisdom tells me that if you put all of your trust in God, you cannot fail with Him. He will take care of you in times of need. Nobody ever said start trying to get everything out of God. But what is most important is to know that you have a personal relationship with Him. That means that He knows you by name. Somehow God Himself links these words together to make sure we understand that all wisdom must come from Him. He makes it clear that His wisdom is hidden, but the believer can find it as long as God Himself reveals. *1 Corinthians 2:7: "But we speak the wisdom of God in a mystery, the hidden wisdom that God ordained before the ages for our glory."*

Father, thank you for the beginning of wisdom. Thank you for the wisdom to believe in my heart that Jesus is the Son of God and that He died and rose from the dead. Guide me to lead my family in wisdom. Guide me in understanding through thy Holy Spirit as well to please you Lord. Thank you for all the days of life and eternal life. Lord, I praise you, in Jesus' name.

GET WISDOM IN YOUR HOUSE

PROVERBS 9: 1: "Wisdom has built her house, She has hewn out her seven pillars."

Wisdom can tell you that your house is the central focus of ministry. Of course Jesus must take first place and take root in your life. Every need to start at the first level of ministry in your house, He will provide. Jesus never leaves anything undone. You want a complete household, and then ask God to restore the house so it is pleasing in His sight. No one needs to run to church and start giving up everything they have and leave their house out with no concern. Do not just leave your house just hanging. Why should I minister somewhere else before nurturing my family? Well, keep the focus on the family once you have taken it to the Lord.

Your very first step is to become a man and woman of God for His purpose. Once you have done that, then focus on your family with even greater vigor. Seek God to help increase your faith. The old you has some focus but the new you, a child of God, will have a better opportunity to minister at home. Start your practice at home and watch how the Lord moves in your life. This does not mean forget correcting your children. In fact teaching, correcting, and nourishing them is a ministry itself. Start at home with love and kindness.

This scripture points to the fact that wisdom lacks nothing. It represents completeness in the will of God. The seven pillars appeal to so many. The number seven reminds us that God always completes what he has began. It is God's business for Him to complete what He purposed for life. He does not leave anything undone. When He acts, He blesses us in tremendous ways that we can never repay or even imagine. This wisdom in your house should reveal a house that is working on complete happiness and joy. Wisdom is also a way of saying you are acting in perfection to satisfy your house. God's house is still His house. But you need to know that He is able to recover you and bless you in your house.

A well-respected and friendly couple fought like cats and dogs, always at each other's throats. They were trying to impress others and were full of excuses as to why the marriage was not working. It got so bad that it came to point of taking each other to court. But you need to understand that God shows up in any courtroom and can change the heart of everyone involved, including the judge. God has wisdom that He gives the judge. The Lord can even give you wisdom before the courtroom. He can reconcile your marriage before you get to that point. You need to develop a sense of trusting the Most High God and developing a heart of wisdom.

A good woman who is in love with Jesus will demonstrate that wisdom works because she is responsible for her house and she possesses the attitude of a helpmate to her husband. More importantly, she has learned to submit and surrender to Jesus completely. When doing so her character changes for the good of the family and the ministering that God has laid aside for her.

Any time a person has to deal with sin, God will immediately restore you from that entanglement. He wants you in His kingdom. You need wisdom so that you will not punish yourself with guilt and self-denial. God helps you to look up to the hills from whence cometh your help. God's wisdom will carry you over and help you to live in the blessings. Trust Him completely.

Father, thank you for your wisdom in my house. Lord, give my children understanding. Help me lead and make a difference in my family.

WISDOM IS THE PRINCIPAL THING

PROVERBS 4:7: "Wisdom is the principal thing; Therefore get wisdom. And in all your getting, get understanding."

Wisdom is extremely important to life's survival. Wisdom is vitally important to those in leadership roles appointed by God. King David wanted his son, Solomon, to know the importance of wisdom. He knew that his son would be his successor and he wanted him to be prepared because it was hard being a king in those days. He faced so much adversity and so many tests by God that he needed to pass to be pleasing in God's sight. A person in a position of pastor or bishop must have wisdom to lead a congregation appointed by God.

Moses was definitely one who was appointed and ordained by God to bring God's children out of the bondage that Pharaoh had put them in. It took wisdom to go on such a journey in Egypt, but the key to it is that wisdom follows you. At one point Moses did feel he had the ability to speak, but because of God unfailing wisdom, He assigned Aaron to go with him to speak on behalf of God to the king. Wisdom is what makes people listen. Although sometimes they still do not listen. If you want wisdom, you must pursue it. You must ask God for it. When ask God for wisdom, according to His purpose for you, you get wisdom.

Wisdom defined means the quality or state of being wise. It also means knowledge of what is true or right coupled with good judgment. Another meaning refers to scholarly knowledge or learning. You want the principle thing in all matters. When we talk about the principle it refers to the most important part of a particular subject. You will not have wisdom if you do not understand or obtain knowledge in particular subjects or matters. Wisdom implies that you have to know something to have wisdom. Many families experience different things and the solution sometimes varies and is somewhat different in so many cases. Therefore you must have an anointing on your judgment toward situations.

The scriptures teach us about King Solomon who was said to be the wisest man who ever lived, besides Jesus of course. God said there would be no one else like Him in wisdom. Most people remember the decision King Solomon made between two women who claimed the same baby. These two women both spoke up to the King stating that the baby belonged to each one them.

The woman whom the baby was not related to was willing to allow the baby harm just to prove her point. The other woman had a different view. I believe we missed her judgment as well. She even displayed some wisdom. When King Solomon said to cut the baby in half, he knew exactly what was going to happen. Someone would step up because of their heart and bond to the baby. You see the original mother spoke up and told the king to spare the life of the baby. Not only that, she told the king give the boy to the other lady. The king knew that the biological mother's instinct would take over to ensure the utmost safety of the baby. God shows us over and over again that the truth will always come out.

Lord you know the principal thing in our lives. Give us the wisdom to know when you are speaking to us. Help us to take your advice in our lives. When we find ourselves in those predicaments like King Solomon, help us to be calm and full of wisdom

GET WISDOM

PROVERBS 6:16: "These six things the Lord hates, Yes, seven are an abomination to Him: A proud look, A lying tongue, Hands that shed innocent blood, A heart that devises wicked plans, Feet that are swift in running to evil, A false witness who speaks lies, And one who sows discord among brethren. My son, keep your father's command, and do not forsake the law of your mother. Bind them continually upon your heart."

When people learn the power of love, it helps to overcome the power of hate. As longs as people keep their minds on the Lord instead of meditating and entertaining evil and hate, then will they get their blessings. God is warning us to not walk in pride, hate or any manner of evil. Walk in love so that you will win souls. Walk under the influence of the Holy Spirit so that hate will not grip you.

God wants us to know the seven things that He hates. He wants us to keep our focus on His loving kindness and His character. Listen to what God is saying get wisdom to overcome—a proud look that makes you feel like you are above God. He is saying don't just concentrate on your image, know who made you from speaking a word. He wants to remind us that our eyes have an impact in our lives because of how we see ourselves. In some case people see themselves higher than God. When you take a word for each statement, apply it.

I was in a group study that covered different variations of being a good employee in an environment that supported wounded soldiers. In that class they emphasized goals. We normally make goals to remind us of the individual achievements we want to make. I believe that if you replace negatives with positives and evil and hate with a word of success and wisdom, then you will be able to make an impact.

Try something like this: breaking a proud look—keep your eyes on the Lord and not your accomplishments and what you think that you achieved by yourself. Do not lie on others because it is sinful and God sees it rolling off of the tongue of the person telling the lie and the hurt it causes the innocent. Don't murder or take the life of anyone because it is not the will of God that you live with such pain and regret. It is not the will of God that you shed innocent blood. God is able to deliver you out of that situation the enemy lowered you into. Keep your heart filled in the Spirit of Jesus Christ. If you have Jesus inside your heart, then the wicked scheme cannot take root because you are now rooted in the will of God. Remember the story of Moses and Pharaoh, his heart had became hardened for the purpose of giving God the glory without him even knowing it, yet with the intention of pouring out evil upon the children of Israel. God finally penetrated his heart and convinced him at the Red Sea. But it took God drowning Pharaoh's army.

God does not want us to run to evil and celebrate evil. That is what happens when the mind is on worldly things. Do not become a false witness that tell feel good stories that are really lie on someone or thing. Whatever you do, "follow peace with all men because without it, no man shall see God."

Lord, you have the power to deliver me from my sinful ways. Keep me in your sight Lord and take me from those things you hate. When sinful things you hate arise in my life, cleanse me by the power of your Holy Spirit. Give me the wisdom to learn of your word and abide in it. Give me the wisdom to know when to listen. Help me to walk daily in wisdom that I may avoid those evil devices and the sin that tries to beset me and manifest within. My trust is in you Lord. Help me to stand in wisdom.

I pray that you keep my family and friends and me clean of these seven things you hate. Turn my life around so I can be pleasing in your sight. All praise to you, Lord Jesus.

CHAPTER 10

LORD, ORDER MY LIFE

ROMANS 5:19: "For as by one man's disobedience many were made sinners, so also by one Man's obedience many will be made righteous."

Once God's people began to understand processing His order into their individual spirit, man then, and only then, will each believer begin to walk in power of His righteousness. When you begin to walk in righteousness because you made a decision to subject yourself to the will of God's transforming power in obedience, the Holy Spirit will embrace it and bless you in tremendous ways. God wants us to be obedient and submit to His authority and purpose for our lives in every way.

We do not submit partially, but submit all of ourselves. It is the power of the Holy Spirit that enables us to walk in obedience and reveal to the Father our commitment to Him. Obedience enables us to be true worshippers and honor Him in the Spirit. Our Lord makes us righteous by our conversion in the spirit of Christ and in our hearts and minds. The Lord takes hold of us and keeps us out of the evil ploy, manipulation, and sin's grip. Having been made righteous, we begin to reap the harvest because of our obedience and sowing. The righteous lives for the uplifting of the Kingdom of God. Therefore the Lord orders our lives.

God will also begin to show His people the blessings of the Lord in more abundance. His blessings flow more and more each day in our lives because we believe in the power of His word and His will and promises through the scriptures. It is amazing how people still avoid the most fundamental requirement of God. God spells out in so many scriptures and in so many ways. The first thing in pleasing God is obedience. Why? It is because obedience demonstrates our individual love for God and His love for us as well. Obedience is top priority in pleasing God. It is because the fruit of the spirit—commitment, sacrifice, humility, holiness, and relationship—are all factors of obedience. The Holy Spirit helps us to be validated in God's eyes with these types of spirit traits.

It is because He said to "love with all your heart and all your mind and all your strength." Obedience is necessary to have order, and everything that follows is for the glorification of Him who called us out of darkness. Walking in the Spirit of the Lord will enable you to be obedient and worship Him with all your heart. Your walk will become faithful and life will be better because he will become real in your life like never before. Anything on the outside is not of God and has no bearing in your praise life. You will become one who walks with praise on your lips and in the depths of your heart. You will be the one who worships in total admiration and glory to His righteous name. This will be because now you know Him.

There is an order that no man can stop from God. Man is incapable of stopping your servant heart. Man is incapable of stopping your stewardship heart. Man is incapable of stopping the anointing on your life. Once God ordains it, man just needs to say, "Lord what do you want me to do? How can I serve to glorify you Lord?" Otherwise man will think that he is God.

There is an order in the home. The man must be the priest in your house or else you are open to the gateway of hell in your house. If a wife is not submissive to her husband, then the house is out of order. You are blocking those multiple blessings that God set out for you to have and to overflow in your life.

Then there is the seed planter in the house. God gave man the ability to plant seed. He gave man the right to plant seed so that He would raise an heir in his house. You can look at Abraham's story and see that the blessings on Abraham it was significant that God had already planned on giving Abraham a son and heir. This simply means that God was waiting on Abraham to be obedient in faith and at the same time trust Him.

One of the things that I learned about God is that if you trust Him, and wait on His promises, you are in for blessings of a lifetime. You will overflow in the blessings of the Lord because He never goes against His promises and the blessings that are laid up for you and me. Not only you will be blessed, but also your entire house will be blessed. I am telling you right now is the time to trust Him completely for order, promises and blessings.

God still orders the house in other respects. You remember God giving Adam a woman. He gave him a woman in holy matrimony, a sealed marriage. Adam was so powerful that he announced that this woman is bone of my bone and flesh of my flesh. Adam was signifying that they are one under God in their marriage. This expresses covenant marriage. You see God did not stop there. He gave the woman the ability to birth. There is no other human being with that capability. Then Jesus told a woman that every male that comes forth from her womb is blessed in Jeremiah 1: 5. I just wanted to tell you that the birth process is never over and has the purpose to bruise the head of the serpent while the Lord is still blessing us. It was the Lord who gave the gift that He gave women.

Father, you made us righteous. I will trust you to walk in righteousness. Help me by the power of your Holy Spirit. Order my steps in your righteousness.

FAMILY SURVIVAL

GENESIS 4:1-11: "Now Adam knew Eve his wife, and she conceived and bore Cain, and said, 'I have acquired a man from the LORD.' Then she bore again, this time his brother Abel. Now Abel was a keeper of sheep, but Cain was a tiller of the ground. And in the process of time it came to pass that Cain brought an offering of the fruit of the ground to the LORD. Abel also brought of the firstborn of his flock and of their fat. And the LORD respected Abel and his offering, but He did not respect Cain and his offering. And Cain was very angry, and his countenance fell. So the LORD said to Cain, 'Why are you angry? And why has your countenance fallen? If you do well, will you not be accepted? And if you do not do well, sin lies at the door. And its desire is for you, but you should rule over it.' Now Cain talked with Abel his brother; and it came to pass, when they were in the field, that Cain rose up against Abel his brother and killed him. Then the LORD said to Cain, 'Where is Abel your brother?' He said, 'I do not know. Am I my brother's keeper?' And He said, 'What have you done? The voice of your brother's blood cries out to Me from the ground.'"

Family is so precious and crucial to have and belong to. We mess up from time to time, but the fact remains we need our families and we need God to lead each person in the family. You know how it is when you see a television show that projects the images of a loving family. It makes your heart warm and you want to act better. You do not want to portray what you see in the acting sense. You want the real family love. One of the most important points of the family is the role they play in each sibling's life. Everyone is a keeper of the rest of the family. So stop feeling like you are the lost sheep of the family. God never said it. At the same time, no one really wants to be the leader of the siblings.

It may come down to it because of difference of personalities and attitudes that you will have to take hold of the situation and lead. But when we remember Momma and her love in our hearts get back on track. We need to be reminded of how to survive as family members.

The family must be a focused family. Family members must be introduced to Jesus as Lord and Savior. There will be more confusion if you do not have Christ as the center of your life. When you begin to focus on Jesus as the center of your life, prayer, and worship time, then you have come to a point where you are pleasing God. He loves it when we give Him all the glory. Focusing on your family as Adam and Eve should have done more of, but you do not blame them. God casts that kind of judgement.

Take life with your brother serious enough to love him more by giving him the word. It is the key to that Jesus demonstrates. Jesus Himself offers that greatness that you can receive, salvation through His word and His power. Family matters because of the blood of Jesus that washes us white as snow.

In GENESIS 1:1-10: God reveals to us, "In the beginning God created the heavens and the earth. The earth was without form, and void; and darkness was on the face of the deep. And the Spirit of God was hovering over the face of the waters. Then God said, 'Let there be light'; and there was light. And God saw the light that it was good; and God divided the light from the darkness. God called the light Day, and the darkness He called Night. So the evening and the morning were the first day. Then God said, 'Let there be a firmament in the midst of the waters, and let it divide the waters from the waters.' Thus God made the firmament, and divided the waters, which were under the firmament from the waters which were above the firmament; and it was so. And God called the firmament Heaven."

It is a blessing when you know that this rain is coming from heaven. It is God who sends the rain for the earth and the welfare of people. It is good that God gives us the waters in the seas and oceans and all through the land. He blesses us with the abundance of rain. Let the rain flow to remind us constantly that He blesses us more than the rain flows and He has more to give.

Father, thank you for the beginning of wisdom. Thank you for the wisdom to believe in my heart that Jesus is the Son of God and that He died and rose from the dead. Guide me to lead my family in wisdom. Guide me in understand through thy Holy Spirit as well to please you Lord. Thank you for all the days of life and eternal life. Lord, I praise you, in Jesus name.

SUBJECT TO GOD'S AUTHORITY

ROMANS 13: 1-7: "Let every soul be subject to the governing authorities. For there is no authority except from God, and the authorities that exist are appointed by God. Therefore whoever resists the authority resists the ordinance of God, and those who resist will bring judgment on themselves. For rulers are not a terror to good works, but to evil. Do you want to be unafraid of the authority? Do what is good, and you will have praise from the same. For he is God's minister to you for good. But if you do evil, be afraid; for he does not bear the sword in vain; for he is God's minister, an avenger to execute wrath on him who practices evil. Therefore you must be subject, not only because of wrath but also for conscience' sake. For because of this you also pay taxes, for they are God's ministers attending continually to this very thing. Render therefore to all their due: taxes to whom taxes are due, customs to whom customs, fear to whom fear, honor to whom honor."

The Constitution of United States of America was written under the authority of men who had been persuaded by God to write about rules and order in a new land. They had to set the foundation of the country under the influence of God in the document. That meant to set slaves free, follow government orders, and make specific demands by law in order that these articles will be enforced to fall into place for the common good and order of the people and Nation.

They wrote the preamble, the Bill of Rights, and the twenty-seven amendments that serves as the law for this nation. The Constitution was designated to be the law of the land, but it still did not turn out to be a perfect system of government just because of the writings. It took men to go to war to set this nation free from its own inadequacies and sinning nature to finally shape a nation for its own welfare and propriety. We need sometimes to glance back at what happened to be reminded of freedom's cost and the freedom gained. People died for freedom. We should always think of the goodness of our Lord who set things in order in man's heart and mind to begin the freedom process and healing process. Government should never think that it is free from God. Therefore faith and politics are integrated because God made everything and everybody. Most people have some of the same thoughts, dreams, and hopes when it comes to peace and prosperity. They have a common bond when it comes to loving their neighbor.

Shaping the views and character of its citizens is extremely necessary in every country and in every household. The people make the government. The people are the centerpiece after God. Shaping faith and character is essential and you cannot go without it and be truthfully successful in Christ. In fact, failure will approach every time in the absence of faith in God. Faith, integrity, character, truth, justice, and the love for Christ and your neighbor is what God requires of all of people. They are at the highest of necessity. He will guide us by His Holy Spirit. Make up your mind today to follow His wisdom and blessings for your life, family, and friends.

Faith and politics sounds like something to so many that can never be work out or worked on together. Well it is time to go against the grain, the old belief system is just what it is, a belief system. It has no weight or bearing except being out of touch of reality. Politics may survive without sound faith in God. But Godly order and the appropriate politics must have God at the center to survive. I believe that this country is surviving and setting new standards that are making a difference. Politics may be the procedures, laws, and government controlled resources and spending. The deficient and the economy are elements that are a huge focus. We built it as God gave it. We should not worship it, nor get off track with the Lord. We had faith in it all these years. Keep having faith that things will get better. Make sure that your faith is in God first.

Faith is a spiritual belief system that each person takes on an individual belief and personal relationship. For example, with me, I believe whole-heartedly and with all my mind, soul, spirit, and strength that God is God and there is no one like Him. I believe that all of my blessings come from Him alone. I believe that He even allows others to bless you by blessing them. I believe that God sent His Son, Jesus and He lived on earth thirty-three years and died and rose from the grave on the third day. I believe that He died for my sin, my imperfections, and disobedience. It is important to have faith because it puts you at a level of wise thinking and knowing that Jesus is your Savior and Redeemer who loves you unconditionally. Faith connects you with God and therefore your political role becomes much more trusted and you become much more confident in what you are doing for the church, community, and the world. Blessings, honor, and glory are unto our Lord. Amen.

BREAKING THE PRISON MENTALITY

MATTHEW 25:36: "I was naked and you clothed Me; I was sick and you visited Me; I was in prison, and ye came unto Me."

It is what you do in life that counts the most. If your actions please our Lord in Heaven, then you are on the path that God wants for you. God is pleased with you when you are fulfilling the purpose and plan for your life that He mapped out for you. For the majority of people that are snared or being held back for whatever reason, it is time to break that prison mentality. Break it by force. Take everything that God has for you by force in Jesus Christ. This does not mean be violent and go out fighting to draw blood. Let the Lord fight your battles. He will see you through.

It is what you do for the ministry of Christ Jesus that results in everlasting blessings and rewards. We should never seek to be recognized for, or gain from, our service. We should serve for the love of God. What you do for the ministry is how you think of yourself because it affects your daily decisions and choices in life and the ministry. You want to make life count regardless of what it looks like at this present moment in time. Make your life the best life that God has to offer. People will not think of you like you do yourself, so get ready to make changes to please God. The service in God's kingdom matters more than you and I could ever imagine in our minds. God is infinite in wisdom and mystery. God is infinite in His Glory and Holiness. His rewards are far greater than you and I could ever dream of. I am so glad that He is unlimited in the blessing of grace and love.

I just could not help thinking about the movie Saving Private Ryan. It was a war story. It seems that warring is one of the top issues that stimulate a certain amount of violence in our communities and worldwide. It was a story of young man who served in war. It just so happened that he had other brothers serving in the war as well and they all were killed in war. He was the last remaining son alive; the army calls it "sole surviving." He was the only son left to carry on the family's name.

The commanding general sent out a special task force to locate him and bring him home to his mother and family. War mentality is similar to prison mentality in so many ways. They both are elements of sin. They violate peace efforts; they get infused with enemy tactics and strongholds. If you are not careful, your mind can remain locked up in those elements and moments of war and imprisonment. I never forgot that one scene that still sticks with me today while viewing Private Ryan's rescue on the bridge in a heated battle. The actor Tom Hanks, starring as the commander of the special task force in his dying words, he said to PVT Ryan, "Make life count." No wonder millions watched the movie.

Today come out of your prison and make life count! War can be a prison and a stronghold that keeps you mentally hurt and damaged. But you can overcome all things by the power of the Holy Spirit. Even if war causes hurt, death, pain, suffering, you have a healer and a comforter to help you through all of your times experiencing them. Remember Romans 10:9 no matter what happens in life. You have eternal life with Christ Jesus after this life is over. The effects of war and anything that has affected you or makes you feel like you are in bondage has no power over you. All the effects of depression or PTSD and any other setbacks and hindrances in your life are prisons. But they do not have the power to hold you back forever.

You have an advocate strong and mighty and His name is Jesus. You can break the prison mentality by His name and authority. You can break the war mentality that left you injured. You can overcome all wounds and hurts at the deepest of its core. With all your might, call on the name of the Lord. He is our strong tower, He is our shelter in a storm, and He is the one who rocks us in the midnight hour when no one else is there. He is the God in sends His angels to guard us in times of trouble. Trust Him right now.

You and I can always break the prison mentality by our submission and witness for Christ. You work for God to witness to the lost and to help restore those who need a helping hand. You have a mission in life today. You might as well get up and get moving in your witness before the Lord. Jesus was talking about what people do counts as though they did it for Him. You see what we do for others give God the glory and honor. God sees the good heart of your good deeds.

True, one of the most common mistakes in society is to have a prison mentality. There is a prison mentality that keeps so many men down in the pits of hell and locked up. The same mentality keeps men away from worship time to the Lord. There is a prison mentality that keeps the household down and under constant attack of the enemy. There is a prison mentality that is expected by the enemy and some people, it is sad to say, keep falling into the same traps. This prison mentality is demonic because it tells men and women that there is no better life on the outside of prison bars. It tells everyone a lie about the Lord. It will make you believe that God cannot break your chain and shackles.

Evil will make you believe that your life is over. But your life is never over because you have been redeemed, washed in the blood of the lamb. God wants you to get up and start making a difference in life today. Let God work a work in you that even those that look down on you will be baffled in amazement of what you give to the kingdom of God. Let them see what you contribute to society. Life is not over yet, stand up man! Stand up brother! Stand up you preacher! Stand up Christian soldier! Stand up women, stand up child of God, you have work to do for the kingdom's sake.

How do you break the prison mentality? You break it by the power of prayer. The scripture says, "men ought always pray." You break the prison mentality by meditating in the word of God. This should get millions of people saved and delivered into God's kingdom. You break the prison mentality by serving God in prison and wherever you are in life. You can be on the moon and still serve God. Your ministry in Christ Jesus is not limited by your condition. The only limits you have are the ones you accepted from the enemy and yourself. That is not God. So denounce it today in by the power of the Holy Spirit. God does not operate that way. You break the prison mentality by acknowledging Jesus as Lord and Savior. Once you get God on your side, there is nothing that He will not do for you. He can fix anything. You should ask to attend programs such as church service to keep you from falling. Fellowship in the Spirit and the power of His love.

Bless His name because Jesus breaks every power that entangles the mind, soul, heart, and strength. What I mean by that is He can get inside us and change us in every area of our lives. If the prison mindset is what you have, He can take it away. If you believe that Jesus is Lord of your life, He can strip you of any wrong mindsets and wrong heart conditions.

God has a ministry for everyone. Never think that you have been left out. Just because someone says it, does not mean it is true. In God's kingdom, work will never run out. Jesus said, "When I was in a condition, you took care of me. When I was in the hospital or at home on my sick bed, you visited me. When I was locked up for my mess ups, you visited me." You are not in the prison anymore. Break the prison mentality with the spirit of Jesus Christ in your heart today. God is able to deliver you and me.

NO BARS HOLDING ME!

Are you a prisoner for Jesus Christ? Make every effort to become a prisoner for Him. Be a slave for Christ to do the ministry marked out for you. You see the real question is are you a prisoner for Christ, or are you a prisoner and slave for the devil? You already know. It is not a surprise for you. Examine yourself to determine whose bars you are behind. Make up your mind that you would rather be slave and prisoner of Jesus Christ. Ask the Lord to take hold of your spirit, soul, mind, heart, and life. Ask God to take hold of you like He did the Apostle Paul. God took His life and transformed it. Saul at that time was in denial. He was in a spiritual prison that had him deceptive for the devil. We know it because he was killing Christians.

See, being behind the wrong bars can either help you or break you. Take full advantage of seeking God to do a complete makeover in your life. God will put the right ethics and morality inside a man's heart. Ask God to keep you as you try to work things out. If you want to get bold, get up and call on Jesus, and expect Him to do what He said He would do.

GOD IS KNOCKING AT YOUR HEART

MATTHEW 7:7: "Ask, and it will be given to you; seek, and you will find; knock, and it will be opened to you. For everyone who asks receives, and he who seeks finds, and to him who knocks, it will be opened."

Every time you get an opportunity to open your heart to God, do it and see what happens. Every time you hear God speaking to your heart, allow Him to do a work on the inside of you. It is important to understand that God is always working on the heart of man. The Holy Spirit is always at work in the lives of both the believer and the unbeliever. He wants to convince the unbeliever who Jesus is and what the advantages are to surrendering to Jesus Christ as Lord.

The question you have to ask yourself is what do you want in life? Jesus can help you with anything. Have you asked Him a question to your situation? He said ask, and it will be given to you. He did not limit anything because He already knows what you will ask for. Maybe one good idea is to ask God to help you accomplish your dreams and follow your destiny. If you ask and believe, then you need to trust Him. Faith in God is the solution to those things you ask of God and receive. If you ask God for a new house because you need it, the God we are talking about supplies all of your needs.

If you need your marriage to work because of distractions and enemy attacks on your marriage, God is the God that put marriages together in Corinthians 7. He will work on your marriage according to His purpose for your marriage.

Seek after God always because He is first in your life. If you had challenges or barriers in the past, make Him first and seek Him always. If you are searching for the Spirit of God in your life, make sure that you have accepted Him into your heart first. Some people believe that God is just with them. The Bible declares that God saves us by His grace in Ephesians 2:8. When you know that you have been saved by grace. Seeking Him is always in the forefront of your mind because you know that God hears you and will answer you. Why are you seeking God? You seek God because you need Him to bless you. You seek God because you need someone to trust completely and with total authority and confidentiality.

You need to see God because your life depends on it. You see the Bible declares that the enemy comes to kill, steal, and destroy. The Bible tells us that the enemy is like a roaring lion seeking and roaming this earth to see whom he may devour. The scripture says in Psalms 27, that *the Lord is my strength and my salvation, whom shall I fear? The Lord is the strength of my life, of whom shall I be afraid?* The power of His love is what saves you and me every time. Seek Him with all your heart. Isaiah says seek Him while He may be found. Today is your day to know Him better.

God is always knocking at the heart of man. He is knocking at the door of your heart to come in and stay with you. You just like everyone else have an entrance in your heart that God can come in and sup with you. He will come in and change your heart and transform you into the image of the person He wants you to be. Yes, God is just like that mailman knocking at your door to give you new mail that you receive so easily. You receive that $10,000 dollar check. If someone opens a door for you to become a millionaire, an actor, song artist, dancer, or any assistance of value to you including income, you will receive it because you believe that you deserve it. Well that is what Jesus is saying; you deserve the best at all times. You deserve to have Jesus in your heart. He is knocking to come into your heart.

In Romans 10:9, He says, *"that if you confess with your mouth the Lord Jesus and believe in your heart that God has raised Him from the dead, you will be saved."* He is more important than all the other opportunities and blessings that you and I have gained in our lifetime.

In fact, he is the reason for you gaining all your success and any accomplishment that awarded blessings.

STEP OUT !

GENESIS 12:1-3: "*Now the LORD had said to Abram: 'Get out of your country, From your family and from your father's house, To a land that I will show you. I will make you a great nation; I will bless you and make your name great; and you shall be a blessing. I will bless those who bless you, and I will curse him who curses you; and in you all the families of the earth shall be blessed.'"*

One of the most common mistakes in life is not listening to God and acting in obedience and faith to God. When He speaks to us about taking specific steps and actions in life, we must be ready and conform to what He asks of us. It is because we have conditions and specific circumstances that keep us in a place where we need to depart from. God might be telling you today to step out of your condition. The questions for you are do you hear His voice, and will you obey God to get your blessing and glorify Him as well? The answer for you and I should be a resounding, "Yes Lord, I will obey. I will step out of my conditions."

Abram at a time in his life heard God's voice and moved by faith and obedience. It was his time to move. We may not move perfectly in obedience, but if we move, God sees and rewards us because He knows why we are moving, why we are acting obedient. It is our destiny by faith to act in faith and accordingly when God speaks. He already knows! Nothing is a surprise to God, our Father. Stepping out of your condition to get your blessing is one of God's priorities for your life. The top priority is acting in faith and obedience to His order. Today, for every Christian, the priority is to first get salvation. The simple step of opening your mouth in confession and opening your heart is a form of stepping out of your condition. Ask Jesus to come into your heart today. Then your faith walk will begin.

Abram was later rewarded for his faith and obedience in God. One of the things that impressed God so much was Abram's faith to say goodbye to any opposition in his life, to any thought of comfort or his comfort zone mentality, to any condition that had bondage. Yes, it meant existing false God, any relative that did not see God the way he saw God. They have not had the same experience with God, talking to them the exact same way and moment in time. You do not stop loving your relatives. You just do not have to live like anyone. You have been transformed to walk in the image of Christ. You have been born again.

Sometimes in life you have to strip yourself of things that are holding you back. Other people may not understand, nor comprehend what is going on with you. But you need to know for yourself what God has for you. God has for you what God has for you. No one can take it away with his or her mentality or any kind of way. They may not understand what you are experiencing in Christ and that is fine. They might not understand the joy you feel in your heart because you know that you heard God speaking to you. They just don't know what you are experiencing!

They may never know until you depart, taking the nearest exit route to get away from them that are holding you back. God wants His people to develop an attitude of stepping out in faith and on His word. His word is your path of life. His word will deliver you and enable you to prosper.

You may have heard plenty of people talking about stepping out. The problem is they develop the when, where, why, and how are you going to do it mentality. Those questions are fine, but if you use them to make an excuse, then you will miss out on the blessing God has for you. One thing is for sure, get yourself out of the picture of God's power, meaning "do it yourself" attitude. Do not misunderstand, you may have to do some things to get things going. But you must operate under God's influence. If you are going to do anything that will succeed, you need to do it because of God and under the power of the Holy Spirit. Your moment and timing and intention must be because of God. Abram strictly moved because of God.

By reading this scripture, it tells me that Abram had to have a heart to move strictly for God's purpose. One thing for sure is that when you step out and obey God, there has to be blessings in store.

I look at many of the churches today and most of them step out when it seems like there was no hope and no help from anyone else. But they trust in God. You are not going into any ministry unless you are trusting and having faith in God. People have started small ministries to mega ministries and the attacks still go on against the church. But God's ministry continues in the power of His might.

I believe God sees the worship inside us and that worship belongs to Him. God sees the faith inside of us and that faith belongs to Him. God sees the glory that you have to give Him, and you and I must give Him the glory. It is not yours, not one measure is yours or mine, and it belongs to our Lord, redeemer of our souls.

Today, I want you to know that your obedience and faith in Christ Jesus is far better than any prophet or any other person in the Bible. We need to have the hope in Jesus' return just like we have to believe in His resurrection from the dead. You see my friend Jesus moved by faith when He carried the cross on Calvary. He did it for me and you. He did so that we could one day see that His faith in His Father was stronger than even Abram's when He moved in accordance to the voice of the Lord.

I remember the days of warfare, fighting a fight that was not mine. Have you ever fought a fight that was not yours? I stepped between two brothers because they were blood brothers, and got hit in an effort to stop the fight before blood was shed between those two brothers. But whatever happened between those two brothers was relational and within the family. So even though blood was shed, pain was inflicted and feelings were hurt, there was still reconciliation between the two. Why was that so? They still had faith in the love inside of each other because they were blood brothers.

They knew that they came from the same seed, same father, and the same mother. Home is where security exists. Jesus reminds us that He is the one who shed the blood that covers us that brings us into the family of Christ Jesus. We are the family that have salvation and will reign with Him in eternity. If it had not been for the blood of Jesus, where would we be? He makes us blood brothers and sisters in Christ. So we must live the life of love, joy, and peace in pure holiness.

There are other warfare moments like serving in Iraq or Afghanistan where the bullets are all around your head. They will kill you without hesitation as sure as the midst and an open target. It is important that every soldier knows that God loves him or her more than they could ever imagine, no matter where you are. He loves you in and out of battle, at home, and wherever soldiers are located. He loves you when you retire and throughout the remainder of your life. He will shower you in love more than you will ever know. God also wants you to know that your faith can still stand strong and that you can still step out of your situation when you get out of the combat zone. He will preserve you for a set time and set reason.

Your life is not over and it will not be over because you are a child of God and a servant of the Most High God. So today stand to your feet and stand tall and confident, full of faith in Jesus Christ with the purpose predestined for your life.

Jesus is showing us a land that we can posses. He is pointing out things that we need to do to glorify Him. Has God shown you anything yet? Has He shown you that He will order your steps if you just step out on faith. The same Jesus will bless you just like He blessed Peter for stepping out of the boat to walk on water to Him. You have got to believe just like Peter did for that moment in time. He knew it was Jesus! Can you feel Jesus in your life? If you step out and feel like you're sinking sometimes, Jesus will reach His hand out and pull you up so you will not drown. Blessed be His righteous and Holy name.

GOD AT THE NARROW GATE

MATTHEW 7: 13: "Enter by the narrow gate; for wide is the gate and broad is the way that leads to destruction, and there are many who go in by it. Because narrow is the gate and difficult is the way which leads to life, and there are few who find it."

One of the most critical skills to have in the military is the ability to maneuver and negotiate obstacles and challenges on the battlefield. Therefore it is absolutely of the highest importance to have land navigation skills to complete every course and mission that you will be faced with in the future. Before you are tested, you usually get trained on what to do in order to know your direction on a map. A map has several gridlines, several north translations and features that you must know in order to get through and pass the test. If you want to be successful in finding your way home, you must be able to read a map. Then you must have the confidence to know the path home. It reminds me of entering the right gate or the wrong gate. If you enter the wrong gates, you could easily end up in the devil's court.

Night land navigation is much more difficult than day time, especially when there are other tasks involved. It adds more stress because you have to have more thought and execution movement to complete it at 100 percent. Routes are so extremely dark that you may not be able to see the hand of your leader, not to mention your own hand. We like to think that you could see God's hand directing you. Our God has different ways to direct us while we are on the path.

It is sometimes at the gate where you get some directions to which location and path to take. The gate also represents the place we call heaven, a place of thanksgiving, a place of worship, and a place of deep adoration and exaltation, a place where we travel in spiritual style to get there. The gate represents a place of entry. Psalms 100:4 states, *"Enter into His gates with thanksgiving, and into His courts with praise."* What a blessing to be able to do so every single day of your life. We should always enter the presence of God with thanksgiving because of what He has already done. Another scripture says, *"The gates of Hades shall not prevail against it,"* (Matthew 16). Satan, hell, and all of its demons can never stop the church because Jesus already defeated him. Jesus is eternal and has all power in His hand. His glory is forever and ever.

As a believer of Jesus Christ residing in your heart, evil will be unable to stop you for whatever purpose God sets out for you. The enemy may delay you and try to imitate you, but it is all a façade and false imitation. You need to know that you are a child of the Most High God. You need to understand it clearly in your heart, mind, and spirit.

Our God allows us to see something in this wide gate so we can get an understanding of reality. The wide gate is the gate that can lead you to hell. It is a real place, but not for the believer to visit, not for the believer to worry about, only those who do not believe in Jesus Christ will end up in that place. Tell all of your friends today that they need to accept Jesus as Lord and Savior. We denounce and rebuke every measure of Hell and every evil spirit that presents itself against the saints of God and the blessings of the Lord. We confess and profess the name of Jesus to rebuke and destroy all attacks of the enemy. Hell is a permanent place of residence to those who do not believe. We pray that they change their mindsets to believe in Jesus Christ as Lord and redeemer.

The narrow gate is the gate that leads to heaven, eternal life. Anyone who puts forth the best effort can remain on this path of the narrow gate. They just need to have faith and trust the Lord with all their heart and lean not to their understanding, but acknowledge Him in all their ways and He will direct their path. Most people never try to stay on the narrow road because they experience a roadblock that might deter them. They experience potholes and deep ruts that they find themselves in after taking wrong turns and traveling on the wrong paths and routes. God wants you to get on the best highway so you can enter into the best gate.

The military is located throughout the world. Large populations enter daily to get to a required destination. Every soldier that is currently serving and those that have retired for various reasons travel daily to get to military installations as well. Most travel to the military base because that is the place of duty. Some, on the other hand, travel because it provides a sense of security for jobs and shopping centers. What is so important about the installation, along with its high security, is the fact that you have to have an identification card to enter the main gate and all military gates because they have the same level of security and restriction for access to enter. If your identification card is not stamped and approved and authorized by the proper agency, guards at the gate will not allow you inside.

This gate is the proper gate for military soldiers to enter to get equipped for battle and to plan engagement against the enemy. In this gate, you stay on the right track to defeat all the arrows that the enemy throws at you. In this gate, you have the capability to put armor on and fight back. In this gate, you get prepared for war that is happening on the outside. Here you have all the resources needed to be successful. When you function out of your atmosphere and environment, it may not be to your benefit. That is why it is important to remain on the right path and entering into the right gate. You would not enter into the enemy's gate unless you had been prepared to do battle. You would not enter the enemy's gate unless you were totally equipped to destroy the enemy and his foes.

They may even have some wrong ambition that will deter them. I want you to know today that Jesus moved ever barrier, roadblock, and experience that got in His way to die on the cross. We do not have time to let something little or imaginary impede our visions and purpose of Jesus Christ our Lord.

The wide gate is symbolic of the path leading to hell. Stop and take an assessment of where you are in life. What are you doing every day to progress in the Kingdom? Who are you serving every day? We all need to know that we serve our risen Savior. Do you even know and care about where you are destined to go after this life is over? Sure you are, everyone dreams of a fantasy place. That place we often dream of is paradise. I never hear people saying that they want to go to hell. It is because God designed us to want Him and to want to live with Him forever. Today, ask God to remove the scales from your eyes so that you can get back on the narrow path that leads to heaven.

The key to getting through the main gate of Jesus Christ is repentance, obedience, sacrifice, and believing by faith that He is the Son of God. He is the only true and wise God that delivered us from God's wrath. It is high time to tell friends and family about entering into the narrow gate. It is the gate where Jesus will bless you before you enter and while you are entering.

GRACE HELPS YOU SEE

JOHN 9:13-15: "They brought him who formerly was blind to the Pharisees. Now it was a Sabbath when Jesus made the clay and opened his eyes. Then the Pharisees also asked him again how he had received his sight. He said to them, 'He put clay on my eyes, and I washed, and I see.'"

You heard that expression before, take off the blinders so you can see. Now you should feel better when the blinders come off. Because when the blinders come off, the truth is revealed and acknowledged.

Today is the day to take your blinders off! They can be removed whenever you are ready on this day. Jesus is waiting to enter your heart right now. That is exactly what happened to the Apostle Paul when he experienced Jesus during his wicked runs to murder. A conversion was waiting on him. So get ready! You will know that you are ready to run for Him in service as soon as you accept Jesus as Lord in your life. In fact the only way you are truly ready is when you accept Jesus as Lord and Savior in your life.

He will be the one to give you permanent vision. Your eyesight and your vision will be restored for the remainder of your life and nothing can change it. Barriers and all kinds of obstacles will be removed. Start trusting in the power of the Holy Spirit.

I know living with the natural body you can see things and they seem so clear. But when you operate in the spiritual realm, God is showing you things that defy the order of the natural realm. He is the God of both supernatural and even the natural because He made us. I, like so many other people, have difficulty explaining it all. There is just no way to tell it all. One thing for sure is that God is in charge of the supernatural things that occur in our lives. He is the God of miracles. For things that we cannot control, nor understand, He is there to show Himself strong. He defies natural order because He is the Creator of all things.

A blind man was brought to the Pharisees because they were disturbed at the fact that Jesus had healed a man who was blind all of his life until He met Jesus. The Pharisees did not misunderstand the miracle Jesus had done. They were jealous and felt betrayed by the people because Jesus had gained so much fame for His ministry of healing and delivering people. Jesus had proved Himself to be the Son of God. All of the evidence needed was present. However, the Pharisees ignored it because of their interpretation of the law.

They ignored it because of the reputation Jesus had gained by the people. Sometimes in life when you are doing the work of God and you do well at it, jealousy strikes the heart of people you know or may not know. Jealousy strikes at the core of nerves and individual pride surfaces because the enemy is busy. All this jealousy and thinking that they were supposed to enforce the law over the miracle working power of Jesus had no substance and no way of glorifying God.

Jesus tells us in Mark 2:27-28 that the Sabbath was made for man, not man for the Sabbath. Therefore, the Son of Man is Lord of the Sabbath. Another way of putting it, do not worship the Sabbath day, but worship on that day and not let what God need from you be blocked by religious beliefs of the Sabbath. The only true and wise God is not about to let someone suffer because of the opinions of others. He does not let a day go by that His healing touch is not involved in.

If you go to the hospital on the Sabbath Day, you will find that the Savior is there healing and blessings those that need His touch. If you go by the nursing home where people are lonely because time is going by and their loved ones may have already gone, Jesus is there. If you go by homes where people are not able to get out of bed, Jesus is visiting that person on the Sabbath.

Mark 3: 1-5: "And He entered the synagogue again, and a man was there who had a withered hand. So they watched Him closely, whether He would heal him on the Sabbath, so that they might accuse Him. And He said to the man who had the withered hand, 'Step forward.' Then He said to them, 'Is it lawful on the Sabbath to do good or to do evil, to save life or to kill?' But they kept silent. And when He had looked around at them with anger, being grieved by the hardness of their hearts, He said to the man, 'Stretch out your hand.' And he stretched it out, and his hand was restored as whole as the other."

Jesus heals again. This time He entered the synagogue and a man was there who had a withered hand. Jesus was under watch at this time by the Pharisees to see what He would do. And it is just like Jesus not to abandon anyone. He will not let you go broken when you call on Him. Jesus asked the man to step forward with His withered hand. He told the man to stretch out his hand. And he stretched it out and it was healed even better than the other.

The Bible says that He never sleeps, nor slumbers. He is always on watch, looking for someone who needs a miracle. You see it was on the Sabbath when Jesus opened the eyes of the blind man. He will open your eyes anytime you need Him to. He will remove the scales of darkness from those that have the Pharisees' mentality. He will remove the spiritual scales that work to keep you in darkness, working in sin. Millions of people today need a touch to see again. They are missing abundant blessings.

You heard the story of the mule stuck in the pit. The owner never thought for a moment to leave his mule so he stayed all night, digging the hole wider and trying to pull the mule free. He knew if he left that mule in the hole, he would just die. He also knew that the mule had a special place in him. You see when we fall into a ditch or a pit, God has a special place for us in His heart. He is there no matter what the situation may look like.

CHAPTER 11

NEW SIGHT FROM GOD

Acts 9:9-14: "And he was three days without sight, and neither ate nor drank. Now there was a certain disciple at Damascus named Ananias; and to him the Lord said in a vision, 'Ananias.' And he said, 'Here I am Lord.' So the Lord said to him, 'Arise and go to the street called Straight, and inquire at the house of Judas for one called Saul of Tarsus, for behold, he is praying. And in a vision he has seen a man named Ananias coming in and putting his hand on him, so that he might receive his sight.' Then Ananias answered, 'Lord, I have heard from many about this man, how much harm he has done to Your saints in Jerusalem. And here he has authority from the chief priests to bind all who call on Your name.'"

Ananias spoke to God saying that this man, Saul, could never become a Christian because he was murdering Christians. In his mind this was absolutely impossible for a conversion to have happened with this man Saul. How could a murderer be changed so instantly and be proven in God's eye? Only God has such answer. The living God can do anything. He reminded him that Saul was a chosen vessel. God's power worked on Saul inside and on the outside.

Ananias was surprised that God would select someone who was once an enemy of our Lord and God's Saints. Saul had been a man who killed habitually because of Christianity. He hunted Christians down like dirty dogs to the death. Thank God that He still used Ananias to bless Saul through the Lord. This man whom God selected continued the remaining of his life in the powerful anointing, grace, and mercy of God to write two thirds of the Gospel. He went on several missionary journeys to witness to unbelievers and believers and later ended up establishing churches along the way in his missions. God can change anybody for His glory. God can change the worst of human life and dignity that the enemy tried to still. His compassion fails not. His power and authority can never fail. His power is all eternal and everlasting. He is flawless, infinite, perfect, infallible, and all mighty. His mercy endures forever.

There is always someone in life that God leads us to for the working of His ministry. When the Lord sends you to that person to receive you, let them receive you because it could be of the Lord. However, always be aware that it is God who chose you before the foundations of the world. He already gave you sight before you came into the earth. Sooner or later more people will have gained their sight by removing the scales and use the power of Christ to witness. God is able to use anybody whether spiritual or non spiritual. I believe that you can never be limited by your past, any mistakes, any hurts, any handicap, or thing that seems like it may be blocking your from prospering and being successful. Do not let anything hinder you because you are a child of the Most High God.

When I was a young child, my mother use to say, "Put the record on for me baby!" She was referring to the old 45-sized records that they used in the 1950s, 60s, and 70s. She would want me to put on music artists like B.B. King, the Temptations, and Ray Charles—the old school singers. They all had amazing talent. But there was something unusual about Ray Charles. He was legally blind. I must admit that when I saw Jamie Foxx playing the role of Ray Charles, it brought back memories of this legendary artist who captured the minds and hearts of people through several generations. What set Charles apart from other artists was his amazing talent demonstrated under disabled conditions. Most people would have given up on life and hope. Certainly many people would have allowed their condition to overcome them.

Charles captured the heart of millions of people with his singing and piano playing talents while having a blind disability. He could even pat his feet at the organ and sing like no other. But I believe even today the majority of his fans never really saw him as blind because he never performed like he was blind. To some, blind means the inability to see from the lens of your eyes. Blind means unable to see the break of day. Blind means lacking the ability to see you're in walking from point A to point B. Blind is a condition that disables a person and sets limitations. I never knew Ray Charles' spiritual condition, whether he knew the Lord or not, but the attitude he portrayed would make one believe that He knew about the blessings of the Lord. Because he demonstrated a zeal and thirst to sing and play skillfully for millions of people weekly and yearly, he demonstrated that there is no limitation.

Christians should have that ability to sing praises to the Lord with a zeal that demonstrates a witness unlimited and unparalleled to any other. Christians should sing with a heart of melody that will reflect the light of Christ and impact millions influencing them to surrender to the Lord.

Music touches the soul as so many of us already know. We get excited about so many songs. Life is good when you're dancing and having so much fun. Christians can reach out to help in touching souls and impacting to the point where people will say Lord please anchor me, please come into my heart. Please forgive me for backsliding, and all of my sins. In order to be effective in the Christian life and the community in this world, people who need to know the Savior, we must allow our scales to fall off from our eyes.

When Ray Charles sang, one would think that scales had fallen off because it appeared that nothing was ever blocking his view from performing his art. He moved to new levels in his career of singing. We as Christians should do the same. We should move to new levels in Christ Jesus our Lord. Whatever your scale of hindrance is ask the

Lord to help you in allowing it to fall like the Apostle Paul's experience. The scale can fall and you can see again and be active in the Lord by serving Him alone.

GOD OPENS SECOND CHANCES AND MORE

Acts 9: "Saul! Saul! Why are you persecuting me?"

Thank God that He allowed me to have a second chance at life. When I was a young boy growing up, there were opportunities to do things too easily that would cause harm to me or even take my life. I am grateful that He heard my cry and He saw my frailties and weaknesses that could have stolen my life. There were times that I had bullets flying over my head in a neighborhood that had no tolerance for peace.

It was my choice to visit that place called the "bottoms." It was my choice to visit places across town that had gang violence and could have easily engaged in stabbings and more shootings at the drop of a dime. There are second chances for everything that God allows for His glorious purpose. It does not change just because you come into the ministry and call yourself a minister or servant of the Most High God. Trouble still comes your way and mine. So open your eyes and seek God for a second chance at life. You are not dead yet. But you can die to sin and be born again.

What do you think the Apostle Paul said when he heard the voice of Jesus? He said who are you Lord? Although he did not have a relationship at that time, he still acknowledged Him as Lord. God called out and I believe that then Saul, now Paul, believed that something spectacular was about to happen to his life that would transform him for the remainder of his time on earth.

The Apostle Paul was open to a second chance. He has been given a second chance to set the record straight. Jesus gave Him a second chance to follow Him under obedience. Jesus gave Him a lifetime of ministry to substitute the pain and suffering he has caused Christians. He was a killer, a man filled with hate, but God intervened and no longer could he hate and kill. Jesus had put into process a new man who would shake the kingdom with giving due glory to God. He would set forth and ordained the Apostle Paul to be fearless and truly committed to preaching the gospel throughout the world. This Gospel is to be preached that all captives are set free. God opened the door to a second chance for all that call on the name of Jesus. It's time to go to your prayer closet and start seeking Him for you. It is your time for a second chance as an individual to impress God. God is waiting for you to make a move so He can bless you. Do not wait on man or else you will be waiting too long and you may miss the timing of God in your life.

Listen to His voice when He says move. No matter what happened in your life, God can change it for His purpose and for your good. You have a second chance to preach this gospel and help deliver the lost. You have a second chance to be successful in the community and be a positive role model. You have a second chance at your marriage. You can shake the devil off of your marriage. It's yours because God fixed it and ordained it for you to live a good life—long and joyous with your loved ones. You have a second chance at serving the right God. Who is your God? Are you caught up on religion and do not understand that you have been blinded by Satan and his demons. Cast them out of your life right at this moment.

Call the Lord and be moved in the power of deliverance. You have a second chance at accepting Christ as Lord and Savior. Do not wait another day! Read *Romans 10:9-10: "That if you confess with your mouth the Lord Jesus and believe in your heart that God has raised Him from the dead, you will be saved. For with the heart one believes unto righteousness, and with the mouth confession is made unto salvation."* Say this! Lord Jesus, I repent of my sin. Lord, come into my heart and save me. I believe that you are the Son of God and that you bled and died for my sin and rose from the dead. I thank you Lord for everlasting life.

GOD HELPS US STAND!

Jude 1:24-25: "Now to Him who is able to keep you from stumbling, And to present you faultless before the presence of His glory with exceeding joy, To God our Savior, Who alone is wise, Be glory and majesty, dominion and power, Both now and forever. Amen."

God is able to keep us from falling. Have you ever fallen down hard? Have you ever failed a test in your life that was important? Have you ever failed a mission that you knew had to be completed? Have you ever fallen accidentally and it was difficult to get back up on your feet? Some of us have fallen and everyone around us have seen a physical fall. It always seems like a sense of embarrassment because you did not keep your balance, instead you appeared to be clumsy and unbalanced. Even through the embarrassment, we still get back up.

Have you ever fell to the bottom of life because of an addiction to a certain drug, drink, or a type of medication, or just anything in general? Have you ever fallen spiritually from a relationship with Jesus Christ? Have you ever chosen anything or anyone above Jesus Christ? Ephesians 6:12-16 tells us that there are principalities and rulers of darkness. The Apostle Paul says, *"For we do not wrestle against flesh and blood, but against principalities, against powers, against the rulers of the darkness of this age, against spiritual hosts of wickedness in the heavenly places. Therefore take up the whole armor of God, that you may be able to withstand in the evil day, and having done all, to stand. Stand therefore, having girded your waist with truth, having put on the breastplate of righteousness, and having shod your feet with the preparation of the gospel of peace; above all, taking the shield of faith with which you will be able to quench all the fiery darts of the wicked one."*

Many people have problems in their lives with drug habits and alcohol consumption, which leads to so many improper actions and a wrong lifestyle. All in fact need help in those struggles. Many people have fallen to adultery and fornication and just all sorts of sexual relations. Some people fall from their self-made empire that seemed strong and invincible. Some people have desires that take them to places that can lead to a fallen state of life in general. There are so many good things in life to live for. This life is worth living. God gave us this free life and now He is offering salvation free. Salvation is free living eternally. God looks to bless rather than be bothered with the evil one. He removes that issue of life. God already knows that the enemy is on a personal rampage to destroy His people. We are told to be watchful in our lives but we need the Savior watch over us. We will mess it up every time unless we trust in Him. God is on your side to blesses you in ways unimaginable. The continuation of Ephesians in chapter 6:17-20 says, *"And take the helmet of salvation, and the sword of the Spirit, which is the word of God; praying always with all prayer and supplication in the Spirit, being watchful to this end with all perseverance and supplication for all the saints— and for me, that utterance may be given to me, that I may open my mouth boldly to make known the mystery of the gospel, for which I am an ambassador in chains; that in it I may speak boldly, as I ought to speak."*

In the movie Fallen by Denzel Washington, it was portrayed that an evil spirit was loosed and was on the attack against any and all people everywhere he could attack. The enemy sought to kill, steal, and destroy the lives of people in every business it could reach. The enemy was on duty to take away life. In his movie, it was revealed that the enemy desired to go to one place; it showed us that the enemy was always looking for a host, the entire mind, and spirit of a person. Many people were falling into the enemy's trap. It appeared to me that the enemy was like a roaring lion seeking whom he may devour.

It appears in large that the enemy was searching for empty vessels, those that did not have Jesus Christ on the outside. At the same time, the enemy was looking for saints as well. It is important to know that in the enemy's mind, if you do not have Christ inside your heart, you are an open target and set apart for a fall of the enemy. Jesus Christ can keep you from falling.

We need to know today that Jesus can keep us from falling. When the enemy comes in like a flood, God is there to take hold of the situation. He has a standard that stops the enemy in its tracks and rebukes and sends it back to the pits of hell. You have an advocate strong and mighty, who is our Lord God. You see, the Bible reminds us in Jude 24, *"Now to Him who is able to keep you from stumbling, And to present you faultless before the presence of His glory with exceeding joy, To God our Savior, Who alone is wise, be glory and majesty, Dominion and power, both now and forever."* You see He has been keeping you your entire life. He has kept many people for 20, 40, 60, 100, and some over 100 years of life on this earth. His grace and mercy is from everlasting to everlasting. God with His own infinite wisdom and blessings will present you faultless before His very presence. Accept Him in your heart today and have a trusting relationship with Him that will last in eternity with Him.

What was the Lord saying when He said, keep you from falling? He was simply saying that any danger in your life, I will keep you from it if you trust me. If the attack is so massive and has he potential to overpower you, God will still keep you under the shadow of His loving care. When the attacks get so heavy on your back, I will be there to remove the enemy attacks. You see God controls all things. You remember what happened to Job. God allowed the enemy to attack him to almost a breaking point in life.

The enemy was allowed to strike him with sores, and pain, and take away his family members in death. God allowed it! God always knows exactly what He is doing. He never allowed Job to fall and die. He specifically told the enemy, do not touch his life. When God speaks and gives orders, power is released beyond measure. The enemy did not touch Job's life, he touched the things that mattered to him most. But God blessed him more abundantly that what he previously had. God kept Job from falling.

God can keep you from falling into deep hurt. It is more than just falling and getting scratched up knees. It is more than falling and getting a hurt ego and pride, it is more than falling and getting your reputation stained and your name mocked. It is a fall that will take you to hell without release. God keeps you from that fall. It is a fall you take that changes your life to a new destiny because now you know Jesus saved you from hell. You just have to trust in the Lord with all your heart and lean not to your own understanding. Acknowledge Him and He will direct your path. You have to accept Him as Lord and Savior. He already redeemed you and me with His precious blood. But you still need to get on the right side of the track.

Listen, the Lord will hold you up more than friends will. You still need to have some friends, but no one on earth can do you like Jesus. He is a comforter when you need Him. He is love when you feel unloved. He is the one who keeps you in perfect peace. He is the one who visits you in the midnight hour. You see when you're lonely He is there. When you are suicidal, He will change your mind to think and know how to live life abundantly. He will remove the thoughts in your heart and mind. You need Jesus just like me and everybody else. You are not an exception to the rule.

Today, make a decision in your prayer requests to Him that He would keep you and your family from falling away from Him and not in the hands of the adversary. Live a new lifestyle in the Kingdom of God from this point on. You will not regret it because you will reign with Him in eternity. He loves you right now and forever. Blessed be the name of the Lord.

GOD'S POWER WORKS INSIDE

EPHESIASN 3:20: "Now to Him who is able to do exceedingly abundantly above all that we ask or think, according to the power that works in us, to Him be glory in the church by Christ Jesus to all generations, forever and ever. Amen."

God is able to do exceedingly abundantly above all that we ask or think, according to His power that works in us. He is able to do things that are impossible to us. But we need to understand that His power works on the inside of us and that He can do anything inside and outside. His power works at all times. We need to realize that we are speaking of the God who created all things from nothing. His power is at work on the inside of the believer right now. He is working out every plan by allowing you to move under His authority and power today.

He is working on your mind and mine at this very moment. If we could even imagine what He has put inside our minds, the capability to expand to a level beyond human comprehension. God's power is not limited by any stretch of imagination, nor at any time, nor in any way. Whatever the situation is, He has already worked it out in the life of the believer. He works out those that are called in His righteous name. You are the one who is blocking those particular blessings in your life or that particular mission He has set apart for you. He will send you whether you like it or not because it is for His purpose.

Everything that God wants done, He will complete it through you or whom He has chosen. You want God to do it all for you! He has already done what is needed for you. You just need to start claiming what He has already delivered to you. Start giving Him all the glory due Him because He has already blessed you in abundance. What about you giving Him the glory?

There certain things that He wants you to do. One of them is move when He says so. One of the books I am working on now is called "You Can't Stop the Move of God." It will target all the people who are feeling down and lost and confused. It will move those who know its time to make a move. It will tell those who are suppose to bless that you are to start receiving your blessing and stop holding yourself back based on people's attitudes and opinions.

You need to start telling yourself they don't count, especially if they are not blessing you in the Lord. I was just speaking with a leader in the church who has a ministry and several ministers under him that it's time to be fruitful.

There can be twenty-two ministers, or fifty-two, or even one hundred plus under your watch, but the fact remains to whether they are being truly mentored to or just stagnant. Are they just checking a box to appear holy and righteous, or are they key players in the ministry? A strong ministry will develop people and start sending them out beyond the four walls. It is time to take what God has taught them to be disciples and be fruitful in God's Kingdom. It is in the move of God that we please Him.

Another one is that you are responsible for activating your faith. Do not let your faith die. Do not let your faith depend on someone pumping you up in church. Do not let your faith be dependent on false gods and images. Do not allow yourself to get caught up on things that are in darkness. Do not allow yourself to get placed into a pit and not get out. Do not allow your faith to be approved by someone else. God is your approving authority in faith, truth, spirit and word. The flesh is the flesh.

The scripture reminds us that there is no good thing in the flesh. Your faith is the same kind of faith that God was looking at when He saw Abraham's faith. So start walking in the faith God destined for you. It is approved by God and you will not it if you have a relationship with Jesus Christ.

Another one is that you need to believe in God when He ordains something because it will come to past. If you truly believe, you will push and press your way to the victory that He has set before you. Living in victory is part of the abundant life. You will start receiving the benefits of victory. Those benefits are the abundance that God is pouring out in your life. You just need to reach up, reach out and get it. Then giving Him glory will be easy for you. Stop holding back on God. He has filled you in abundance. I always find myself holding back. The God of creation, the ruler who sits on the throne in heaven has already blessed a brother to bless another brother.

At one particular time in ministry, I found myself stuck and at a standstill in ministry. I start seeing people play the same tired, wicked ministry games in the church. I started seeing people in different areas of my life acting in ways not pleasing to God and it was a turn off. In my mind I was saying, I don't want to be involved in this mess. I started believing that I could be ministered to at home watching evangelists preach the gospel. The word is his word and no one can change the word of God. At last, I was at a distance. But the fact of the matter is we all need Jesus to straighten out those matters of the heart. We need Him to help us to be obedient. I need Him to help me be obedient to the call of ministry and family.

You and I both have the power to change our own situations as they occur. We can change as fast as God moves in our lives. We just need to allow the Spirit of the Lord to work a good work on the inside. If you do not enjoy being down and depressed, call on the Lord and change it. You have Him on the inside of your heart! You should not be walking depressed anyway. There is enough of God for everyone to have. You just need to count on Him. Depend on Him. You need to know Him for yourself.

It is time to stop limiting God in what He can do. You may have had a situation of drugs and relationships ups and downs, but it is not too much for God. People may have run out on you. You thought they were going to love you the rest of your life. You better get it together and stop waiting on folks to love you like they are God. No one can fill you will abundantly love and His pure love like He can. The same God we are talking about is the one who called the world into existence and created Adam and Eve and all human existence. He gave life in abundance. He formed societies. He formed states and cities. His power was working then in us and on us. His power is still working for the change of our lifestyles.

I am telling you that if you want to see God work, use your faith and believe that the Holy Ghost will work it out. What do you think is impossible for Him? The scripture says that nothing is impossible for Him. If you think that a disease is more powerful than the Lord, think again! He cleansed men who had leprosy. He restored sight to the blind. He even raised Lazarus from the dead. He raised a little girl from the dead. God has the power to give life again. He can restore and bless you in ways unimaginable.

People in the music industry use what they have to produce record labels year end and year out. They trust that the power of singing in them exists, and that it will never fade away. Why can't you as a believer and you who are lost believe that God can put His power in you and that His power will never fade away? His power can and will produce something great and spectacular in you that you will glorify Him and witness to the world that Jesus is Lord.

The Apostle went on journey after journey to please God. He encountered the worst-case scenarios. He was even snake bitten. But the power that works on the inside kept Him alive to overcome that snakebite and all the people who came against the work and testimony of Jesus Christ through His servant Paul. When things get so bad, you need to trust that God's power is working. Remember, He sent His Holy Spirit to work in our lives. There is nothing more powerful than God's Holy Spirit working on behalf of the believer to give God all the glory through us. That, my friend, is the abundance that we must give back to God. Bless His righteous name.

AUTHORITY TO BIND

Acts 9:14-18: "And here he has authority from the chief priests to bind all who call on your name. But the Lord said to him, 'Go, for he is a chosen vessel of mine to bear my name before Gentiles, kings, and the children of Israel. For I will show him how many things he must suffer for my name's sake. And Ananias went his way and entered the house; and laying his hands on him he said, Brother Saul, the Lord Jesus who appeared to you on the road as you came, has sent me that you may receive your sight and be filled with the Holy Spirit.' Immediately there fell from his eyes something like scales, and he received his sight at once; and he arose and was baptized."

Something like scales fell from the eyes of Saul so that he could receive his spiritual sight for the ministry of Jesus Christ, our Lord. His life had begun a new course. God blessed the Apostle Paul to be a chosen vessel. He chose him to bear His name before Gentiles, kings, and the children of Israel. This means that He would be faced with ministering to many people of authority and those that were lost, those looking down on, those calling him names lower than dogs, and those rich in their own eye, even those that claim to be righteous in Christ, those who did not regard God as being the only true God, those that kept people in bondage, and of course His chosen people of Israel.

So then, the Apostle Paul would have many missionary journeys to bear the name of Jesus. Yet be reminded that bearing Jesus name on mission has a cost. The cost is to suffer for His namesake. The cost is persecution. But above all be ready for His return to bless you when He pulls you in the air to forever be with Him.

It takes God to change things in our lives. It takes God to move us from sin to righteousness. It takes God to move us from sin to servanthood. It takes God to restore a man to be on God's side rather than evil's side. God can use anybody He desires to use for His kingdom.

When God sees you any way you are, even in your worst condition, He can still chose you because he alone can and will restore you. All you have to do is ask and receive is blessings in your life. Some people have been a destructive or deceitful, but God still chose them and He is waiting for the next person to ask for deliverance. Believe this, He can change you from destructive to witness for His namesake. He can change you and me from our worst state of heart and mind to become one in the fivefold ministry.

When God wants you, He will get you. He can change your daily habits to serve Him. He can remove you bad habits and make you live with the best good habits. Think about it, you do things to please everyone else, but do you please God? He will not hold it against you. He will just choose you then you will choose Him. He has the power to do anything regardless of what man says.

The Apostle Paul had bad habits. His habit was to kill Christians, but God stepped in and changed his evil habits and life. Then God made the Apostle one of His chosen men. Do you want to be one of God's chosen men? Ask God and look for an experience to happen to change you right now for the glorious purpose of God. Ask Him to remove the scales from your eyes so that you can see like He did for the old man Saul to be translated to the Apostle Paul. Then you will become a light to the world as a witness to the one and only living God to bear His name.

Later it would be Jesus who said in Matthew 18:18-20, *"Assuredly, I say to you, whatever you bind on earth will be bound in heaven, and whatever you loose on earth will be loosed in heaven. 'Again I say to you that if two of you agree on earth concerning anything that they ask, it will be done for them by My Father in heaven. For where two or three are gathered together in my name, I am there in the midst of them.'"*

YOUR CALLING AND ELECTION

2 PETER 1:10: "Therefore, brethren, be even more diligent to make your call and election sure, for if you do these things you will never stumble; for so an entrance will be supplied to you abundantly into the everlasting kingdom of our Lord and Savior Jesus Christ."

Peter wanted to let people know that your salvation is not based on a good life. He also wants them to understand not to become complacent in the ministry to the point that they might listen to false doctrine. Peter is saying, do not allow yourselves to get complacent and just accept anything and any type of doctrine, but receive and accept the doctrine of Jesus Christ our Lord and Redeemer.

You have to work to develop yourself in the Lord when it comes to His doctrine or any service. The word will work on you and through you. But you must remain in the doctrine of Jesus our Lord, especially if you received your calling. The Holy Spirit will guide you into truth and keep you on the path of righteousness. The Holy Spirit will help you to be diligent in your calling. He will help you through the hard times and even strengthen your calling and election for service in the Lord.

An entrance will be supplied for those who hold onto their calling and election. Child of God, keep on standing on the word of God. He will never let you go. You can count on it with Jesus! He loves His people. He loves those that are called according to His purpose. Hold on to your calling. Remember what the word tells us. The enemy comes to kill, steal, and destroy. If you have a calling, you need to understand that you are God's child. You do not belong to the enemy, but the enemy will come at every angle to destroy you. He will try to kill, steal, and destroy your calling.

Your mission is to be ministered to by the Holy Spirit. Your calling is to be for the Holy Spirit to protect. You have to use your mouth and tongue and speak things into existence by the power of the word. That is why God put the Holy Spirit here. He is your guide. He is your protector. He helps you speak the word with power, authority and boldness. God is still the Most High God and is able to do what He has already predestined for your life.

So you received your calling! How do you know? Was it a burning desire on the inside of your heart? If so, don't let anything stop you from your calling. God is the one calling! Rest assured; if He is calling you, you are in for blessings of a lifetime. Remember how Jesus called the disciples. He chose one by one and taught them about the ministry. He did not turn them away to be lost. He did not look down on them to hurt them. Jesus wanted men to build the kingdom of God. He has already chosen more disciples than men can even imagine. Yes, you are correct, you are one of His disciples.

You can find out by asking yourself, have I been serving God? If you are a servant, you are one of His disciples. You do not have to try so hard to become a disciple. You just need to know that Jesus called you to missions and be obedient and faithful to the call. Remember, there are so many callings in service for our Lord. So you do not have to get bogged down on just what you think. Continue in your daily walk to seek the Lord for counsel. You need the Holy Spirit to teach and guide you to become an effective witness. The word mission means that you have service to do in God's will for your life. There is a place for you.

It is the expressed blessings in the ultimate sense of serving the Most High God.

The Apostle Paul lived one of the most dangerous lives on earth. He was a murderer who went about killing the people of God. Then it became his time to have the "script flipped." He became a servant for the Lord because the Lord chose Him. He was a mission-minded servant. He was a man on a mission regardless of what anybody said about his calling and service for the Lord. It was the Lord's anointing that rested on the Apostle Paul while traveling to Damascus. It was His anointing that kept him as he served all of his years. His life was never the same. God changed his life, just like He can change yours and mine even more.

One of the things I think about is the military mindset and the service. In the military, we always maintained a high level of mission-minded attitude. If you reject it or allow it to diminish, then the ball would drop, meaning that important mission and tasks would not be accomplished. People would suffer because of that. Then someone will start the blame game. But in Christianity and serving God, no one can point the finger at anybody else. You have to be a man or women of God for yourself. It is your relationship. The Apostle knew because it was him that God confronted while on the road to Damascus. God changed his heart and mind that one moment. It takes a heart change to become a mission-minded servant. Remember this visitation was the beginning of the scales falling from the eyes of Saul's conversion to the Apostle Paul.

Another important point is the fact that the Apostle Paul was led by the Holy Spirit to make his election sure. God said that he was a chosen vessel. So then God was the one who elected him. It was not a man who elected him. God wanted Ananias and anyone else to know that it was His choice. That is powerful because we know that God wants us to make the choice to surrender our lives to Him, to serve Him, and worship and praise His righteous name. We need to understand that our election is also by God. He knows who wants to be one of His before they even attempt it.

When the people elect a president, or a new government representative, they know if that person wants it bad enough. They know because of the debates, and the constant campaigning, and advertising to win. They know because of the constant theme or slogan that they are consistently using such as, "Chose me, I will be the best president or representative because I will do this for you," "I will represent you and get the best results."

God wants us to have that kind of attitude. Christians should aim to get the best results in God's kingdom. When you get born again and have the type of experience, the scales have fallen from your eyes and your heart, you will also start campaigning and advertising for God. You will put off the old you in your mind and set your sights on things above because in you are the blessings of God.

Today, make our Lord you new focus in life. Make Him the center of your life. Make your faith walk the center of life in Christ Jesus. Once you make Him the center of your life, blessings start flowing in abundance. You will start seeing things different in your life and all around you. You will start to love people better than you used to love. You will start to put your marriage into a better perspective and focus in your heart. Life is just better all-around in Jesus Christ.

Open your heart right now in your private room, in your secret place, and give your life to Jesus! You do not have to wait on anyone, just do it today so you will have eternal life. Eternal life means living with Jesus forever. It is a free gift and opportunity. Nothing can beat it! Blessed be the name of the Lord who reigns forever and ever. When Jesus spoke in John 17 about His disciples to the Father, the meaning of it was extremely clear.

EXPERIENCE YOUR CALLING TO THE END

Matthew 10:1-4: "And when He had called His twelve disciples to Him, He gave them power over unclean spirits, to cast them out, and to heal all kinds of sickness and all kinds of disease. Now the names of the twelve apostles are these: first, Simon, who is called Peter, and Andrew his brother; James the son of Zebedee, and John his brother; Philip and Bartholomew; Thomas and Matthew the tax collector; James the son of Alphaeus, and Lebbaeus, whose surname was Thaddaeus; Simon the Cananite, and Judas Iscariot, who also betrayed Him."

When the disciples were called, they were about their daily business. Jesus walked about and selected them. They did not know that He was coming to choose them to become followers after Him. They did not know that they were destined to be some of the greatest Christian men that ever lived. They did not know that their lives were about to change, that they would be known in later generations.

They did not know that their ministry and calling would be extended until the end of time. They did not know that over 2,000 years later men would be preaching the gospel that they wrote inspired by the power of Jesus Christ Himself. Men today might as well get ready because you will be called out by the Lord to serve similar to these men. The Holy Spirit will help you serve God to be pleasing in His sight. There is a call for men and women to serve. God knows who is His and He alone opens the ministry for His glory to be revealed. Men put limits, but God opens doors for you.

These men became the disciples of Jesus of Nazareth. Jesus specifically called them and did not need someone on earth to call them. It was not of their doing. It was not that they were self-proclaimed. They had to be obedient to the call. That is what it took on their behalf and that is what it takes on yours and my behalf. It was because of Jesus and the power of the Holy Spirit in their lives that they accepted the call.

You have got to be ready for such an experience, but if you are not ready, He will equip you for it. He is the only one who can truly prepare you for the ministry. It may be difficult to know your complete calling in your life, but Jesus knows exactly why He called you. In your calling to serve Jesus, you need to know what He is saying to you daily. In order to do so, you need to get a prayer life, and start fasting, and submitting under His authority. If you do not believe that He is speaking to you, then it's time for you to get on your knees and pray some more until you get a breakthrough. Pray like Daniel prayed if you have to, but pray. God can hear you. If fact it will be a good habit if you start praying three times a day or more. In being a servant for the Most High God, our Father, you need to stay in constant communication. Pray is one of the primary means. His word is another mean. Worship and praise is another means of communicating to God.

Too many people are beating themselves up about what their calling is or whether or not they have been called. You know if you should be a preacher, a deacon, usher, or any area of service for the Lord's house and missionary. Others may have some insight through demonstration of your calling and ministry, but God and you are the central focus. Use the gift if you want to please God. Jesus called twelve and no one knew that He was about to call that twelve. Nothing is standing between you and God's calling but you and the enemy. Those are easy obstacles. Just rebuke the enemy and trust God. Trust Him more than you trust anything else. In fact, the best way to look at it is to trust God more than you trust you. That does not mean that you should not use your brain. It means that God is more powerful than you and your flesh. The Apostle speaks of the flesh always getting in the way. Whenever you try to do right, you end up doing something wrong because the flesh keeps on getting in the way. No matter what the problem appears to be, you stand the test of time. You hold on to your calling. If it is one thing you know that you have, that is your calling unto the Most High God. Blessed be His righteous and Holy name.

GOD SEES YOU MINISTERING

HEBREWS 6:10-12: "For God is not unjust to forget your work and labor of love which you have shown toward His name, in that you have ministered to the saints, and do minister. And we desire that each one of you show the same diligence to the full assurance of hope until the end, that you do not become sluggish, but imitate those who through faith and patience inherit the promises."

God sees you are willing and able to minister and He will reward you. The Lord sees your obedience to the call to serve Him. He has your rewards and inheritance laid up for you in heaven. He will bless you anywhere because you chose to be one of His. What a thought! One of His! That means you are no one else's property. No one else controls you. No one else can bless you like Jesus. You have Jesus, the Son of the living God on your side. He is the one who holds all power in His hands.

Jesus will not forget your obedience to the faith and to His call to serve. He wants His Saints to maintain hope in their lives in the spirit. Hope will bring you through it all. You have to know that God is with you during your service. Listen to what the apostle is saying, you have ministered to the saints, and do minister. Too many people believe that the church is the only place to minister. God has news for you! It is not the only place to minister.

God wants you to know that it is easy to allow yourself to get discouraged. God has not forgotten about you, our families, nor me. God sees every good work that we perform under His anointing.

In the early years of Christianity, people thought that good works was the final solution to salvation, getting to heaven. But God did not design it that way. The path to heaven is simple yet there are things that try to prevent you. Repent of your sin with a sincere heart to our Lord Jesus Christ is the way to get to the Lord our God. Confess with your mouth the Lord Jesus and believe in your heart that He is the Son of God and you will be saved (Romans 10).

Some days are harder than others in this life. Thank God that we do know why. We know that days are hard because the adversary seeks to destroy those that follow Jesus. We know that this flesh also has days when it will not submit to the voice and moving of Jesus. Sometimes the flesh gets over emotional and misled with false inner wisdom.

There are thousands of movies that have so much creativeness within them. It takes a person with a creative mind to develop them. Some weekends are advertised on television as movie marathons. Movies are poured out left and right, hour after hour, day after day. New titles are birthed and show rapidly, faster than ever before. What strikes so many people is the ability to imitate a developed script by himself or herself or someone else. It takes skill to put yourself into another character and project it as you being so real and persuasive. It takes skill to be so diverse and flexible with script adlibbing and maintaining posture and different identities.

The other important piece to it is the level of commitment and diligence toward the performance in entertainment. Please understand there is nothing wrong with possessing those great skills because I believe so many movies do make extremely valuable points in life. Some make you cry, some make you laugh, and some even make you frown and wonder. The point is that there are thousands of imitators in those movies that impact and influence society in ways that God can use them. For the Christian community, we must be imitators of the faith of the gospel of Christ. We need to be committed to Him even higher than actors are committed to their work on screen. I think it is time that followers of Jesus started launching out into the deep to catch fish just actors do. In Hebrews 11, God illustrated through the Apostle Paul the heroes of faith that touched God's heart in the work of the ministry as good imitators and the list goes on throughout the Bible and even today with His saints. Glory to His righteous name.

Today is your day to have an outpouring of life into the ministry. Let your light shine through your life in the ministry that was assigned to you. Ministry comes in different ways. Everyone just needs to understand that it is under the operation of the Holy Spirit.

Who comes close to being the imitator of the faith? You and I are the imitators. We witness throughout the world, in our communities, and right where we are at the moment. God is everywhere and His eyes see all things. When you need help, He is there.

CHAPTER 12

PEOPLE ON FIRE

ACTS 2:36-47: "'Therefore let all the house of Israel know assuredly that God has made this Jesus, whom you crucified, both Lord and Christ.' Now when they heard this, they were cut to the heart, and said to Peter and the rest of the apostles, 'Men and brethren, what shall we do?' Then Peter said to them, 'Repent, and let every one of you be baptized in the name of Jesus Christ for the remission of sins; and you shall receive the gift of the Holy Spirit. For the promise is to you and to your children, and to all who are afar off, as many as the Lord our God will call.' And with many other words he testified and exhorted them, saying, 'Be saved from this perverse generation.' Then those who gladly received his word were baptized; and that day about three thousand souls were added to them. And they continued steadfastly in the apostles' doctrine and fellowship, in the breaking of bread, and in prayers. Then fear came upon every soul, and many wonders and signs were done through the apostles. Now all who believed were together, and had all things in common, and sold their possessions and goods, and divided them among all, as anyone had need. So continuing daily with one accord in the temple, and breaking bread from house to house, they ate their food with gladness and simplicity of heart, praising God and having favor with all the people. And the Lord added to the church daily those who were being saved."

There are thousands and thousands of people that are on fire for the Lord; ready to serve just like the apostles were once they knew that God sent the Lord Jesus. Once they saw His miracles in the lives of people. They knew He was and is the true deliverer. People are used by God in different types of ministries and the Holy Spirit is there as a guide to help them stay on the right path. It's amazing that God would chose men to serve in so many different capacities. When I think about someone being on fire for the Lord, I think of the men that have fixed in their minds that they will not be moved by carnality and those that that block ministry and those that place obstacles in the road. When God puts the fire in you, no man can put it out. You might as well start telling everybody you know that you have the fire inside your heart from God and for God to witness to the world through you.

In Acts 2, when the Day of Pentecost had fully come, they were all with one accord in one place. And suddenly there came a sound from heaven, as of a rushing mighty wind, and it filled the whole house where they were sitting. Then there appeared to them divided tongues, as of fire, and one sat upon each of them. And they were all filled with the Holy Spirit and began to speak with other tongues, as the Spirit gave them utterance. For people to be on fire for the Lord, they need to be filled with the Holy Spirit. God is the one behind the infilling of the Holy Spirit. None of this takes place without Him directing it. Our Father in heaven has full control of distributing power under the Holy Spirit. He alone sets His anointing on the life of the believer. He awaits those newly transformed that He might do a good work in them.

When you set your heart to be on fire for the Lord, God will make room for your gift. You do not have to worry about not being used. There is a ministry everywhere! There are all kinds of ministries as well. You just have to step out of your comfort zone and your rigid way of thinking. It is time for new ideas to be blended with old ideas and of course new ideas in its original meaning as well the word never changes is what you always have to remember. Millions of books are written to persuade you or encourage you and that find as long as it's directing to the word of God. The word of God stands forever.

One of the primary reasons that this book is written is to reveal that the eyes of people can be opened and will be opened so that they can be on fire for the Lord. Open your eyes to see what God wants for you as a servant. Ask the Father in your personal closet to open your eyes that you may see what He desires for you. The intent is to get you to act on it now so that spiritual scales can fall away from the eyes, heart and mind so that you will be filled with the Holy Spirit like the apostle who waited for promise of the Holy Spirit. Your fire comes from Him. Your commitment and sacrifices of service comes from Him. He helps your acts of obedience. Your power to heal and witness to the glory of the Father comes from the Holy Spirit.

It is vitally important that you do not allow your dreams to be stripped from you by the enemy. You hold on to your dreams and visions just like Joseph, son of Jacob. He never let His dreams go until the Lord revealed to him and as a result Jacob's name was changed to Israel. Joseph never let go and as a result he became second in command of all of Egypt. He was highly favored because He stayed on fire for the Lord. He walked in the Spirit of the Lord and everyone noticed him. What you do for the Lord is what God sees. You just stay on fire in whatever you do for the Lord. He will be pleased with you. Make it personal.

I love the story of the Hebrew boys. They would not give in to anything. The King could not strike fear into their hearts in any way. They knew whom they stood for and whom they worship. These men were on fire to the point that they were willing to go into the fire and die for the Lord. They put their lives on the line for their belief in the one and only true God. The Bible says that they were put into the fiery furnace and it was turned up to the highest point but God showed up and there was a fourth man in the fire. That fourth man according to the scripture was the Son of God. That is just like our Lord Jesus to be there to rescue us. No harm or danger was done to these men. I tell you when you are on the Lord's side; He knows what to do to help you.

In this chapter, Peter demonstrated a boldness that revealed the fire burning on the inside to preach the gospel and as a result of the Holy Spirit in filling Him and the others who waited, blessed in salvation hundreds of people. Peter's preaching under the power of the Holy Spirit and helped to deliver 300 people on that day and moment. It was the fire of God burning on the inside to perform the purpose and will of God. In His sermon He said, "Repent, and let every one of you be baptized in the name of Jesus Christ for the remission of sins; and you shall receive the gift of the Holy Spirit.

When you make a decision to repent and turn your life around, then will you know that God is working in your life. Once you experience the blessings and know for yourself that God is your ever present help in times of need—your power source—you can do all things through Jesus as the Apostle Paul put it, "I can do all things through Christ who strengthens me." That means you can preach the gospel, you can teach the gospel, you love through the power of Jesus, you can accomplish any mission you put your heart with the help of the Holy Spirit.

Get on fire, saints, that we might be pleasing to Him who sits on the throne in heaven. Get on fire, families all around the globe, to give God all the glory due His name. Your fire might be different from my fire. Nevertheless, it is still the fire of God burning inside you to let loose and surrender to help someone turn his or her life around. Get on fire, God's witness, because you will turn the world upside down. You are chosen and appointed to do the will of God. It is His manifold wisdom that will carry you while you help to deliver a person out of darkness to this marvelous light. Your light will shine as you demonstrate the fire within you.

Saints, the fire we possess by the Holy Spirit is more powerful than wild fires. We have more power to speak the word and prayers of deliverance for those that are captive. No wonder those Hebrews confessed that their God is God and they do not bow to, nor serve, any other god. We need to speak that kind of faith with fire from our tongues and heart.

Today, make sure that you have repented of your sin, been baptized, and received the gift of the Holy Spirit. He will help your with your zeal, readiness, ambition and vision for the Lord in your heart for the glory of the Lord. God has set His promise in His word for you and I to take hold of all the promises. God's blessings are reasons why we must give Him the glory and thanksgiving in all things. May the praise be given to the name of Jesus, forever and ever.

PROMISES OF GOD

HEBREWS 6:13-20: "For when God made a promise to Abraham, because He could swear by no one greater, He swore by Himself, saying, 'Surely blessing I will bless you, and multiplying I will multiply you.' And so, after he had patiently endured, he obtained the Promise. For men indeed swear by the greater, and an oath for confirmation is for them an end of all disputes. Thus God, determining to show more abundantly to the heirs of promise the immutability of His counsel, confirmed it by an oath, that by two immutable things, in which it is impossible for God to lie, we might have strong consolation, who have fled for refuge to lay hold of the hope set before us. This hope we have as an anchor of the soul, both sure and steadfast, and which enters the Presence behind the veil, where the forerunner has entered for us, even Jesus, having become High Priest forever according to the order of Melchizedek."

When God makes a promise, no one and nothing can make Him go against His word of promise. He is the one who establishes and works out promises in our lives. You see God made it extremely clear that His promises of blessings in Abraham are sealed promises. He swore by Himself. God knows that in His holiness and glory, His promises are perfected and no one can break them nor stop the manifestation of His promises. He sees the promise before anyone. He reveals what He desires for His people.

You have to allow the Holy Spirit to open your eyes to see what God has done in the spiritual realm and His manifested glory on earth in your life. When He opens your eyes is when you will begin to see the promise of God manifested before you. Even when you think that you do not see God's promises, they have already come to pass. God cannot lie. God is in control of His personal will and He also knows the natural will of men.

The Lord God's promises are similar to a contract agreement between two or more people. But God's agreement is more binding and perfect in every possible way. In the contract agreement, you make specific agreements and by no means do you break it. Many people have an agreement with a car dealership. You may have purchased a 2009 BMW, which means you signed a contract to pay up each month a specific car payment. If you are late, creditors could come after you and not to mention the mounds of late fees. If you are late more than once, you could be facing repossession.

If you go through some or all of that, then you are breaching the contract. God will not and He cannot go against His own word. He will never breach His covenant and promises for your life and well being. He is the God who provides. His promises are guaranteed. His promise is more than a guarantee of having money in the bank.

God wants us also to be patient. Patience can test character and the entire person. You do not have to rush anything. When the Lord tells you something, no matter how many years go by, how many months go by, or even how many weeks and days go by, He will live up to His expectation. It is time to be patient in the things of your house and watch blessings start to overflow in your house.

God has two immutable things that He deals with in Hebrews 6:18. God declares His oath and His promises, meaning He is unchanging. God is truth and He cannot lie. You can be secure about God's promises. He seals it with the fact that we are anchored in His hope.

We are anchored in His promises. We are anchors with more power than the anchors on the largest sea vessels combined that stop the flow of vessels in full force flow. So when He speaks there is absolute assurance that He will accomplish what He set out to do. He will not go back on His plan for our future. Once He set blessings in order, expect to receive them in multiples.

The Lord God wants us to know that the High Priest Jesus anchors our souls. That is one of the actions in securing the promises of God. We do not need a priest to go before God for us any longer. Jesus paid it all. The veil (curtain) that hangs there to separate the holy and the most holy place is no longer needed. Jesus died and rose and now is seated at the right hand of the Father. Jesus is in the presence and will of the Father continuous. This is good news for everyone to know. Jesus did it once and for all. He saved a sinner soul like mine. May we always remember God's promises and oaths.

PROPHESY SAINTS WITH POWER

1 CORINTHIANS 14:1-4: "Pursue love, and desire spiritual gifts, but especially that you may prophesy. For he who speaks in a tongue does not speak to men but to God, for no one understands him; however, in the spirit he speaks mysteries. But he who prophesies speaks edification and exhortation and comfort to men. He who speaks in a tongue edifies himself, but he who prophesies edifies the church."

Our goal as Christian believers is to give God all the glory and honor. We must edify Him in all we do each moment of our lives. We may not be able to give all that is due to His name, but we can try in this lifetime through expression and acts of faith with our ability to serve. We need to use what God gave us. When God gives you the ability to prophesy, then prophesy! If He gave you the gift to teach, then teach.

God is looking for Christians that are in the pursuit of their gifts, ready to activate what God has given you. God wants all of His people to understand what it is that He has for them. He continues to pour out His word for more understanding and blessings in your life. You must know what God is saying to you to activate His destiny for your life. Prophecy means having the ability to call what the future has for you. To prophesy allows men and women of God to speak of things to come, to communicate God's message, provide correction and insight to future events, warnings and corrections by the power of the Holy Spirit.

King David had a prophet to advise him. Each time Nathaniel the prophet visited David and revealed to him things that the Lord desired him to know. He even revealed to King David of his sin that caused him to send Uriah to the front line. It is important to understand that that God was looking for a man whose heart would be an honorable heart. So then the prophet was to help King David to learn to walk in the path pleasing to the almighty God. God wanted him to be a godly King. One of the things that was important is that God used these prophets to express edification, exhortation, and comfort. They did this through their messages from God. Before that Samuel had revealed to him that he would be King by the power of God.

King Saul had a prophet; Samuel was his advisor during his kingship. The prophet Samuel warned him of his disobedience toward the Lord when he did not destroy the entire camp. Saul had one of the poorest excuses—it is almost always, "The people made me do it." If we say, "The people pressured me and made me do it," we might as well look forward to being delivered to hell as well.

The Apostle Paul makes it clear that prophecy (preaching) is necessary because it benefits the church in ways that we can't even imagine. But only God can give such gifts. We all are looking for someone to encourage us in areas of life. Our first priority of encouragement should come from the Lord.

Ezekiel 37:4: Again He said to me, "Prophesy to these bones, and say to them, 'O dry bones, hear the word of the LORD, God reveals Ezekiel's spiritual gift. He had to go into a valley and speak to dead bones. When he speaks to these dead bones, they were supposed to rise up from the dead and be covered up back into their life form; but this time as a strong and mighty army. It's amazing what God can do in His power. It pointed out several important factors. One is that if God gives you the gift to prophesy.'"

Please read 1 Corinthians 14:1-40. It blesses us to know that God wants to let a dying world know of His saving grace and what it takes to demonstrate and convey understanding.

OPEN YOUR EYES

2 KINGS 6:16-17: "And Elisha prayed, and said, 'LORD, I pray, open his eyes that he may see.' Then the LORD opened the eyes of the young man, and he saw. And behold, the mountain was full of horses and chariots of fire all around Elisha. So when the Syrians came down to him, Elisha prayed to the LORD, and said, 'Strike this people, I pray, with blindness.' And He struck them with blindness according to the word of Elisha."

God has something for you and you need to receive it. So open your eyes and your heart to received it from God. You starting point might be to pray like Elisha did to open the eyes of the young man. What caused that to happen? God's love for his manservant did. Elisha's faith had also played a vital role. It was the man of God who told the young man to open his eyes. God has a vision for you. Even better, God has a sight for you to see when your enemies cannot comprehend. Get on God's side.

He wants you to open your eyes and see the blessings set forth for you. When the enemy makes it seems like God will never show up, it's a lie and do not fall for it. God is sovereign and omnipotent. God knows everything and can be anywhere at any time. Stop allowing manipulators tell you the opposite of who God is. Victory is for you in ways unimaginable. Open you spiritual eyes to see. Start seeing your Blessings from God. Do you see anyone else trying to give you a blessing? Open your eyes, God has something special for you and you will never be the same again.

The promises of the Lord are for you. God has blessing waiting for you to grab hold of them. He has blessings laid up in heaven for you. You no longer have to wait on anyone to make you fill complete. You just need to do what Elisha did. He prayed to the Lord to open the eyes of the young man. When you pray, the Lord will show you things that you can only see in the spirit realm. In fact, we need to understand that only God can show things that he wants revealed. He just might do it directly or use somebody. In this case, he waited for Elisha's prayer request.

Elisha did something else remarkable in his combat strategy. He asked the Lord to strike the enemy with blindness and the Lord blinded his enemy. Almost moment by moment people allow the enemy to strike them with blindness, and disease, and hurt, and shame, and guilt, and so many things that keep them in bondage. If only they could learn to call on the name of Jesus and ask Jesus to strike the enemy like lightning. Ask God to strike Him with a bolt of lightning just like he was kicked out of heaven to hell. Lord if you could just strike the enemy enough to get off of the back of your people, they can start witnessing to the lost. Ask, "Lord if you could just strike the enemy with blindness to keep him away from family and my wife. Keep my faith determined and true to you Lord."

Tell everything and everyone around you to move for a moment. Tell them that you are about to express your faith in the fullness of God inside you. You need to say in your mind, excuse me, and move for a moment. I have to claim my blessings by faith. You have been in my way long enough. If you want to walk with me and get your blessing, let start moving into the presence of God right now at this very moment.

It is important that you know that God is on your side. The Bible says that the battle is not yours, but it is the Lord's. No wonder so many Christians lose at warfare with the enemy. There are many who should never even go to battle because of their lack of knowledge and strategy and tactics. The Lord should employ all tactics. A wise king will win. A foolish king or servant will lose each time. Find out what a wise King is. What you need to understand is that God already has you covered. Look what God did for Elisha when he prayed unto the Lord. He was supported and covered with chariots of fire all around him. God had placed His heavenly army around the protection of His children. God has a way of fighting your battle for you.

THE VEIL SPLIT

John 19:1-24: "So then Pilate took Jesus and scourged Him. And the soldiers twisted a crown of thorns and put it on His head, and they put on Him a purple robe. Then they said, 'Hail, King of the Jews!' And they struck Him with their hands. Pilate then went out again, and said to them, 'Behold, I am bringing Him out to you, that you may know that I find no fault in Him.' Then Jesus came out, wearing the crown of thorns and the purple robe. And Pilate said to them, 'Behold the Man!' Therefore, when the chief priests and officers saw Him, they cried out, saying, 'Crucify Him, crucify Him!' Pilate said to them, 'Take him yourselves and crucify him, for I find no guilt in him.'

When Jesus died on the cross and rose from the dead, veils in temples split from top to bottom to fulfill prophecy written in Isaiah. The veil splitting in the temple signifies that the gap was now bridged. Our relationship with God is now restored because of the precious blood of the lamb. It symbolizes that each person can approach God through the precious name of Jesus Christ. You can cross over the bridge now. He completed the mission to bring you home to God. I thank God that He made my understanding clear. I see the death of Jesus as a way to reveal to all people that Jesus defeated death and made Himself available for all men. No one can find fault in Him. He was perfect then and He is perfect now. Give Him glory! In 1 Corinthians 15, the scripture tells us that He took the sting out of death. It reveals that Jesus lifts the veils of all people who accept Him. He also lifted the veil of those who have not acknowledged because His power is infinite. They of course just have not acknowledged Him as their personal Savior. He is made Himself available for all people. I believe not only was the veil split for salvation, He remove the veil from the eyes of those who walk in darkness and blindness. Now you can call on the name of Jesus. He removed the veil from the eyes of everyone so that they could have the opportunity to be free and see what He has done in His glorious ways and blessed salvation.

The veil was split because everyone needed, and still needs, to know that Jesus is Lord of all creation throughout eternity. He defeated the enemy and at the same time gave us life everlasting to reign with Him.

What was so significant about the veil? A veil can be used for so many things. One of the most common uses of a veil is in marriages when a bride is presented to her groom. She is covered up to be presented as a gift from God. She is supposed to be treated as precious and should be honored by her husband. The relationship should be a mutual one in marriage. Your marriage can be absolutely made in heaven. She was ready to take on the meaning of becoming a bride. It is funny in a wedding the man always lifts up the veil to kiss her acknowledging publicly and intimately that He has excepted her and she has accepted him. Not only did the veil get lifted to signify their unity. It is a symbolic means of unity with God in their marriage. He is the head of their marriage.

Jesus makes this so significant to them because all believers are transformed into His image and likeness. We possess the love and tender kindness that Jesus has. Jesus wants us to know that we are His bride, the church.

The veil was so significant because it is known to have been a curtain hung in front of the temple room called the most holy place, a place reserved by God. This veil separated the holy God from sinful people. This place was only entered by His grace and His authority, once a year, on the Day of Atonement. The high priest had to enter in on the behalf of the believer for our sin. He needed to always take a sacrifice. Jesus came along and died for us as the perfect sacrifice for God. There is no requirement for the old system anymore. When Jesus died on the cross and the veil split, He reconciled us to bring us back into relationship with God as His children.

What is so key and central about these four gospels is that they involve the resurrection? They all prove that the resurrection happened and bare witness of it. The veil lifted from the resurrection simply means that all people can see with their eyes and heart that Jesus rose from the dead with all power and authority. The veil was a indication that the world had been united to Jesus. No more division from God. Sin was lifted from people transferred to the body of Jesus and crucified on the cross. Everyone was made free instantaneously by the power in the blood of Jesus.

What touches so many people the most is when they see the crucifixion. You then hear the effects such as why He loved me so much. In the carrying the cross, He demonstrated love unconditional and eternal. In carrying the cross, He knew it took someone to carry so many others living in sin. To destroy the works of the devil and at the same time give life back to a dying world. We hunger to know Him today because of what He has done for our families and us.

I can't help but to think of His love pouring out in incredible amounts daily that nothing else can equate to. The Lord's love is so powerful; He forgave even those that crucified Him. He forgives those who have rejected Him today. His love is so perfect, it changes you instantly. His loves never changes. I always like to associate something with the rain that God gives us. It is His love that gives the perfect picture. In His perfect timing He sends the exact person to the exact moment through the exact circumstance that He might get the glory.

My mind takes me to a story that happened with a friend a few years ago. James had been a unique soldier with various hardships. James was also that stellar soldier who was on the fast track. He would volunteer for any mission and complete it. One of James' favorite stories in the Bible is the one of the crucifixion of Jesus Christ (John 19). James had dealt with all the missions that he went on in Iraq and found out that he would finally come home. Well, when he came home, he found out that he had a tumor in the back of his head and he had developed some type of gangrene in his knees. Not only did he have those things to deal with, he was evaluated with PTSD and anxiety. But James, through the comfort of his beautiful wife and family, received more tragic news. His mother had died by having a massive stroke after a long time of suffering with a heart problem.

Whenever death and pain enters the life of a believer and a nonbeliever, God is always there to comfort.

When I discover or hear about stories where a soldier or anyone that served the armed forces and came home to discover different problems, not only does my heart and prayers go out to them, I believe that it is when the outpouring of His love is revealed at a level even our minds are unable to comprehend. James felt like he was been crucified, but he did not understand anything about his suffering. Sometimes people lose hope and stop believing because they are unable to explain what God allowed to happen. The Lord God never stops loving you and your family. He is the one who helps you through the tough times. When the enemy comes to shatter your hopes and dreams, He is still there by your side.

Today, look at the love of Jesus on the cross and imagine that love being poured on you right this minute. Ask God to soak you and bathe you in His love. Ask the Lord to get intimate with you regarding His love. You need His touch of life to move on in life. He will not limit you. He will truly balance your life in the storm and deliver you from the elements of evil. God's love is more than all the gallons of water that rain for a lifetime. He loves us more than the water He made for Noah's ark. Rain the kind of love that is being poured from the heavens as we speak. Just like God waters the planet, He waters and bathes us in His loving kindness. He will do all soldiers the same. He is in the blessing business of showing His awesome love to soldiers and family members.

James' friend Mark had an amputated leg and right arm due to an IED explosion. He was surprised to see his best friend because the last thing James had heard was that Mark was missing in action in Iraq. Thank God that He sits on the throne in heaven showering us in His love of compassion on a daily basis even when we do not ask. God is in the midst of things that we do not see. God is love and His love and mercy last forever.

James is now a stronger believer because of his experience with God touching and restoring his life. He is now a full believer. James, through all of the pain and agony in his life, now witnesses in the local community, around town, and in his local church. James realized that there are some places in his life that God wanted to access and help you dream a dream you have been waiting and desiring in your heart.

He lives forever and He lives in my heart. When Jesus carried the cross while wearing twisted thorns in His head and bleeding in abundance, He thought about me. He thought about every city, state, home, church, the lost, priest, pastor, teacher, loved one, family and His remnants.

The crucifixion represents suffering by suffocation. No one can ever forget the boldness and the humility that Jesus had given to every soldier to make sacrifice. We need to spread the word even if it overflows in the lives of people.

UNVEILED RESURRECTION

MARK 16:1-20: "Now when the Sabbath was past, Mary Magdalene, Mary the mother of James, and Salome bought spices, that they might come and anoint Him. Very early in the morning, on the first day of the week, they came to the tomb when the sun had risen. And they said among themselves, 'Who will roll away the stone from the door of the tomb for us?' But when they looked up, they saw that the stone had been rolled away—for it was very large. And entering the tomb, they saw a young man clothed in a long white robe sitting on the right side; and they were alarmed. But he said to them, 'Do not be alarmed. You seek Jesus of Nazareth, who was crucified. He is risen! He is not here. See the place where they laid Him. But go, tell His disciples—and Peter—that He is going before you into Galilee; there you will see Him, as He said to you.' So they went out quickly and fled from the tomb, for they trembled and were amazed. And they said nothing to anyone, for they were afraid. Later He appeared to the eleven as they sat at the table; and He rebuked their unbelief and hardness of heart, because they did not believe those who had seen Him after He had risen. And He said to them, 'Go into all the world and preach the gospel to every creature. He who believes and is baptized will be saved; but he who does not believe will be condemned. And these signs will follow those who believe: In My name they will cast out demons;

they will speak with new tongues; they will take up serpents; and if they drink anything deadly, it will by no means hurt them; they will lay hands on the sick, and they will recover.' So then, after the Lord had spoken to them, He was received up into heaven, and sat down at the right hand of God. And they went out and preached everywhere, the Lord working with them and confirming the word through the accompanying signs. Amen."

Unveiling the resurrection has been completed by the power of God already. He has removed our blinders to see Him raised from the dead. It is called unveiled resurrection because He rose from the dead with all power, and everyone now has eyes to see what took place in the tomb. You can visualize it in your heart and mind and spirit. True, we may have not been physically there, but God, by His Holy Spirit, reveals it to us what we needed to see and lock into our minds and hearts.

He has set everyone free and made Himself available to be approached with all of our issues of life. He allows us to approach Him now with the sin that tries to entangle us each day. We no longer have to go to a priest in the natural body or in the spirit. Jesus is our priest forever so then we can go to Him with thanksgiving and praise. We can go to Him and worship before Him. When Thomas saw Him in person after He had risen, that is when Thomas began to believe and then He could see what happened in the grave. There are some people who do not believe that God had raised His Son Jesus from the dead. They will argue you until you turn colors, some until the end of life. You do not have to argue. God is God and nobody can change Him.

The resurrection is our priority after Jesus destroyed sin in His body. I'm telling every sick soul, and lost and confused person, that Jesus has already redeemed them. You see our mission as the Holy Spirit leads us is to unveil every aspect of Jesus to those who have not accepted Him as Savior.

In the resurrection, the stone was rolled away from the tomb and Jesus rose from the dead and departed out of the grave. So then a key fact is that the veil of the resurrection stands for Jesus being raised from the dead with all power in His hand. His clothing (veil) remained in the tomb so that witnesses could see it and know that He left the grave. So many people still miss it. Nothing could keep him from the grave. His cloth was evidence that the power of God had resurrected Him and left His garments. Jesus rose from the grave that they laid Him inside. God unveiled His Son Jesus to prove the He was the conqueror and the restorer of life and eternal life. God unveiled His Son to be the one who everyone would be drawn to and felt loved in the midst of His presence. For too long people have been missing the resurrection right before their very eyes. It is time that every saint walks with a new attitude, knowing that it was He who gave life a new meaning. Resurrection is the most powerful piece in man.

I believe the next unveiling of Jesus' resurrection was when the tomb was open, and the stone was rolled away. It was open for all to see. Today, it is still open for all to see. Get up and go and see if you do not believe. He is not there in the tomb where they laid Him. It was important to Mary to find Him because, in her heart, He was so precious and she knew He was the Son of God. Jesus was raised and given all power in His hands. His Father entrusted the power of everything—all existence, all creation, every mind, every heart, every soul, everything that had breath, all the animals, plants, oceans, stars, planets, galaxies, famous people, water, rain, snow sleet, the sea world, fish, oceans, rivers flowing, ponds, gold, silver, coal, mercury, diamonds, and all things. If you can think of it, God owns it and placed it in the possession of His Son, Jesus.

He is the same God who gave everything to Adam, all dominion and all power. The resurrection is what redeemed us from the wrath and the sin that beset us. The blood in the death of Christ Jesus is what redeemed us from sin and the wrath of God. What God wants is people to be resurrected from the pride of life, the sin that keeps us entangled.

LET YOUR REQUEST BE KNOW

PHILIPPIANS 4:6-11: "Be anxious for nothing, but in everything by prayer and supplication, with thanksgiving, let your requests be made known to God; and the peace of God, which surpasses all understanding, will guard your hearts and minds through Christ Jesus. Finally, brethren, whatever things are true, whatever things are noble, whatever things are just, whatever things are pure, whatever things are lovely, whatever things are of good report, if there is any virtue and if there is anything praiseworthy—meditate on these things. The things, which you learned and received and heard and saw in me, these do, and the God of peace will be with you. But I rejoiced in the Lord greatly that now at last your care for me has flourished again; though you surely did care, but you lacked opportunity. Not that I speak in regard to need, for I have learned in whatever state I am, to be content."

Think on Godly things and observe the blessings of God in your life. He alone is the image that we must keep in our minds. Allow Him today to take over your mind more that areas in technology, substance, and life in general. It is important to have Jesus Christ at the center of your mind because everything is being taken to the big screen, Internet, radio, iPods, iReports, YouTube, Facebook, and methods of email, Twitter, AKO, Hotmail, Yahoo and increasing technology. Nothing is wrong with having these excellent tools of now necessity and convenience for communication and enjoyment. God blessed us with these tools. Don't let any of it separate you from God. Instead use it to glorify Him and receive more blessings.

More ideas and images are moving at an alarming and extremely fast pace. What is so fascinating about the big screen movie theater and technology itself is that almost anything goes on television and in some the other areas. America needs to improve on censoring programs for young adults and small children. We still need to keep our future generations protected and nurtured in the word.

Do not forget about prayer and supplication. It is the fastest of all communication tools and the most effective for life's benefits in the spirit.

One of America's favorite pastimes is at the movie theater and viewing DVDs and CDs at home on the big screen or computer. All kinds of movies are being developed. You might love to watch sports, dramas, action thrillers, horrors or some comedy type of show. I enjoy good drama and comedy. One thing for sure, the association with evil does not mix with good spirit-minded folks. Avoid that kind which will tear you down. Horror is the worst thing to watch in my opinion because what you watch goes on the inside of your mind to a certain extent. If you do not believe me, ask all the people who watched the exorcist years ago and observe their response. Better yet, ask the question of how did it make you feel then and today? For me, without even knowing God as my personal Savior, it made me know that evil exists, then and today. Your spirit will pick it up.

It is vitally important that all people especially be informed that what you watch affects your spirit and your life. If you watch horror, then you start feeling the effects of horror. Yea, you might not think so now. But if you remember horror over the last 10 years ago, then you can identify what is being said here. You heard what the saying, what you put in your body is what you get out. Be careful what you take in, because it may try to take you over. Teach your young children in a way that they should go. Teach them about the thoughts of what Jesus wants them to have in Philippians 4, to think pure thoughts. I want to make it perfectly clear that Jesus has all power to denounce any spirit on your behalf. Trust Him today.

I just wanted to tell people that images of what you see on the big screen could be etched into your mind and your heart for life. So why pay for something that will cause you nightmares and a troubled spirit just because you decided to watch a two to three hour movie. Please understand that movies have impact and what you view has impact.

The writer of Philippians says to think on these things. Let all your thinking be absorbed with the thoughts of entering into God's court with thanksgiving and giving Him the fullness of praise.

How do we get ahead in the movie industry? We exalt God with making movies to reflect His image and His glory. We want Him to have all the glory in what we do. God, our Father, is pleased when we put forth the effort to please Him. Train more actors to demonstrate the Lord and His time of blessing people. Reveal to them the image of God.

Here are four types of areas in our lives that we should apply the use of imagery. Jesus Himself, start seeing Jesus for who He really is, the Lord of Lords and King of Kings; the word, see the word for the power, and authority, and truth that exists within and in mystery; worship, see yourself worshiping God before His throne; marriage, meditate on the love in the marriage and keep your vows before God, anything else outside should have no bearing; people, love them and witness and treat with respect just like you want respect; praise, see yourself lifting up your hands in heaven and on earth with a completely open heart and mind and spirit unto the Lord of Lords; and finally be fruitful and a blessing to others, remember God's kingdom belongs to Him and He alone gets the glory and honor and power forever and ever. So bless someone even when you think it hurts. You will get blessed in return. Start seeing yourself planted in the right place to please God. Why have images of Jesus? It is who He is that fascinates and turns our spirits on with His word and mystery.

The world talks about His marvelous way of touching and healing and loving people with an everlasting love. To know Him and the power of His resurrection is enough to want more images of His glory inside our lives. His resurrection says it all. Because it was the resurrection, Him getting up from the grave, that caused the final victory and defeat of all enemies. Today, you can be assured the Jesus is Lord over all creation.

The word is another type of imagery. Imagery is like presenting a picture, painting a picture in your mind. Every time you watch a television program, some images stick with you, they never leave. That is why it is so important that you get the word in you. Keep Hebrews in mind, it says that the word of God is as powerful as a two-edged sword. The word of God is seen in John the Baptist also as a forerunner. He knew that Jesus was coming and He worked the work that God had prepared for him. He announced that Jesus would be coming to save His people.

One of the most important parts of life is to know when you have pleased God. When you know that you have pleased God then you can be content. The Apostle Paul speaks that he was content in whatever state. Of course that state is the mind of Christ without having the wants of society. He was fully aware that Christ Jesus, the same one who delivered Him from evil ways would take care of all of his needs. If your life has peace and you know that God has filled you with the Holy Spirit and you are aware and fully conscience of the fact that He is your God, then you should have a certain level of contentment about your life in Christ. The Apostle also reflects on a fully trusting relationship in Christ. There is no guessing game about who Jesus is and what He means to the Apostle Paul and all the Saints. Lock Jesus in your everyday thoughts. Use the method of imagery to reflect on Jesus and His word in your life. Use imagery to walk with Him daily.

DON'T GIVE THE ENEMY OUR SOUL, FIGHT BACK!

MATTHEW 22:36: "Teacher, which is the great commandment in the law? Jesus said to him, you shall love the Lord your God with all your heart, with all your soul, and with all your mind. This is the first and great commandment."

Give all of yourself to God now. Give the praise to Jesus. If the enemy keeps on your track, start praying and praising God. God will be there to rescue you. Talk to some saints who know the power of prayer. In His commandment, in Matthew 22:37, *"Jesus said to the lawyer, you shall love the Lord your God with all your heart, with all your soul, and with all of your mind.*

This is the first and great commandment. Imagine surrendering to a God who holds all the power. Give yourself entirely over to God. That will be the best thing that ever happened to you.

You can stop worrying; you know the scripture, "Be careful for nothing." You can start an obedient walk with Christ Jesus, walking in the Spirit like it says in Galatians 5:16, *I say then walk in the Spirit and you shall not fulfill the lusts of the flesh.* What a combination!

Love your God with all your heart and walk in the Spirit. This is exactly what you need to do to avoid giving the enemy a piece of yourself. When you give of yourself to God, you make an impression on God that glorifies His righteous name. People give of themselves all the time to others they do not even know. It's good to give to the needy and poor, those that are suffering, God ordain the power to give to them. People give money to orphanages and some never even say a word. People give to local churches to build for the kingdom and what God placed on their heart for it. People give because it their gift to do so.

I believe giving is of God's highest priority. John 3:16 says, *"For God so loved the world that He gave His only begotten Son. For whosoever believeth in Him shall not perish but have everlasting life."* Look what Jesus gave. He gave His life for a ransom. He gave His life that we could be free. He gave the blood that covers us from the wicked sin.

Jesus already did what He told us to do. He did much more than we could for Him. His love is for all mankind. To express our love for Him is good, but we need our guide the Holy Spirit to help us. One thing for sure, if He commands it, and I accept it with obedience and faith, I will be able to walk in His commandments. Trust the Lord with all thy heart and lean not to thy own understanding and He will direct your path. Start worshipping the living God and you will be blessed in salvation and repentance.

Most soldiers are familiar with commands. Military commanding generals and command sergeants majors, they echo commands throughout the armed forces daily and never allow anyone to get in the way of those commands. These authority figures can call soldiers to attention by a command and they listen and adhere to it. They command their organizations and people listen and respond. These commanders have the ability to write orders and all soldiers must obey these orders. If soldiers to not obey, they will receive some form of judicial punishment for disobeying orders.

When our heavenly Father gives out the command, "Love Him with all your heart, mind, and soul," He definitely means give Him more than a piece of you. Give Him the best of you because He has already blessed you and the enemy can't take it away. If you have the give the enemy anything, you speak the word of God so that it will flee back to hell with all of its demons. You do not have time to mess around. You have a mission to do. God is faithful to deliver you. God is faithful to take care of you.

But if you just cannot stop yourself from giving of you, then speak the word and the enemy will flee. If you cannot contain yourself from certain action, start praying in the spirit to break the bondage of it. Habits have to be broken in the spirit because some have deeply rooted themselves to your deepest part of mind and heart. You must have the help of the Holy Spirit. Give all of yourself to Jesus Christ the Son of God.

PRESS IN JESUS NAMES

PHILIPPIANS 3:13-14: "Brethren, I do not count myself to have apprehended; But one thing I do, forgetting those things which are behind, and reaching forward to those things which are ahead."

What is your goal in life? Are you pressing for a particular prize in life? Jesus was the first person that I can see clearly pressing for a mark. His mark was different. His goal was different. It was simply to save a dying, defeated world in sin. Jesus started reconciling us in the very beginning. He saw our past and came from heaven to fix us, to bridge the gap that had separated us. Thank God that Jesus pressed His way with the cross, death, burial, and rose from the dead.

What past thing haunts you? You do not have to keep on going down the same past. For some reason you want to see what you can't change and you wonder how things could have been better and at the same time you are recalling that past and dwelling in it daily. You wonder what that relationship could have been like with that person but must have the courage to get over it. You say things like, we could have had beautiful family! She loved me so much! Now you are at a place of repetitive voices speaking to you about old love versus new love vs. lost love. But then you realize the amount of hurt you went through. Then you realize that how God delivered you through the pain. That is enough in itself reason to magnify His righteous name. Glory is to Him because of His tender mercies and power and gratefulness.

We always have memories and past issues that rise up and make us meditate on that stage of life. Don't give it a second thought. After all are they thinking of you? Your life needs to go on and face Christ's loving gift in your life. Getting a grip on your life is the biggest step you can do. If you do not have it, someone else will certainly try to take your life. The enemy comes to kill, steal, and destroy. Jesus said I came to give your life and give it more abundantly.

If we think those positive thoughts, we can make it through those difficult storms that rage all night long that sometime seep into the next day of life. Yes, most people have those raging storms at night even when rain is nowhere in sight. One thing I love about Jesus is when He calmed the storm while in the boat with disciples. Jesus simply said, "Peace be still," and all creation could have stood still. We know that the storm ceased and His disciple was amazed at Him.

It is a blessing to know that you have Jesus who can stop storms in its tracks. So since we know that He can stop storms in its tracks, we ought to know that he can heal past hurts, new hurts, and direct us, and place us on a firm path. Then He guides us all day long so we do not fall completely. So do not feel apprehended, captive to the past because you have a king to rely on.

You have God almighty who rules all of heaven and earth. You need to look toward the future pressing your way by the power of the Holy Spirit. When anything arises against your spirit, tell it, "Jesus is Lord." I am standing on His word and His promise. He will never leave me, nor forsake me. Bless His holy and righteous name.

Lord, you know that I need you. So I have to say thank you first for all of your goodness. Keep my mind stayed on you, Father. Remove dark thoughts if they arise. Clean my heart from any hatred that was caused in the past and spilled over to now. I claim recovery in the matchless name of Jesus. I claim a clean heart and mind in the name of Jesus. I cast any unclean spirit from the midst of my family and friend. I give you praise Lord, in the name of Jesus. Amen.

THE SPIRIT FLOWING IN YOUR LIFE

Psalms 1:1-3: "Blessed is the man who walks not in the counsel of the ungodly, Nor stands in the path of sinners, Nor sits in the seat of the scornful; But his delight is in the law of the Lord, And in His law he meditates day and night. He shall be like a tree planted by the rivers of water, That brings forth its fruit in its season, Whose leaf shall also not wither; And whatever he does shall prosper."

The Lord is the one who blesses according to His perfect will. Obey His word is one of His highest orders because it proves to Him that you are planted in His word and His word is planted in you. The spirit will flow in your life if you obey him. When He blesses, He makes the rivers flow in your life. Those rivers that flow in your life filled will continue to multiply for He is the living water that you are rooted in. God is looking for men that will stay the course. He wants men that will stay on the path of obedience to receive His blessings. He wants us to stay the course even when it gets difficult, hang in there. He is certainly against the destructive path of rebellious attitudes or disobedience. He will change it.

Adam was blessed, but then turned his focus to disobedience and the world became as you see it now, sinful. A world of sin that God's only Son could change and set us free. Once you have truly become obedience, you will line up with God's word because you will experience the power to know Him as Lord. Your scales will have fallen from your eyes then you will begin life again. You need to hurry and began to see things as they really exist. Reality in the spiritual realm is important because your life depends on it and eternity is for you, child of God.

Have you ever seen a river flow? Have you ever seen the speed in which they flow? God has the answers. He makes them flow with just the right amount of speed and the right amount of force. Rivers flow for several reasons. They have to carry things from one point to another. They are design to carry things at the bottom of the river to another place. They are designed to clean out certain places by taking the unclean to the ocean so it could be eliminated.

Have you seen the power in the flow of a river? It carries and cleanses. It shapes and molds, it builds and designs, rivers are in the Garden of Eden. They carry blessings in the life of the believer. God made it so. God shows us rivers to show us blessings. The river can flow in your life. God is behind causing your river to flow. He wants to bless someone. There are more rivers to flow that we can imagine. God controls more rivers than what we see. You can get wet in the natural river of water. But you will get blessed. Do you know about rivers flowing in your life? When the scales fall off, then you will see the rivers flow.

A strong current has power to move things out of its path and cause devastating destruction. God shows us the power of His flow and that He can cease it as well in a moment. His Holy Spirit flows in our lives day after day. The power of the Holy Spirit is far greater the imagination and surely far greater than water on earth. He controls the waters, the rivers, and seas, and oceans.

CHAPTER 13

GOD HOLD MY TONGUE

James 3:8-10: "But no man can tame the tongue. It is an unruly evil, full of deadly poison. With it we bless our God and Father, and with it we curse men. Who have been made in the similitude of God. Out of the same mouth proceed blessings and cursing. My brethren these things ought not be so."

God spoke and He made things pleasing in His sight. God spoke and life began. Heaven and earth was created. God spoke and life began. Everything that came out of His mouth was pleasing to Him and for His glorious purpose. God revealed His identity to us through His work of salvation and the words He spoke. He reminds us of our destiny to walk in His image. We were made to speak blessings and not curses. He gave us this tongues for the proper use. The tongue is an instrument to be used for God's glory and edification. The tongue is powerful and carries the word of God and the word of God is powerful than a two-edged sword, that pierces even the very asunder of the soul. The word speaks life and death to us.

Acts 2: 4 speaks of tongues of fire in Pentecost, it says, and they were all filled with the Holy Spirit and began to speak with other tongues, as the spirit gave them utterance. Don't you know that If God shows us symbolically and actively the power of tongues resting on His people, then changing them while at the same time manifesting His power, He can do the same to you and anybody else. He is in no respect of person. No one is above anyone to Him. He will empower all His people for the uplifting of His kingdom. He poured out the Holy Spirit then, and the Holy Spirit will work on behalf of the Father in all circumstances. Listen to what really happened. The tongues of fire resting on them and they spoke with their very tongues. They did not speak damages and hate; they spoke edification to the Lord. They spoke different languages, but all languages were for the edification of the Lord. It was the Holy Spirit that was the guiding power enabling these people to get their blessing. He is the controller on God's behalf.

The Holy Spirit will help us learn self-control in our lives and with that little member in our mouth. The tongue is powerful. Every time we say things negatively and harshly, we give in to the enemy's delight. The good news is that we have the Holy Spirit to guide us through life. The Holy Spirit is our best help. The Holy Spirit gives us power to fight against the work of the enemy. The Holy Spirit will help me and you have a tongue that blesses people and not curse them. Try saying something positive about someone. There is power in that little member in the body called the tongue. If we allow the Holy Spirit to work in and throughout us, we will avoid lashing out to hurt someone, gossiping about a situation, or even speaking hatred. Backbiting would cease; all the negative words will cease. It is the Holy Spirit who will help us with anything we allow Him by the power of faith. Trust Him today in your life.

God can do anything with the tongue. He can use it for His glory. Speak the word using that tongue. Speak prayers with that tongue. God will purify your hearts to help us to speak according to our identity in Christ Jesus. People will know us by the way we speak. God is not asking us to be flawless because He already knows that we are sinful. He already knows that we can do better. God did provide His love to just let it be called love. He provided love to be imitated and expressed like His never-ending love.

The Father delights in people speaking blessings in the lives of others. Why not speak blessings in the lives of people? It does not cost anything but to open your mouth with blessings rolling off your tongue is pleasing to our Lord. Praise to our Lord who give power.

HONOR THE LORD

PROVERBS 3:9: "Honor the Lord with your possessions, And with the first fruits of all your increase."

Everything we own already belongs to God. He blessed us just like He said He would under Abraham. I am blessed to know this because my possessions are His possessions. His blessings continue to overflow in our lives. It is so important those who act blind and skeptical seek the Lord's face and get into His presence. There is a scripture that will help all believers to honor God by acting obediently. It is a test of the heart. It is to see what really is in your heart. Is it honoring God or is it honoring self? That is a personal decision for everyone. Your possessions could cause you to get blessed even more if you act under obedience.

The God we serve owns the abundance of everything. There is nothing anywhere that He does not own. So in our abundant life, He wants us to give first fruit. What is this first fruit? The first fruit is the best of all you have. That does not exclude anyone or any church. This scripture refers to giving God your first and best. It is one way of showing that God has first place in our lives. We acknowledge that He is the one that I will honor and be obedient to. It also illustrates obedience to His will.

There was a rich man who had his own issues with the money he had in his possession. Jesus Told him to give the money away and he had to ponder on it and had many heart troubles with it. You can't turn money into being your Lord. But you can make you heart turn away by thinking That it is more powerful and needed more than God is needed in your life. Take away the first fruit and submit it to the Lord and then watch the increase in multiples in your life. God is able to help you break that bondage, that stronghold that constantly tries to ride you. You are not broken. The circumstances that you are in may have you appearing and acting like you are broken. The enemy will not have a laugh today! This time you speak the word with blessing authority. We know that the enemy delights in seeing saints suffer especially when he believes he crippled your faith. There are many people that are rich right now. Watch what happens to those that are rich when they begin to see with spiritual sight. You can also view first fruits as something like. When you get blessed, you owe it to God. If you get blessed with a million dollars that is a fruit blessing from the Lord to you. He always gives. In fact, He never stops giving. All we really have to do is look around and see what He had done in our lives and even in the lives of others.

He deserves a portion of our fruit because He is the reason why we were blessed in the first place. The Lord worked on me to make me understand that all I have belongs to Him anyway. If we leave this earth tomorrow, it still belongs to Him. Everything to everyone is on loan status. God freely gives and God looks to see the heart of man and his giving attitude.

GRACE IS ALL YOU NEED

EPHESIANS 2:8: "For by grace you have been saved through faith, and that not of yourselves, it is the gift of God.

Faith and grace are two of God's holy blessings and power sources. Most people wonder what is this so called grace talked about? Grace is unmerited favor. No one could ever earn it nor work for it, regardless of your efforts in society. It is unmerited favor in your life that only God can provide. We never had a right to see this blessed gift of grace from our Lord, our penalty was death. But He washed us as white as snow in the power of His love.

When someone is truly saved, they have the ability of sight to see these holy blessings called grace. They see the evidence of it in their lives. Since you are a new creature in Christ, you see basically all good things in life associated with His grace. Your scales have fallen off. It is by the grace of God that we live day to day, breath to breath, and moment to moment, love time again and again. He did not have to give us any time nor any chances. But He is the God who never changes.

We deserved His wrath because of our sin nature. In grace, He took away sin that we may live according to His perfect will and love toward one another. You see in grace, you get favor that no man could ever give you. Grace never turns its back on you. Grace never ceases blessings in your life. Grace has the perfect mix of God's love to sustain you and help you to grow all together. We are speaking of God who is all-powerful and sovereign.

God has perfecting ingredients in his grace. We do not know it all, but we do know that the power of love is in His grace. We do know that His glory is in His grace. We do know that His healing power is in His grace. We do know that salvation is in His grace. We do know that eternity is in His grace. We do know that restoration is in His grace. We know that He is sovereign, omnipotent and omnipresent. Grace is in it all. He blood released grace on us. His love and grace both exist to will us into His loving hands. Those perfect ingredients are love and faith that we continue to experience.

There will be some times in life when the enemy will make your mind think that there is no grace. It will seem that way because all of hell appears to have entered your life. At the same time the enemy is playing tricks in your mind. Many people have felt that way before.

When you are anointed, the enemy has someone to go after. Even those in Christ sometimes feel heavily burdened. But they shouldn't allow heavy burdens, nor the tricks of the enemy, fool them, especially if their minds are stayed on Him. Remember, grace did not come because we called on it. Grace was given because the love God sheds abroad and He first loved us. So it is by grace that we are saved and not of ourselves, it is the gift of God and not manmade. Praise and glory be to His holy name.

GOD'S LIGHT OVER DARKNESS

2 CORINTHIANS 4: 6-7: "For it is God who commanded light to shine out of darkness, who has shone in our hearts to give the light of the knowledge the glory of God in the face of Jesus Christ. But we have this treasure in earthen vessels, that the excellence of the power may be of God and not of us."

God commanded the light in the beginning of creation. He has the power to put light in the hearts of man. God knows the darkness that is in each man's life. He knows exactly what we need. He knows that glory will be given to Him through people. He commanded light to bless us. There are many illustrations that can be used. He made light in the world when there was darkness throughout. He even made the day and night.

He made light in man's body to represent Him as the life giver. He put the very thought in man's mind to invent the light bulb currently used in every home, business, and building throughout this world. It was His power of given the intellect and ingenious ability to think of such product and invention. Light is in this world all around us. When we see the sun and the moon, we see the evidence of light that only God can create in the sun and the moon. He is the God who made those elements of this world. In your home, each time you walk in a dark room, you hit the light switch and a beam of light penetrates the darkness in that room. We see again the power of His light breaking through the darkness.

Would it be something if everyone called Christians could let this light shine and penetrate through us to be effective witnesses in this world? It is the light that penetrates so powerfully that it forces evil spirits away. When we walk in the light, He wants us to share His Holy word to a dying world. We may be clay vessels, but the power of Christ rests upon us to do the will of our Father. This light that He has granted us remarkable faith to serve Him. Other lights may have blinded many people. It may have been a light from a distant place that keeps on putting you in bondage.

Our primary purpose is to let people see Christ Jesus through us by walking in the light. Jesus made that statement that no one can shake it. He said, "Let your light shine that they may see your good works." Once you become a new born Christian, there is a walk that you must take.

SEED EXPERIENCE

LUKE 8:10-12: "And He said, to you it has been given to know the mysteries of the kingdom of God, but to the rest it is given in parables, that seeing they may not see, And hearing they may not understand. Now the parable is this: The seed is the word of God. Those by the wayside are the ones who hear; then the devil comes and takes the word out of their hearts, lest they should believe and be saved."

When you become a seed sewer, you might as well get ready for the enemy to put forth his best tactics to steal the word from your heart. Once the enemy thinks that he took it from your heart, then he wants your mind and your confession to be destroyed as well. The enemy will try to hinder, block, steal, and conceal your blessings from God every time.

You need to know that this foe is not concerned about taking your blessings. You are the target. You are like the fertile ground that receives new seed. The enemy does not want the word (seed) in your heart, nor your mind. If you get the word, then you have the power to call on Jesus. When you get the word, which is the seed, the enemy hates it and will try to demand you to step down.

I never understood those that thought everything was okay when the enemy comes your way. I am so excited about the power of His word. I remember working on a farm with all of what you see today—

chickens, cows, snakes, and horses. I rode until the horse bucked me off. On the farm, I learned how to be disciplined in working in so many areas. My father was responsible for placing my brothers and me on the farm to work.

One of the most important things I learned on that farm, working under the heat, was plowing the ground at the right time to put seed in it. When you plow the ground, you will always need a strong mule, dependable plow, and or a good tractor. During those years, tools were available, but Mr. Brown was old school and depended on that mule he talked to day and night. Sometimes as a human being, or little youngster, I would watch him and be amazed how that mule responded to him even after a long day of plowing. I watched Mr. Brown talk to that mule in the backyard many times. The point is, Mr. Brown was a man who knew the power of planting seed and the cost associated with planting seed. Although he left us to be with the Father in heaven, he was a remarkable example on how to plow to plant seed, ensuring the best outcome. Because he was wealthy in his ability to plow and plant seed, others would be wealthy as well, along with the farm owner. I believe that we need some new ground to plow and plant. We need hearts that will receive the power of God's word penetrating on the inside and manifesting inside out.

That farm has a special meaning in my life because it always left the power of the seed in my mind. I did not know then but I know now that the seeds in one watermelon come from the original seed that was planted. God has a way of multiplying seed from the original seed. I never forget eating all of those watermelons and hoping not to swallow those seeds. Either God taught us and saw us through those times.

Believers have to be cautious of what can happen if you allow the enemy an inch. Watch out for those who have fallen to the wayside. And watch for yourself the enemy attacks who claims to have striped us of our freedom in Jesus Christ.

PRAISE GOD!

PSALM 150:1-6:

Praise the LORD!

Praise God in His sanctuary;

Praise Him in His mighty firmament!

Praise Him for His mighty acts;

Praise Him according to His excellent greatness!

Praise Him with the sound of the trumpet;

Praise Him with the lute and harp!

Praise Him with the timbrel and dance;

Praise Him with stringed instruments and flutes!

Praise Him with loud cymbals;

Praise Him with clashing cymbals!

Let everything that has breath praise the LORD.

Praise the LORD!

David spells out that the saints of the Lord must give Him glory and have joy in doing so. This has to be one of the simplest Psalms to obey, but if we allow the enemy to defeat us, then we would be letting God down. In this Psalm, saints have a specific position in praising God. We are to have the heart of praise like a warrior going into battle. Our praise to the Lord is that of one who is confident in defeating the enemy on every front. God is our strength in all things. We shall praise His righteous name.

Praise destroys those strong holds in the lives of people. Praise works faster to destroy enemy attacks. Praise defeats the enemy in a moment's notice. The enemy may not even know what hit him. God is on the throne and He loves for His children to praise Him. Do you want victory in life over all the defeat you were up against? Well, it is time you start doing what Paul and Silas did in the prison. You know what happened when they praised our King of Kings and Lord of Lords, the chains in prison were broken, the doors were open to set them free. The prison guard received a change of heart. When praise goes up to heaven, we get God's attention and He is ready to pour out blessings that we have no knowledge of.

Start thinking about praising God with all of your heart, mind, soul, and spirit. Give yourself to the Lord. Let yourself go into the presence of God with full praise, filled in the Holy Spirit. Just call His name with adoration and absolute reverence. It is time to be set free. You know what Jesus said when Lazarus was in the grave. He said loose Him and let Him go. I am sure you want to have the experience of a lifetime in your heart. Start bowing before His throne and know that He is real in your life each and every day. Praise Him and watch the enemy flee from you. If it seems like he keeps on bothering you, continue in your praise and put all of your heart and spirit in it. Trust the Lord with all your heart and know that you are in God's presence. Love the Lord and worship Him and speak His word and watch the enemy flee. Give God all the glory.

GOD IS IN POSITION

ISAIAH 40: 21-22: "Have you not known? Have you not heard? Has it not been told you from the beginning? Have you not understood from the foundation of the earth? It is He who sits above the circle of the earth, and its inhabitants are like grasshoppers, Who stretches out the heavens like a curtain, and spread them out like a tent to dwell in."

No matter where you are in life, no matter what position you hold or what you think or do, God is still on the throne in Heaven. He sits high and looks low, always expressing who He is in with everlasting love and joy. He will not be moved from His throne. His throne is forever and ever. No matter how hard or difficult something may be, He will not be moved. No matter how your heart may feel when it is stepped on, God is still on the throne. No matter how friends may put you down, and how much you feel hated, God is still on the throne. No matter how sadness may creep into your life, God is still on the throne. No matter what attacks you have been under, God is still on the throne.

No matter how much you been cheated on and lied to, God is still on the throne. No matter how death may have impacted your life and dealt you a blow, God is still on the throne. He is looking at you right now with wide-open arms of compassion. He is on the throne orchestrating your life for His marvelous plan for you and me.

God is so powerful that He sends us signs and wonders and always a message. He has a message through Isaiah that history itself is coming to a close. He made it. History and all of time is God. No wonder the writer asked the question, Have you not known? If you have never worshipped God in your life, then you need to get with it because life will happen. Eternal life will happen. God sits on the throne and every true believer desires to see His face and bow before Him with complete individual exaltation. The word tells us that He sits above the circle of the earth. God shows us that whatever and whoever, He puts in place will come to pass.

When God allowed soldiers to deploy to Iraq, He already knew that the dictator would be captured and put away for his evil deeds. God already knew that top position would become vacant because those put in places have no praise for the provider of the blessings. You can be a well-known CEO and not give God the glory. The same God that people neglect giving glory to, is the same God who can remove the CEO from that position and promote someone else. He still sits on the throne. God is telling people that He is the one to worship and glorify.

In the eyes of the man who thinks He has it all but neglects the will of God in his life, has the opportunity to make God his Lord. You see God can touch Africa, God can touch the United States, God can touch England, the British, and God can touch Australia. God can touch every kingdom on earth. God can touch every hiding place that man may think He can hide in. God can touch every facet of society and every class man made or unmade. God has the eyes that are everywhere. Nothing is unseen by Him. He sits on the throne and sees us as grasshoppers.

God knows exactly what we need and where our minds and hearts are. He can make a way out of no way. He cools the mountains. He orchestrates the running rivers. He designed the sun and all of the stars above. He even positioned them that they would be perfectly aligned. God who sits on the throne made the heavens. He designed it just as though He were a home designer. He has more skills than HGTV. He has more decorative ideas than any homemaker. God still sits on the throne and can never be moved from His place.

EYES WIDE OPEN

GENESIS 3:5: "For God knows that in the day you eat of it, your eyes will be opened, and you will be like God knowing good and evil."

It was sin in the Garden of Eden that caused our eyes to be wide open. Eve could not see beyond the manipulation and deceit of the enemy at that very moment. It was her husband Adam who had the power to deal with that old serpent on the spot. Because of one disobedient act, all of our eyes are wide open. Our eyes were not opened to be like God, as the enemy tried to manipulate, instead they became open in a sin nature. Man will never hold the sight of what God sees and does. Man is not God and will never be God. Man is the substance of what God made to live in the harmony of what God designed for him. One mistake that the enemy did make is that the Lord God through His Holy Spirit did create us to have our eyes wide open for many reasons.

GENESIS 3:7: "Then the eyes of both of them were opened, and they knew that they were naked; and they sewed fig leaves together and made themselves coverings."

Our eyes do not have to be wide open to sin like in the garden. But it can be open to recognize the tricks and maneuvers of the enemy. Our eyes can be used to the advantage in giving God glory throughout eternity. Our eyes are to be watchful for His holy and glorious return to earth. Thanks to Jesus who washed us clean. Now our eyes can be wide open to recognize what God wants for our lives and for His purpose. I like the words the Apostle Paul stated, "We walk by faith not by sight." Even with our eyes wide open, we still need to walk by faith. Your eyes might see something, but do you really have faith for it to be manifested in the spirit. Your eyes have the power to see what God has for you and your family for the edifying of the ministry.

One of the most important things in life, along with your eyes, is the ability to listen. Everyone must learn to listen to God's voice only. The enemy is filled with lies, tricks, manipulation, and devices that can easily cause you to turn. Do not listen to anything that the enemy says to you. You take all of your commands and the word of God directly and strictly from God. That is one the reasons why the Lord wants us to be in direct relationship with Him. Because if you get into a relationship with someone else that wants you to be on their course of life, then you no longer listen to God. The Lord wants you to listen and keep your eyes wide open. It is time to walk in the spirit and see in the spirit.

It is time for people to start having their eyes wide open to their environment. There are many things happening all around us and you need to be on watch and in touch with reality. Be watchful in that Jesus Christ will return from the heavens to claim His own. Be watchful as the elect of God rebuking the snares of life by the enemy and the will of the flesh. The will of the flesh is powerful if you do not put it into subjection by fasting and praying.

You must also be watchful because the enemy constantly seeks to kill, steal, and destroy lives in the ministry and those that are babes in Christ. Hold on to God's unchanging hand for your life. Be careful for the enemy specializes in trying to manipulate everything he possible can. As soon as you see it happening start praying because praying puts the devil on the run. Prayer is our direct connection to the one who sits on the throne forever and ever. Call on the name of Jesus because His name makes the enemy flee because there is power in the name. Start counting on Jesus to be the one who helps you in all circumstances. He will make a way out of no way.

When you think that you are unable to see the things around you, ask God to open your eyes and make it visible and plain with understanding. When you start to prosper in your ministry, with money, with friends, with material blessings, with the abundance of life, the enemy will start raising its ugly head in your life, trying to break down or destroy a happy home. We all must be watchful.

No matter what it is, start praying in the spirit and call on the name of the Lord, Jesus Christ so that the enemy will flee. Rebuke Him entirely. When you know that the enemy has started his attacks, you can start singing praise to clear the atmosphere. The presence of God will overtake the enemy if you trust Him during your worship and praise sessions.

What do you really want to see? My heart's desire is to see Jesus glorified and serve Him entirely. Your eyes can be opened to so many things in life good or evil. We want to see a hard move of God in the lives of His people. We want the word to be revealed to those who have not accepted according to John 1:1-12. Come back to Jesus. You have lived out there long enough. Start pressing your way back in. Ask God to open your eyes by removing the spiritual scales.

WRITE THE VISION

Habakkuk 2:2-3: "Then the LORD answered me and said: 'Write the vision And make it plain on tablets, That he may run who reads it. For the vision is yet for an appointed time; But at the end it will speak, and it will not lie. Though it tarries, wait for it; Because it will surely come, It will not tarry.'"

Write the vision and make it plain. You see things that God grants for you as clear as day. Stop refusing the blessing that God has for you. Start speaking it in your spirit that you will be obedient to our Father in heaven. Start confessing with your lips the promises that God has for you. You do not have to rely on someone else to announce it. Just call on Jesus, the Son of the living God. God will bless your vision especially if it is for His kingdom. If you want it, get it. Blessings are for the taking from the Lord. Blessings will overflow in what you do for the Lord as long as you glorify Him.

There are many men who built churches for the uplifting of God's kingdom. They are built for worship and praise. King David had a vision to build a temple for God to place the Ark of the Covenant inside. But God wanted a place where He always dwelt. King David could not build the temple because he had blood on his hands. The temple had to be built by his son Solomon. You see God has the vision over man. God is looking for those who will be obedient and act on the vision He alone set out for them.

When Moses saw the burning bush, his heart was ignited to move toward God. Nevertheless, He moved toward the mountain and discovered it was the voice and the presence of the Lord with a mission for Him. God blessed Moses that day and for days to come. He empowered Moses so that he could tell Pharaoh to let His people go. You see God had a plan for His people. They were to be set free from bondage and prosperous all their days.

Jesus had the vision and made it a plan. His vision was to lay down His life for the world. His vision was to take a ways the sin of the world. Jesus made it plain that He was the Savior of the world. His vision was to cover everyone in His precious blood. For God so love the world that He gave His only begotten Son for whosoever believeth in Him shall not perish but have everlasting life. This vision that God has for us is for an appointed time. Jesus' death, burial, and resurrection were for an appointed time. All praise to His holy and righteous name.

You may have to give up something to make you vision happen. You may have to work hard at some things so be strong in the Lord and in the power of His might. Remember, if the Lord is in it, then it will be successful. Your visions come from God. He is the maker of your inner being and your entire mind. Seek Him for clearer visions. Make your request known to God. You have some visions and dreams inside that must be awakened and manifested to give Him glory.

I watched the picture X-Men origin and the original. It was a movie about people with extraordinary powers. They were known to be mutants, another way of saying deformed, but with powers beyond their comprehension for a while. Then when developed, they realized the force and the vision within. One thing for sure they needed a leader with vision of their capabilities.

DIVIDED KINGDOMS

MATTHEW 12:25: "But Jesus knew their thoughts, and said to them: Every kingdom divided against itself is brought to desolation, and every city or house divided against itself will not stand."

The writer says a "house divided against itself will not stand." You must keep your house in order because your family is yours for the long haul. You are the priest of the house. You are the head of the house. No one else has your authority. No one can take your specific place unless God intervenes. Your prayers keep your house together. Your love keeps the house together. Your worship to the only wise God keeps your house together. It is your responsibility to seek the Lord to remove the immediate attacks of the enemy that desperately wants you to fall to the bottom of the pit.

Your goal is to continue to keep clinging on to God who is master over all. Jesus keeps your house together. You do not need to destroy your own house nor allow anyone else to do it. You set the course in your house under God's mighty hand. You keep the worship flowing in your house. You ask God to bless and sanctify your home each day and give Him thanksgiving from the heart.

One of the most famous homes on the market today is a split home. It has everything you may desire. The design is unique and it is an eye catcher. But the problem is not the purchase of the split home, it is those who live in the home with an unwelcome spirit and how they manifest the evil as opposed to the spirit of the Lord, Jesus Christ. You want to manifest the Lord in the house with His love shining through each person. It is how everyone demonstrates peace and respect and love and compassion in their own house. You never have to show your home life to someone who lives outside your house, you just have to show it to those who live in your house. If you are living a holy life, they will know it. They will also know it by your fruit. Remember whose you are, and who you are.

You are a child of the Most High God and you will reign with Him in His kingdom forever. So stop allowing defeat in your house today. Pray now!

What causes a split house or divided house is the failure to love Christ Jesus back. It is the failure to communicate, the fear of sound counsel, and the lack of trust, not having the mind of Christ, and allowing the enemy to come in and shake up your house. You have to walk in all of the authority of God because you have the Lord on your side. Why play with the devil? He already seeks to kill, steal, and destroy. In the enemy's eyes, you and me are good prey to him. So when you let your guard down, he loves to come in and wreck your loving home in which Jesus put together for you. The enemy wants the Lord to look bad before you and me. That is not going to happen. We know that God has all power and can even control that silly enemy.

A happy home filled with love is what you desire. Don't settle for less. You can make love come forth in your home regardless of the obstacles before you. Every time the enemy puts trip wire in front of you in your house and each room, you will have the ability to walk through and diffuse the situation with the peace of God that surpasses all understanding in your heart and mind. You have an earthen vessel that is filled with power. Also your house is filled with blessings beyond the imagination of all creation including angels and even the enemy. Put your whole armor on and fight back by speaking the word. Tell everyone in your house that you love him or her. Tell them that Jesus is Lord over this family, over this house.

In Isaiah, we are told that Jesus is our counselor. In Psalm 32, He said to trust Him. In Romans 12, He said be ye transformed by the renewing of your mind. In John 14, He said, "In my house are many mansions, I go to prepare a place for you." It is a blessing to know that the enemy cannot disturb our heavenly house because Jesus lives there. He had blessed us mightily. Keep your house on earth in tact ready for the great day of our Lord's return. Allow the Holy Spirit to run your house. Division is not an option in your house. Run the devil out of your house. Do it by calling on the name of Jesus and praying to our God for help. Pray under the anointing at all times when trouble comes your way. We face the enemy and troubles head on because we are more than conquerors in Christ Jesus. Our confidence is in Him.

Father, you are the peacekeeper. You are the reason for living. You are the shelter in storm. You are the one who blesses my house. You are the priest of my house. I magnify you with all of my heart because of your loving kindness in Jesus name, Amen.

THE EYES OF THE LORD

SEES EVERYTHING

Psalm 34:14-20

Depart from evil and do good;

Seek peace and pursue it.

The eyes of the LORD are on the righteous,

And His ears are open to their cry.

The face of the LORD is against those who do evil,

To cut off the remembrance of them from the earth.

The righteous cry out, and the LORD hears,

And delivers them out of all their troubles.

The LORD is near to those who have a broken heart,

And saves such as have a contrite spirit.

Many are the afflictions of the righteous,

But the LORD delivers him out of them all.

He guards all his bones;

Not one of them is broken.

The sight of one bird can amaze us especially when it is going after something it desires like prey. The fact that the eagle can see so far from a distance in the sky a little mouse or some prey is just remarkable. It seems like he can see from miles and when he comes in, he moves with a unique attack mode while zeroing in on it. Why a bird? God chose them to be unique.

We did not have any say so about it. He knew exactly what He was doing and designed them His way. He has specific tasks for them. They help to revolve this ecosystem just like so many other creatures have a purpose in this cycle of life. The scripture says in Isaiah 40:31, *"they that wait upon the Lord shall renew their strength; they shall mount up with wings as eagles, they shall run and not be weary, they shall walk, and not faint."* The eagle demonstrates patience and precision. It also shows a zeal to get what it desires, food for the eaglets. This captured my mind because God is always watching us. The Lord our God sees everything straight from heaven. Nothing is able to hide from His presence. He sees all things. God sees from heaven when tragedy strikes. He is always on His throne.

He never has to leave it. God is present even faster than the eagle fly. God sends an angel or angels when He wants to. He sends angels faster to us than the eagle retrieving its prey. The angels of the Lord fly much faster and much powerful. God gave them a better wingspan and more power in it. He put more power in His angel than all the eagles and birds combined. This reminds His saints that His eyes are all on the righteous. Psalm 34:15: *"The eyes of the LORD are on the righteous, and His ears are open to their cry. For the righteous, we will be able to see Him like never before."*

IN A MOMENT SOMETHING WILL HAPPEN

I CORINTHIANS 15:52: "...in a moment, in the twinkling of an eye, at the last trumpet. For the trumpet will sound, and the dead will be raised incorruptible, and we shall be changed."

Just think, one blink or twinkle of the eye and the entire world could be changed right before us. God is the one who holds all power in His hand. He can do anything. Jesus could return before you can blink an eye. What is this thing called twinkle? One blink, and things could change in your life forever. He could return and pull you up in the air. It is His decision.

Life happens in a blink. You are here one day, and gone the next day. You ever had something in your life that affected you so fast that you did not know it was coming? On the other hand, there are things that happen that you expect to happen. You trust that it will happen. You trust that your heart will beat. This is important because there are people who do not understand that their heart is beating because God allows it to beat. If He took a way one beat, you would suffer. Isn't that beat similar to a twinkle?

It is fast, seemingly unnoticeable, yet you need it to happen to live. We need the last trumpet to sound so that we will rise incorruptible and be changed as the Lord has planned. We are the people of the Lord and He will not go back on His word. Listen to what the Lord is saying. A change is coming and everyone needs to get ready for blessed return of the Lord. You do not want to miss it.

SHOW ME YOUR GLORY

EXODUS 33:18-20: "And he said, please show me your glory. Then He said I will make all my goodness pass before you, and I will proclaim the name of the Lord before you. I will be gracious to whom I will be gracious, I will have compassion on whom I will have compassion. But He said, you cannot see my face; for no man shall see me, and live."

This is one of the manifested glory moments that fills the heart with joy, praise, and exaltation, unspeakable and unlimited joys in the Lord. I must admit that I just held back tears to the best of my ability because of what this scripture just said. Moses was the only man to see this manifested glory of God. We are talking about the same God who spoke the universe into existence. Somehow the God of the universe walked in His own manifested glory to reveal to Moses that He is God. He did not have to do it. He did it because of His love and because of His plan and purpose for Israel. Then there has to be another reason. He built His man Moses up to show Him that He is Moses' God.

You have not worked in vain for me. God made a statement that no other God could. There is nothing with which to compare the glory of God. He expressed His love and compassion. Listen to what God says, I will make my goodness pass before you. Has anyone ever told you that they had a good side that they could use to pass by you? Has anyone ever said they had a goodness that would bless me and be gracious to me? No, absolutely not. The only one who could pass before you and show His glory is God.

I believe that God is showing us that He passes before us on so many occasions and we miss His presence. He passes before us in the midnight hour when no one else is there to see Him but you and Him and His Holy Angels. He passes before us when we are in hurting situations and it seems like there is not one to cry on. He wipes the tears away. He passes before us when trouble comes our way and it seem like the enemy may have the victory. But God passes by and steps right in the situation and turns it around. He is good. His mercy endures forever.

I believe when God shows His presence to you there must be something on His mind. He desires to bless you, mold you, and strengthen you for a journey that seems to be endless. He puts some of His glory on you and makes everything all right. He will never pass by and not bless you. God is always up to something.

Moses knew it and that is why Moses said for God to show him His glory. I believe there are people who don't mind saying show me your glory in the midnight hour, when I need you to touch me. Show me your glory when life seems too hard to deal with.

God, I need you to talk to me. Speak you word through your manifested glory.

CHAPTER 14

THE GOD HOLD ON DESIRES

JOHN 15:7: "If you abide in me, and my words abide in you, you will ask what you desire, and it shall be done for you."

Jesus teaches us about the truth of His promises. He will answer our petition if we stick with Him instead of the skeptics and those that do not believe in His awesome promises. He made it simple to all believers. "If you abide in me, and my words abide in you, you will ask what you desire, and it shall be done for you. He wants us to know Him. He wants to know if you trust Him totally with His word. We need to understand that our God owns everything in this world and the worlds to come. In Proverbs, He said, "If you delight yourself in Him, He will give you the desires of your heart."

He is the Creator and can make anything possible that seems impossible. He is the God of the invisible who makes things come to be. So when you are looking at the impossibilities, God is up to something in your life to turn it around. God is up to something to show you. You might want to take a look right now at your surrounding and your life. Our Father in heaven is capable of supplying all of our needs. According to *Philippians 4:19, "And My God shall supply all your needs according to His riches and glory by Christ Jesus."* We have the word that gives us the answer to all of God's solutions and blessings we have His supernatural power.

The Lord shows supernatural results. He can give you the healing you want. Abide in Him, and allow His word to abide you, and then ask Him. He can visit any hospital and demonstrate His power in miracles. He can raise someone from the sick bed when death approaches. He is the God of resurrection and miracles. There are witnesses to His power. You can read 1 Corinthians 15. People saw people walking the street because of his resurrection power. I am telling you today that if you want the promises of God, abide in Him and let His word abide in you, then ask what you desire. He is the God of resurrection power.

God is the answer to all of our hopes dreams and desires. He can and will fulfill what is necessary in our lives according to His word and purpose. We can count on God to bless us in so many ways. He is blessing us right this very minute. If you are alive, He is blessing us. The same God in Heaven sent us the Holy Spirit to guide us for the purpose of glorifying Him in living our lives. We need a consistent prayer life to keep our lines of communication open to God and to maintain our obedience and humility toward Him. That is exactly why He gave us the Holy Spirit. In Romans 8:26-28, God sent the Holy Spirit to make intersession for us, especially in our weakness. He knows exactly what you and I am in need of.

Believers know that God has the power to control everything from His throne in heaven. I like the attitude that Peter and John had in Acts 3, when they saw the lame man at the gate of beautiful. There were, at a specific moment, three attitudes with a specific person on their mind. It happened when Peter said in *Acts 3:6, "Silver and gold I do not have, But what I do have I give you, In the name of Jesus Christ of Nazareth, rise up and walk."* In that instance, according to scripture, that lame man got up, and leap, and walked, and rejoiced. This man had been there for a while expecting something to happen sooner or later and it did. God blessed Him. Today you can get up and walk out of your lame condition.

DON'T LET POSSESSIONS RULE YOU

LUKE 12:15: "And He said to them, Take heed and beware of covetousness, for one's life does not consist in the abundance of the things he possesses."

We saw every possible type of classic yacht at the river front auction show last week. They had yachts of every size and color. As I looked at the yachts as a spectator, I begin to realize that you almost had to be fitly rich for these types of yachts. I think yachts are wonderful and private. For a moment, I thought I was lucky I realized that I always wanted to take my wife on a cruise in a private yacht so we could have good time.

The problem with that was that you have to make the commitments on providing funding early. In Luke 12, this man was holding on to money and using it as a crutch. Because of this man's actions, He was in harm's way. But when Jesus found out, this man was categorized as a fool. What does Jesus want from me? Jesus requires of your soul. He wants all of our being. Jesus does not want half of us. He wants total surrender. He wants us so He can make us over again. Most people can connect with being made over again. We already know deep in our hearts that we need a makeover. There are too many things that can blind and certainly riches are at the top of the chain.

Today what is needed is a confession to God. We need to confess to God that we have been blinded and we need to be fixed. We need the Lord to know that our possessions are not more important than He is in our lives.

BE A WITNESSES

1 CORINTHIANS 15:3-6: "For I delivered to you first of all that which I also received: That Christ died for our sins according to the scripture, and that He was buried and that He rose again on the third day according to the scripture, and that He was seen by Cephas, then by the twelve. After that He was seen by five hundred brethren at once, of whom the greater part remain to the present, but some have fallen asleep."

The question came up about whether or not Jesus returned to see Pilate after He rose from the dead. He rose from the dead. No one, including Pilate had to validate it for Him—it happened. Neither did He have to revisit old business. If you recall in John 1:1-8, He had come to His and they received Him not and that was in the beginning. Jesus already knew that people were going to reject Him. Pilate rejected the fact that He was the Messiah, Christ in the flesh. Pilate, if you recall, did not want to dirty his hands, but he still turned the Lord over to the mob.

I thank God that He allowed this vessel to use this scripture today with a brother who wants to get back into a relationship with the Lord. The Lord will always have witness. He will never run out no matter what happens. Somebody is going to have to tell of His resurrection. Somebody will have to tell of His saving grace. You can never get away with the most elementary facts of Jesus.

Christ died for our sins. Secondly, He was buried and He was raised from the dead on the third day. It is amazing in God's plan that He could strategically place people to see Him and turn over some of the blessings. 500 people had seen Jesus after His Resurrection. Then there were 12 disciples that saw Him.

ROOTED AND GROUNDED

EPHESIANS 3:17-19: "...that Christ may dwell in your hearts through faith; that you, being rooted and grounded in all love, may be able to comprehend with all the saints what is the width, the length and depth and height—to know the love of Christ which passes knowledge; that you may be filled with all fullness of God."

What do you think the Apostle Paul was saying to the church? Surely He was encouraging them to know that all the fullness of blessings is in the Lord, Jesus Christ. He was praying for the believers in the church at Ephesus that you would be strengthened in the inner man. He was encouraging them to hold on to Jesus who is the one who roots and grounds us in the faith through our hearts. He knows that your heart must be rooted and ground in Him in order to make it through the rough time and even the tribulation period.

There will be some hard and evil things that will approach your life in the natural, and the spirit. But our sweet Savior knows how to rescue us and comfort us all at the same time. He has that kind of power. We, as saints, must walk with the fullness of God in our hearts. I am finding out every day that there are challenges that await us before we even wake up good and go about our business at work. We need the fullness of God to dwell in our heart even to forgive a co-worker or anyone who comes up against you with evil plots and schemes and outrageous and dysfunctional attitudes and behaviors. It takes the love of God in your heart and that means the fullness of Him overcome and forgive on a daily basis.

The Apostle Paul said that we "may be able to comprehend with all the saints what is the width, the length and depth and height to know the love of Christ which passes knowledge; that you may be filled with all the fullness of God." He took my mind back to high school when we had to work out mathematics with a similar type of equation. God is not an equation. He is not complicated. He is the God of multiple blessings and I believe that is why we cannot comprehend the width, length, and depth of His unfailing love. His love is so powerful that it fills the very core of all of our being to keep us in His perfect will.

If you are challenged by anything in your life, if you are lonely or have complications with medical issues, if you have problems with maintaining your faith, if life just dealt you a blow that you believe no one is there for you, please understand that there is nothing more powerful than His love that is already extended to you right at this very moment. God is omnipresent. He is in your presence right now. He knows all about your decision to kick the drug habit, put down the alcohol, leave the world of sleeping around and violating yourself. You are better than anyone else. Today is your day to clean up and cast off the bondage that has been trying to destroy you. Today, you ask God to come into your heart and cast down any other imagination and stronghold. Repeat this. Jesus, I believe and I confess that you are the Son of God and that you died for my sin and on the third day you rose from the dead with all power in your hand by the Father in heaven. May the praise the glory and the honor go to your name o' Lord.

CRUCIFIED WITH CHRIST

ROMANS 6:6: "...knowing this, that our old man was crucified with Him, that the body of sin might be done away with, that we should no longer be slaves of sin."

We must know that all our sin was taken away in the death of Jesus on the cross. Crucifixion was one of the worst forms of execution. Jesus was crucified for us. He hanged on a cross, which caused suffocation. He was nailed to the cross. He had thorns put in His head. He had a spear to pierce His side. Blood came out of His body. He died because He bared the sins of the world resulting in the defeat of sin. His crucifixion stood for eternal love. His blood washed my sin, and yours, away.

We are asked to crucify our flesh that we can walk in the spirit. We are not strong enough to walk alone. We will need our God, the Holy Spirit to strengthen us in our walk. Our lives are not ours. We believe in Jesus. We were created for God's purpose. He wants us to crucify this flesh so that we will not put ourselves, the flesh, before Him. The tendency in life is to almost worship ourselves without even knowing it. The reason why we need to cast off some things in our lives is because Jesus already destroyed sin. It is the enemy and our flesh that raises sin. Listen to what the apostle said, we should no longer be slaves of sin. We do not need to get in these comfort zones where we welcome sin and become slaves to it all over again.

To be crucified with Jesus means to put off the old you and clothe yourself in righteousness. You have to be reminded that you are a new creature in Christ, the old one has passed away. An old thing like an old relationship has to be broken, an old alcoholism issue, drug attack, cocaine, ecstasy, dirty needles, marijuana, and a host of other drugs. If you need to go on a diet, you can crucify the flesh. The Apostle Paul said in Philippians 3:10, *"that I may know Him and the power of His resurrection, and the fellowship of His sufferings, being conformed to His death."* Get your sights set on Him and know Him. He is the only true and wise God. He is the redeemer of my soul and yours.

You can start anytime walking as a Saint. It is a good thing to acknowledge who you are in Christ and allow your light to shine and your flesh to be crucified. Start walking in the ministry as a new creature and new man in Christ. Jesus will not let you go. There are blessings in your walk in Christ. That is what God wants you to do. Walk in boldness and power. Let everyone know who ask that you are a child of the King of Kings and Lord of Lords.

NEW LIFE

ROMANS 6:4: "Therefore we were buried with Him through baptism into death, that just as Christ was raised from the dead by the glory of the Father, even so we should also walk in the newness of life."

You can have a new life in Christ Jesus any time you want it. It is available twenty-four seven. The good thing about it is that you do not have to beg for it, just surrender. You do not have to purchase it because He already paid the price. God already knows your heart's desire. He already knows whether you trust Him or not. If you trust Him, He will bless you. You need to confess that you receive Him then allow Jesus to come into your heart right now.

In baptism, when we see a person immersed into the water who has committed their lives to the Lord, we see a picture of that person being resurrected from the dead. In other words, the old person is left in the water and the new person rises to walk with Christ. He was born again in the water, but he acknowledged the fact that he believes in the death, burial, and resurrection of the Lord, Jesus Christ. I never liked visiting graveyards because it is death all around me. And it sends off an uncomfortable feeling. But I realize now that I am dead. I am no longer who I use to be. I am a new creature in Christ Jesus. The graveyard now only symbolizes that time is up, a new life must start, the past life is gone, and more importantly, I am not who I used to be. I am a new creature in Christ Jesus. The old man was dead and gone—buried.

It is interesting that the Father raised Him up. Sometimes people do not want to hear that; however, they need to hear it. They need to witness what God has for people.

A GOOD FATHER

LUKE 15:15-23: "Then he went and joined himself to a citizen of that country, and he sent him into his fields to feed swine. And he would gladly have filled his stomach with the pods that the swine ate, and no one gave him anything. But when he came to himself, he said, 'How many of my father's hired servants have bread enough and to spare, and I perish with hunger! I will arise and go to my father, and will say to him, "Father, I have sinned against heaven and before you, and I am no longer worthy to be called your son. Make me like one of your hired servants."' And he arose and came to his father. But when he was still a great way off, his father saw him and had compassion, and ran and fell on his neck and kissed him. And the son said to him, 'Father, I have sinned against heaven and in your sight, and am no longer worthy to be called your son.' But the father said to his servants, 'Bring out the best robe and put it on him, and put a ring on his hand and sandals on his feet. And bring the fatted calf here and kill it, and let us eat and be merry."

Thinking of the prodigal son's father who blessed him upon return, most sons are silent and are not looking for anything. When they come to the light of understanding, there are things that are needed to survive.

Most sons are load ambitious, have strong training, and have the desire to achieve, but when they cry for help, it is a different sound. God makes it known to you of the blessing that waits. Man is aware of when he needs to step in and nurture that young blood, son of his regardless if he is a blood son or step son, step in and step up. I discovered that my son is listening, but not hearing, sometimes hearing, but not listening. In other words, nothing effective is happening.

My father was my hero in my life. He took care of seven children and then his brothers and sisters. He took care of more than He had to. He was just a young adult, but his heart led him to bless others. God fixed where fathers have to know when to love and when to keep things in high intensity. You men like the prodigal son need to learn the lesson that you cannot get over the father in your house. Every young man and daughter needs to rely on the wisdom of his or her father. If they ignore the wisdom, there is all types of confusion and mislead life could be the results. In other words, God speaks to your father and He speaks to you as well. One thing you have to understand is the authority of the house and who God orders in your house.

One of the most powerful things that can happen in the house is when a father forgives and grants a kiss. He may not have to kiss as the prodigal son's father, but if he forgives sincerely, God has smiled on him. Today take hold of the word of God. Take hold of the God who has redeemed us from the devils grip. Jesus spoke of His Father in prayer. Let us pray like Jesus did. Jesus said, *"Our father in heaven, hallowed be your name, your Kingdom come. Your will be done. On earth as it is in heaven. Give us this day our daily bread. And forgive our debts, as we forgive our debtors. And do not lead us into temptation, but deliver us from the evil one. For yours, is the kingdom and the power and the glory forever. Amen."*

A ROUGH RIDE

HEBREWS 13:5-6: "Let your conduct be without covetousness; be content with such things as you have. For He Himself has said, 'I will never leave you nor forsake you.' So we may boldly say: 'The LORD is my helper; I will not fear. What can man do to me?'"

There is always something going on in this world that needs some attention whether it's tough love or just plain old roughing it up kind of love. One of the phrases my friend Willie used to use all the time, is "scuff him up." We got some laughs out on that one because it was well needed for a soldier who had no discipline. In those days, you would tell a private first class to pack his wallet one way, and he would pack it an entirely different way. You would tell the private to put the pillowcase on one way, when you returned the pillowcase would be on backwards or on the floor.

Those were the times when soldiers needed to drop and knock out about a hundred push-ups to work and condition their mind. When things got too out of order of discipline, drills would have to get the senior drill sergeant. His entire motto stamped in his mind was to rough them up within the standard.

Another problem is gang violence is on a rise in so many areas in our communities. It seems that it never ceases. Innocent people are always victims of unnecessary violence. You can visit almost any country and find out that someone has a need of help against predators. Sin is like a predator that keeps on seeking who it can take hold of and destroy. You need the word for your protection. This is what you need to do, speak the word and so you can rough that enemy up. Instead of you being on the end of receiving the blow, you shake the enemy up with the word.

You do not have to be victimized any more. Tell the enemy that God's word has you and you are content in His word. It's powerful and cuts through every attack. You have the victory so start walking in it. That will affect him. Stop the enemy under your feet. Saints, it is time to get together and rough him up. Start praying, saints. Make time to pray today, right now, in Jesus' name. Pray until you have a breakthrough. Pray until you hear from God.

When you pray, please understand that the enemy is receiving a blow to the head each and every time. It is time for you to believe that the power of the Lord is at work in your life. When we pray, we pray expecting something to happen and honoring God at the same time. You do not have to worry about being afraid again. The Lord said that He will never leave you nor forsake you. I am content with the blessings of the Lord. Even though I am content with blessings flowing in my life, I still have a mission to witness and serve Him.

There is no need of counting me out of the picture. That is the attitude all of us need to gain. You see in my witness and my service, God is always there. He said I would never leave you nor forsake you. That is exactly how I know it time to rough the devil up. It makes no sense if the enemy keeps attacking you and you do nothing but entertain Him over and over again. Some people walk around moping and crying about what the enemy did to them. All they have to do is to use the faith power that God equipped them with.

It is time to live like you like you are ready to rough the enemy up. If you were in the combat zone, you would put full force and full ammunition to the targeted enemy. Use your prayers. Give God all the glory.

GOD ORDAINED YOU

JEREMIAH 1:5: "Before I formed you in the womb I knew you; Before you were born I sanctified you; I ordained you a prophet to the nations."

The Lord, God knew everything before it happened to you and me. He said, I knew you before you were in your mother's womb. How can you know someone before the seed had even been developed? God is the one who decides what the seed will be because He made the seed in man. We existed in God's eyes even before our time could be manifested on earth. That is a reason to shout because no one else can express such power and make creative miracles come to existence.

God wanted Jeremiah to be encouraged about the mission he would be faced with. God appointed Jeremiah as His prophet to the nations. He wanted Jeremiah to know that all power is in His hands and that He would be with Him in delivering messages from God. So to expressed

His power. He wanted Jeremiah to that He knew Jeremiah before He was conceived.

The Lord has already thought about us before we could even know ourselves, before we even came into the world. He knew everything about each person individually and accurately before we could know anything about ourselves. That is enough to shout about. God knew our hearts and minds and soul and strength before we knew anything about it. What a reason to praise Him and serve Him the rest of your life.

Everyone that God calls has a specific purpose for Him. No one should live life without knowing his or her purpose. If you do not know, ask God. Seek Him with all of your heart and soul and He will answer. The word of God is also the answer. God will bless you through His word. Seek ye first the kingdom of God and His righteousness. When you seek Him, everything else that He desires for you will follow and bless you.

There are several things that God wants you to do and more. You may not finish everything, but set goals in Christ Jesus. Jesus can help you make it through all of your goals. He made you and I before time. He already had us in mind before the world was formed. Not only did He already know us, He sanctified you. He ordained the person He wanted to ordain for His purpose. It means that God has a mission for His people. He set apart specific people for pinpointed assignments.

Do you know your assignment? Do you know where God wants you? Remember, before He formed you and I, He already knew about us. He knew everything about us. He knew our comprehension levels, he knew our intellect, and He knew whom we would marry. He knew the trust level inside our heart. He knew if we would accept Him as Lord and Savior. He knew that He would wash us in His blood for the remission of sin. He knew who would birth out a baby boy and a baby girl or even twins, triplets, and quadruplets. God knew the morning and the days of the year and times of thunder and lighting and the floods of life. He knew how much trouble you would be faced with.

BREACHING ALL LINES OF ENEMY TRAPS

The Apostle Paul breached the lines of the enemy with the aid of the Holy Spirit as he went on journey after journey. I believe. The Apostle Paul had the audacity and the boldness to venture out and position himself where God wanted him. He was led by the Holy Spirit to be a missionary in the field of touching thousands of lives. He was led by the Holy Spirit to breach all lines of the enemy including booby traps laid for him. His goal was to press for Christ and please him.

It was Jesus who blessed the Apostle Paul to become the saint he turned out to be. I think what was important is that God placed His word in this vessel and used Him mightily.

It was the apostle who gave us the word from called grace. In Ephesians 2:8, He reminds that all lines are breached. Because the scripture says we were saved by grace, though faith, and not of ourselves, it is the gift of God. So we have a God that is so kind to give us a gift that the enemy can't breach. Grace can't be altered. Grace can't be shattered. Grace can't be manipulated. Grace can't be stolen or lost. Grace can't be taken away. God owns it and allows us to preach His word so it will not return void. Grace breaches every obstacle of the enemy and every obstacle of man's bondage and fleshly desires. God is good and worthy of all praise. That is exactly why you and I can rest in His grace. No need to worry about anything. We have grace on our side and Jesus to back it up.

In the military, it takes professionalism and training and discipline to spot those booby traps and the enemy IEDs, and those around the corner aiming RPGs and missiles to take on casualties. We have grace to keep us in His perfect will. When in battle, know that when you accepted Jesus as Lord of your life, you became a new creature in Christ Jesus.

We are so blessed because God showers us in grace. You see because we stay soaked in grace by the spiritual rain of blessings from God, we can breach anything in life. If there is a challenge in marriage breach the troubles because you have grace and you have a high Priest who has already blessed you.

Grace gives you the will to survive in any and every situation. Grace carries you to the edge and back. It takes you through all enemy attacks. Grace enables me to grow. It took Jesus to breach all lines of the enemy. Adam could not do it because he had sinned with his wife. All of the old prophets and Jesus' disciples could not do it. It took the blood of Jesus to breach the most fortified and built up area of hell.

The need to minister involves grace. The Lord will prepare all of those like Apostle Paul to run the mission outside. There is always a need for God's ministry. God put order of His ministry in place. When one falls and when one leaves for the purpose of Christ into His marvelous presence, then He alone has the authority to rise up another. You are the other. Do not allow circumstance and other people to get in your way. Seek God and ask Him for directions and purpose for your life. God is always looking for new journeymen like you. He is looking for journey women also. He has a way of sending His anointing through those who seek Him and love Him with an open heart of thanksgiving.

GLORIFY GOD

PSALM 8:1: "O LORD, Our LORD, how excellent is your name in all the earth, who have set Your Glory above the heavens!"

God's name alone has all power to shake kingdoms, shape kingdoms, and loose those that are bound by the grip of the enemy. His name alone declares His glory and strength. His name is the highest name there is throughout creation. Jesus is Lord anyway we look at it.

His name is excellent because there is no one like Him and His glory is revealed throughout the ages. His name is above the heavens because He is the Creator of all things including the stars, planets, moon, earth, and even death and life. He makes the impossible possible. Imagine in your mind that God designed the man and the soul and spirit of Him. All people and everything must bow before Him in full worship. He is excellent, glorious, and worthy of all praise.

So now when you speak of the King of Kings, Lord of Lords, worship and praise Him with all your heart, mind, soul, and strength. He is forever merciful and all loving. Our Lord is the one who is responsible for putting a soul inside of man. He is responsible for putting a spirit inside of man. The scripture says, "He breathed the breath of life into man and man became a living soul." In that process, we became His alone. That is why men must bow before Him in adoration. I believe the excellence of the Lord's name was etched into the minds of men even before they accepted Him. With God's name, everything has a touch of holiness. Man must glorify Him for what He has done and is performing right now in the life of the believer and even in the natural man.

BELIEVE IN THE LORD

John 20:27-29: "Then He said to Thomas, 'Reach your finger here, and look at my hands; And reach your hand here, and put it into my side. Do not be unbelieving, but believing,' And Thomas answered and said to Him, 'My Lord and my God!' Jesus said, 'Thomas because you have seen me, you have believed. Blessed are those who have not seen and yet believed.'"

The Bible illustrates several times that Jesus touched people in different situations. What was so important about His touch? He always made it personal. Healing was a result of His touch. It was His love that restored every possible issue in His touch. His touch in our lives is the key focus. He touched the blind, He touched the lamb, He touched those with leprosy, He touched the hand of man broken, He touched the dead, and He allowed Himself to be touched. He never denies His unfailing love, grace, mercy, and healing power to all people. God desires to touch each one of us everyday in every way of our lives.

You might have a personal experience one day that bounds you to it. But God will deliver you from it because you are one of His and He knows that you trust in Him. It was hard for Thomas for a little while but he came around to understanding it and began to understand who Jesus really was at that time. When Thomas truly understood that Jesus had risen his faith grew instantly. He believed in the resurrection.

The blind man wanted to see and finally found someone who could change the course of his life. When you ask the Lord about seeing, you might as well trust Him because you will be able to see. Your old spiritual scales will fall off. Your eyes will be opened for the first time. Strange things can happen for the first time in the life of the believer. Your life could be different from that blind man's experience. God might have you doing a great work to glorify Him. But He needs you to see in the spirit.

The woman with the issue of blood just wanted to touch the hem of His garment. Jesus noticed her faith. Jesus asked, "Who touched me?" because He knew that someone had touched Him in faith. So He had to speak, "Your faith has made you whole." God wants us to have that kind of faith to know that He will make you whole. Even if the physicians cannot heal you, the Lord will make you whole again. You just need to ask Him to touch your situation, no matter what it is, He has the power to change it.

The men with leprosy had more than they could handle. They saw Jesus and asked for healing. They knew that they were outcasts and no one wanted them around. They knew that their conditions were contagious and had to be controlled or else it would spread. But when they saw Jesus, they knew that all they had to do was ask for healing. Jesus healed them and one of them praised Him and rejoiced for His mighty act. You may have felt like an outcast because of a medical issue or because life just dealt you a blow. Call on the name of the Lord. He is our strong tower. He is our healer.

What was amazing is the fact that when Jesus rose from the dead, he did not want to be touched by Mary because as He said, "I am not ascended yet into heaven," and yet he ate with the disciples to prove that He was in form and that He defeated death. Jesus had gone down into the depths of hell and defeated Satan.

Then you have doubting Thomas, who was instructed to touch the side of Jesus so he could believe. Some people need their belief restored or healed delivered from the doubt and confusion. They need the Thomas experience. Jesus instructed Thomas to touch His side. It was then when Thomas believed that Jesus was and is real and that He rose from the dead. The blessing was when Thomas touched Jesus, and made the statement that would touch the world, "My Lord and My God." Jesus said, blessed are those who have not seen and yet have believed. My Lord and my God, your love has touched me and made me to believe. Ask God to touch you today that you may reign in His kingdom forever and ever.

Sometimes in our lives we think that like the woman with the issue of blood who touched Jesus' garment and was made whole that it was just our touch of faith. But the fact of the matter is that it was faith in Him and more importantly it was His touch that healed her more than her reaching out because the power of healing is in His hand. The power of love is in Him. Blessed be the name of the Lord.

BONE OF MY BONES

GENESIS 3:23-24: "And Adam said: 'This is now bone of my bones And flesh of my flesh; She shall be called Woman, Because she was taken out of Man. Therefore a man shall leave his father and mother and be joined to his wife, and they shall become one flesh.'"

The Bible speaks of marriages that are made by God. God ordained marriages, one marriage between man and woman, period. The other marriage is between God and His church, the saints. These are the only marriages blessed by God Himself in accordance with Genesis 3: 23-24 and Mark 10:6-9, God does not want man to drift into the mindset of what happened in Romans 1:18-32. When people fall or step out of true matrimony, they open the gates of hell into their lives.

The enemy starts to feed off of the weakness of people then they fall for anything the enemy throws at them. The enemy makes it look and feel good, then distorts the mind and spirit to making one believe that whatever the sin is, it's good. You need to understand that the enemy is the author of lies and confusion. He wants to destroy your blessed marriage. The one the priest and both of you vowed to live by. Keep your marriage in prayer and before God at all times. He will bless it. You do not have to allow your marriage and yourself to be a tragedy and victim of the enemy. Instead walk in the victory daily under His saving grace and power of love. You deserve to be blessed by God. Your loved one and all of your family deserve to be blessed. Anyone who believes in God knows that there are tricks all day long and that evil exists to tear you apart. Evil wants to take over you and so we will not have a loving family those that marry outside of God's authority are opening themselves up for evil to take over completely. Those who love the Lord are praying that all people come on one accord and be blessed by God's true marriage principles.

Marriage definitions can be complicated to so many people, but in reality it is not complicated. Too many Christians' marriages fail because they stop trusting in God to lead that marriage. God has to be the center of the marriage. God has to be the center of each individual person life to make it work. So then marriage is defined by your relationship with God. You remember the wedding day. You made a commitment before the wedding day and you made a commitment on the wedding day with perhaps hundreds of people in attendance or a few as witnesses to your statement before God.

You want to know why marriages fall apart? They fail and fall apart because of those who once believed in the power of love from Jesus Christ left the sacredness of their vows. You have to recall that God ordained your marriage. Your marriage is your marriage; it is not anyone else's. Marriage does require attraction and love and affection. You do not stop showing love and affection because you love Jesus. He wants you to reveal your love to one another daily.

Your marriage can be a marriage made in heaven. Do not allow outside forces human or evil to interrupt your relationship. You must work everything out with the Lord. He is your primary and key counselor for all circumstances. Trust Him and He will bless you and maintain your marriage for His appointed duration of your lives together.

THE BEST GIFT

John 4:9-10: "Then the woman of Samaria said to Him, 'How is it that you, being a Jew, ask a drink from me, a Samaritan woman?' For Jews have no dealing with Samaritans. Jesus answered and said to her, 'If you knew the gift of God, and who it is who says to you, Give me a drink, you would have asked Him, and He would have given you living water.'"

God gave us the ultimate gift. He gave us His Son, Jesus Christ. He sacrificed His own Son for all people to destroy the work of sin. God is the only true living and loving God. He is the only one who can give such gifts. After the death, burial and resurrection of Jesus, God gave us the Holy Spirit to help us. It was after the ascension of Jesus to heaven when the Holy Spirit would come to help us with our life issues. The Holy Spirit is our gift that God gave us from Him, to be there when we need a guide and comfort through life.

God planted His Spirit in us when He breathed the breath of life into Adam's body. Before Adam became a spirit filled man, he was just a man in a dirt suit, made by God only. He was fashioned by God. He was made of God with a clay body. God gave Adam the best gift. He gave Him His Spirit to walk in the image of God. So then gifts are one of God's special expressions of blessings in the life of the believer. That is exactly why I stated, if you knew the gift.

One of the things that God wants for His people is to understand that there is no difference between the Jews, Gentiles, and Samaritans. God sent Jesus to wash the sin from all people on earth. In Romans 1:16, the Apostle Paul made a statement that there is neither Jew nor Gentile. He said, "For I am not ashamed of the gospel of Christ, for it is the power of God to salvation for everyone who believes, for the Jew first and also for the Greek." The Apostle Paul, under the anointing of the Holy Spirit wanted everyone to know that the message of the good news. The good news was the news of salvation, which had then, and now the power to change people lives from evil to good. He was not ashamed of the Gospel of Jesus Christ because it has the power to deliver a sin-sick soul from that condition to claiming a place in heaven upon the return of Christ. That is the gift of God for all men sick.

No one was exempted from the salvation that God gave us. No one was too special that they could be turned down. No one was better than the other person in society to receive the blessing of eternal life. If that were so, then Jesus would have had to come as a sacrifice for specific people who could earn their way in the kingdom of heaven. The Lord wants us to know that whoever you are under the sun, He can change your life. The Samaritan woman could not in the beginning grasp who Jesus was. It took Jesus to tell her about herself. He began to tell her that she had five men in her life and now the one she is with is not her husband. With conviction and surprise, she now believes that He is a prophet or somebody that has factual insight.

Much like many other people in this world who believe that someone else is better than you, she was in total amazement. Jesus told this Samaritan woman, "If you knew the gift of God and what He can do for you." It's time to stop searching for the wrong God and the wrong religion. If you get caught up on the wrong God, life will steer you wrong under the devil's influence. That is exactly Jesus is the gift to people. They recognize Him as Savior and life becomes better in that old world.

CHAPTER 15

FIRST SEEK THE KINGDOM OF GOD

MATTHEW 6:33: "But seek first the kingdom of God and His righteousness, and all these things shall be added to you."

One of the most important things in life is to not let life pass you by without you getting the most out of it. Time moves fast and you can miss opportunities and special moves of God that can bless you in abundance. Also God has priorities for your life. His priority is that all of us seek Him. Matthew 6:33 says, *"But seek first the kingdom of God and His righteousness, and all these things shall be added to you."*

Make Him your priority in life to seek first the kingdom of God and His righteousness. So many people seek everything else in life such as new homes, cars, the right companion or spouse, fantasy vacations, retirement and so many other things. But the truth of the matter is that God comes first. The Lord knows who is putting Him first in their lives. He will bless you in the overflow. He will touch your life and make you prosper. Stop listening to those that tell you opposite of God's blessing. Just in case you want to drop a word to them, ask them whom are they seeking in life for self-satisfaction and blessings and inheritance. The inheritance you get from God is eternal and never exhausted. People can bless you, but they bless you differently than God. Continue to concentrate and seek Jesus first and seek Jesus always.

Jesus is the first and the last, the alpha and omega. That means you have everything you need to survive in life. When you get Jesus, you have the beginning of life and the end. He is eternal so He cannot end but we in the flesh and carnal state will perish.

At one point in my life, basic training was the most important event for me to achieve. I have made up my mind that I was going to be a soldier and serve the Armed Forces for several years. My focus became clear in my life. I needed to get through those eight agonizing weeks of hell with those crazy drill sergeants. If I could make through all demanding physical training and the draining mental effects, then I knew that I could now be called a United States Armed Forces soldier. When you know that you are a real soldier, then you know that everything that you sought after was pleasing and rewarding in your life. I can rest now knowing that those years and that training were not done in vain.

I liken the military career to seeking first the Lord's kingdom and His righteousness. I need the help of the Holy Spirit in God's Army. Nothing can be sought after and achieved if you do not have the Holy Spirit working on you. As a Christian today, sometimes I believe that I need to revisit God's basic training camp. I need a special tune-up inside me. I need the Lord to take hold of me and make me over. When He makes me over then I will be able to see the reality of seeking Him first. It will be more than what we think. What is clear to me now is that whatever comes to mind as a desire, a want and even a need, I must put God first no matter what.

There are various kinds of people in the world. Some enjoy the outdoor game of hunting. When you hunt, you are searching for the kill of the game. God wants that kind of attitude in His children.

Some hunters score big point for big game. It this game is game that you keep and eat and transform into trophies. The same happens when you play football and basketball. The best players are highlighted and given huge contracts.

BALANCE YOUR LIFE

HEBREWS 12:1: "Therefore, since we are surrounded by such a huge crowd of witnesses to the life of faith, let us strip off every weight that slows us down, especially the sin that so easily trips us up. And let us run with endurance the race God has set before us."

You can be weighed down and have all kinds of weight on you that is harmful. You want to live the good life. In order to live the good life, you need to be healthy and full of strength. God the Father did not make us to be unhealthy. Set a new goal in your life today to exercise and eat the proper food groups. You will be happier and feel better. You will also live longer.

A proper diet is essential for your health. Take a look at the proper breads, fish, dairy products, fruit, and vegetables. Take the necessary portion each day to maintain a healthy diet. You already know you, and you know how to discipline yourself. If you do not know how to do it, then seek God and a nutritionist to develop a plan. Then stick with that plan. When you start your diet, just think of it as going on a diet for the Lord. You can also look at in a view of fasting, though they are two separate actions. The two key things about both of them is that they result in a breakthrough and a balanced life. You will see as time goes by.

You will live a better life. You can do it. Do not let yourself down. Your health means a lot to the Lord. He gave you this earthen vessel to take care of it, not worship it but to live a good life. I was thinking of the proper diet spoken earlier. When you go on a diet, imagine how you study the word of God. Well use that method of training your body. At the same time, when you are fasting and praying, you will also get a breakthrough if you are vigorously doing it. Fasting gets your spiritual breakthrough.

These other help to balance your life. God wants us to be aligned in His word and not self.

PROVERBS 6:16: "*These six things the Lord hates, Yes, seven are an abomination to Him: A proud look, A lying tongue, Hands that shed innocent blood, A heart that devises wicked plans, Feet that are swift in running to evil, A false witness who speaks lies, And one who sows discord among brethren. My son, keep your father's command, And do not forsake the law of your mother. Bind them continually upon your heart.*"

JESUS' HAND

John 20:19-21: "*Then, the same day at evening, being the first day of the week, when the doors were shut where the disciples were assembled, for fear of the Jews, Jesus came and stood in the midst, and said to them, 'Peace be with you.' When He had said this, He showed them His hands and His side. Then the disciples were glad when they saw the Lord. So Jesus said to them again, 'Peace to you! As the Father has sent me, I also send you.'*"

You know Jesus, the Son of the Living God. He is always revealing miracles and demonstrating His love again and again. Thank God that He is always taking care of us. As I was playing with my granddaughter, I placed her hand in my hand and really just looked to see how tiny they really are.

I was amazed, as always, thinking of how God can do such miracles of creation and birth. I was playing the little game itsy bitsy spider with her and what got me is when she just stared at my hand. I kept showing her my fingers and placing her hand in my hand. Something about that moment just blessed me and struck me in complete awe and amazement of God's gentleness and loving kindness.

I thought about the hand of God. Our Father's hand covers us every time we are in need, and every day that we breathe and walk. Every time we need Him to lift us up from falling into the pits of hell, He reaches out His hand of unfailing love and mercy. Every time we stumble into the enemy's camp, He reaches out His hand to place us on the right path of life. Every time we drift back into the mindset of sinful living, He reaches out His hand to find and rescue the ninety-nine to show His love. The writer says, do not remove your hand from me.

Every time we call on Him in marriage situations, He knows exactly where to place His hand. When Thomas had doubt about the resurrection, it was Jesus who told him to put his hand in the side of Jesus and in the nail prints in His hand. The purpose was so that Thomas would believe in Jesus' resurrection. Then Jesus said that those who have not seen shall surely be blessed. Thomas needed to touch Him to see if He is real.

Today is your day. If you want to find out if Jesus can touch you with His loving hands, ask Him to come into your life. Receive salvation for it is eternal and you will reign in His Kingdom forever. His hand will keep you in perfect peace on earth. His hand will bless you in ways men cannot imagine.

RECOVER UNDER GRACE

2 Corinthians 12:9: "And He said to me, 'My grace is sufficient for you, for my strength is made perfect in weakness.' Therefore most gladly I will rather boast in my infirmities, that the power of Christ may rest upon me."

I was riding in my tactical vehicle being as tactical and technically proficient in my skills as anyone else. Suddenly, a blast, a loud explosion hit the Hummer and flipped it over. There were casualties and too many of them. It was supposed to be an easy day of patrolling the streets of Baghdad. I had my game face on and I was observing every obstacle, scoping out every potential hidden improvised explosive device (IED). Everybody knows now that an easy day can turn into your worst nightmare when least expected. The only thing I wondered about the most was if God truly loved me and where I would go. I wondered if grace was sufficient enough to get me through this war zone.

Some days even in you calmest state of mind, you are saying get me out of this hellhole of mess and confusion. It is already enough to be wondering about if I am going to heaven or hell. It is the grace of God that kept me through and through all the time. It is important that all soldiers recover under grace.

When it rains, it pours and it seems like it will never end. Today is your day to look at the enemy and all of His legions and speak the blessings over your life. Tell God that you need an out pour of His grace.

STRIPPED BUT BLESSED

GENESIS 37:23: "So when Joseph came to his brothers, they stripped him of his robe- the richly oriented robe he was wearing. And they took him and threw him into the cistern. Now the cistern was empty; there was no water in it. So when the Midianites merchants came by, his brothers pulled Joseph up out of the cistern and sold him for twenty shekels of silver to the Ismaelite, who took him to Egypt."

His brothers stripped Joseph so God could use him. His brothers and His entire family did not understand the anointing on his life in the beginning of the message. They did not have the vision or the dreams he had. Joseph's brothers thought that they had broken his spirit.

Instead, they just pushed him into the favor of God. They stripped him down for the purpose of getting rid of their father's favorite son. They did not know that by stripping him of the coat of many colors, they set him up for God's favor and blessings. There is no way to stop the blessings that God has in store for you and me. Certainly, Joseph's blessings were not going to be stopped. When the Lord set something in motion, it will not be stopped by anyone or anything.

Joseph's coat was a representation of royalty. His father gave it to him because he favored him. Joseph's coat reminds us of the rainbow colors. It made me think of the covenant God made with Noah, no more floods and the sign would be a rainbow in the sky. Some see the coat as a representation of a priest. His father saw it as a gift and a blessing for his son, Joseph.

We need to know that God has made all of us royal priests in the army of the Lord. We need to know that when we have family situations, God does not turn His back on us. There are blessings on the way. The robe was a blessing and that is exactly why the enemy wanted to twist things in the family, causing jealousy. It is clear that when Jesus rose from the dead He wore a priestly robe.

Jealousy can cause all kinds of trouble. But when trouble comes our way, He always makes everything all right. He walks with us and protects us. The pharisees were jealous of Jesus because He went about healing, making miracles happen, and teaching disciples. The Pharisees and His own people punished Jesus because of jealousy. His own brothers punished Joseph. No matter how much you feel like somebody has broken you like a slave, keep your head up and look to the hills where you help comes from. Jesus always looked up to the Father when things got so rough. He prayed in the Garden of Gethsemane. Joseph just kept the faith in knowing who his God was during that time.

You have an advocate to take you back from the enemy. You have an advocate to set you up for blessings innumerable. You have an advocate that will help you when someone sells you out. God is always on your side. You can be just like Joseph and be positioned second in command or you can be first in command according to God's favor and will for your life.

Do not give up even if you feel like you have be placed in a pit and sold out. God is on your side and He has multiple blessings for you. You need to know that God strips all of us.

HEARTS ON FIRE

REVELATIONS 3:15-16: "I know your works, that you are neither cold nor hot, I could wish you were cold or hot. So then, because you are lukewarm, and neither cold nor hot, I will vomit you out of my mouth."

God sees everything and hears everything from the throne room of heaven. He knows the ability of the church. He knows the ability of those who proclaim His name. He knows who has backslidden and fallen from the faith. He knows what caused it and who caused it and the situation behind it. God is no respecter of persons. No one can hide. No one can get away with anything. He is omnipresent; present everywhere, and all knowing. He is looking for a church without spot nor wrinkle. God knows the heart of man. God knows the heart of the church.

The Lord wants men to have a heart that is on fire for Him. He said either cold or hot. The point is to go all the way for Him. He wants men to have a servant's hearts that will continue in obedience. He wants men to follow in His will for their lives and the ministry of the Gospel. Do you remember you first time you felt the change and the conversion? You were on fire for the Lord. God is saying do not leave your first love. He was there when you first fell in love with Him. You read the word and were on fire for the Lord. Do not let somebody or something steal your joy and your anointing. The enemy is sly enough to make you think otherwise.

He comes to steal, kill, and to destroy your dreams in the Lord, your service for the Lord. You do not have to stand by and let the enemy snatch you away. Listen to the voice of the Lord. Noah did, he was on fire for the Lord. He built an ark and saved the world from total devastation. Abraham was on fire. He moved when God told Him to move. He moved in faith and became the father of many nations. God has something in store for you. You are a child of the Most High, so start walking in the anointing placed in your life. You might lose some friends. But God is on your side. Besides, no one can get you into Heaven.

VICTORY IS IN JESUS CHRIST!

1 JOHN 5:4-5: "For whatever is born of God overcomes the world. And this is the victory that has overcome the world-our faith. Who is he who overcomes the world, but he who believes that Jesus is the Son of God."

To be born of God already reflects that you have the victory in the Lord for your life. No one can walk victorious without Him. You must be born again to walk in victory. You must have faith to be an overcomer of the world. The world is tricky because it is attractive to so many people. It has so much that looks so good that entices you to live a life without Christ. It is vitally important that you make Jesus the head of your life today. Do not wait any longer. It is like suicide without Him. He will bless you more than you know.

Never let someone tell you that they predict your relationship and victory. You get yourself up and you make it happen with the Lord. You tell Jesus that you want to make a date, time, and place for you and Him to meet. You talk to the Lord for yourself. When you get Christ Jesus in your life, you can tell any and everybody that no one can snatch victory away from you because of who you are now. Make a change.

Don't misunderstand the blessings that God gave us in this world. Just do not get caught up with all the misleading things in life that are not of God. As a soldier in the army, I remember telling about 64,000 soldiers or more about what the Bible says is victory in the Lord. I was absolutely shocked when I was able to tell some of the highest-ranking officers and enlisted that nothing is better than having victory in the Lord. You see victory comes directly from Him.

Our strength, our knowledge, our technical skills, our strategy and planning, our decision making, our creativity, the sound mind, the best of judgment, all of our tactical skills and abilities, all of the future planning and the past reviews of war, all of the war gaming tools and techniques had to come from the one who holds and gives intellect to man.

It must be faith in God that drives senior leadership and subordinate leaders and the soldiers who attack on ground and by other means necessary to secure victory in war and battle. Faith must be the corner stone, it must be absolute ingredient in the heart of man that enables him to survive and secure victory for the sake of peace and tranquility in the land of the free. All believers and all that battle against enemy must overcome every obstacle so that all nations live in a peaceful environment and relationship in foreign policy and trade will be in the best interest for everyone.

Victory is not substitutable when it comes to saints of the Lord. We have it in Christ and will not be changed because He promised it. Victory relies on faith. You must have faith. It can be the faith of a mustard seed. It can be the faith of a person newly converted as long as that faith is true Godly faith. The faith you have whether you are in Iraq, Afghanistan, Africa, Asia, Korea, Kuwait, or even the United States is the faith needed to believe in Jesus and accept Him in your heart as Lord and Savior. Then, you will walk in a continuous life of victory in the Lord.

You can start over from where you are now. You are never too low. Read Psalms 139. God said if you made your bed in hell, He is there. He will not leave you. Certainly, if you have fallen from the faith, God is there to pick you up again. Let the Lord carry you. You just ask the Holy Spirit to ignite your heart that it will be on fire again for the service of the Lord. The Bible says to pick up your cross and carry it. When you are on fire, God will use you in ways to glorify Him.

It is time to pick up your sword again. Pick up your Bible and read again. The enemy has worked hard trying to destroy you. Some of your companions worked hard to keep you down. If they are encouraging you then fine, but if not, you might have to break away. Do not let any one tamper with your soul salvation. Be strong in the Lord and in the power of His might. Stay focused and God will see you through.

Preach the word and be instant in season and out of season. Tell of God's plan of salvation. Be a witness on fire and tell that God loves you more than anybody and everybody could even imagine. Tell them that God listens to a repentant heart. Tell them that God has a plan for them and for you. Remember to keep the faith and let the love of God spread about your heart by the power of the Holy Spirit. Praise His righteous name forever.

FASTING AND PRAYER

MATTHEW 4:1-12: "Then Jesus was led up by the Spirit into the wilderness to be tempted by the devil. And when He had fasted forty days and forty nights, afterward He was hungry. Now when the tempter came to Him, he said, 'If You are the Son of God, command that these stones become bread.' But He answered and said, 'It is written, Man shall not live by bread alone, but by every word that proceeds from the mouth of God.' Then the devil took Him up into the holy city, set Him on the pinnacle of the temple, and said to Him, 'If You are the Son of God, throw yourself down. For it is written:

'He shall give His angels charge over you,' and,

'In their hands they shall bear you up,

Lest you dash your foot against a stone.'

Jesus said to him, 'It is written again, You shall not tempt the LORD your God.'

Again, the devil took Him up on an exceedingly high mountain, and showed Him all the kingdoms of the world and their glory. And he said to Him, 'All these things I will give you if You will fall down and worship me.' Then Jesus said to him, 'Away with you, Satan! For it is written, you shall worship the LORD your God, and Him only you shall serve.' Then the devil left Him, and behold, angels came and ministered to Him. Now when Jesus heard that John had been put in prison, He departed to Galilee."

Jesus began His Galilean ministry after He fasted for forty days. When you fast and pray, you may have a wilderness experience that will change the course of your life. Jesus had experience that was set by the Father in heaven.

It appears that one of the most effective ways to begin your ministry is by fasting and praying. This allows you to seek the Lord and get closer to what Him. Fasting opens up channels of communication between you and God. You get the connection properly when you leave flesh out of the matter at hand. God loves it, as it appears when we put our plates aside for a while. He wants us to fast properly and not publicly announce it. It is personal between you and God alone. God wants us to have breakthroughs. Jesus illustrated exactly what we need to do. We fast and use the word of God for the enemy who chases us daily. We fast to get the mission done if need be. We fast out of devotion to Christ Jesus to let go of things that entangle us and bound us. We fast and pray because we are committed to live a life in Christ Jesus.

Today, ask yourself what is it that I need to fast from that has a necessary hold on me? If you need it each day and can't do without outside of water, then it may have a hold on you. Remember, when you fast, get ready for some attacks as well because you operate in the spirit even more. Also remember that God is on your side whenever you are going through. It is important that you seek God before fasting. Ask the Lord to help you make the right choice. When you fast, you do not have to boast about it and tell everyone. It is between you and God. However, you can let you and your wife and if the community church are fasting together, it is necessary to keep each other in prayer. Seek your breakthrough in Christ Jesus.

HEALING

MATTHEW 9:1-8: *"So He got into a boat, crossed over, and came to His own city. Then behold, they brought to Him a paralytic lying on a bed. When Jesus saw their faith, He said to the paralytic, 'Son, be of good cheer; your sins are forgiven you.' And at once some of the scribes said within themselves, 'This Man blasphemes!' But Jesus, knowing their thoughts, said, 'Why do you think evil in your hearts? For which is easier, to say, 'Your sins are forgiven you,' or to say, 'Arise and walk?' But that you may know that the Son of Man has power on earth to forgive sins'—then He said to the paralytic, 'Arise, take up your bed, and go to your house.' And he arose and departed to his house. Now when the multitudes saw it, they marveled] and glorified God, who had given such power to men."*

This day is your day to get out of the paralyzed conditions of life. It may seem impossible but it is not. It may seem as though no one cares or will help you but that is not the truth. God is able to do the impossible and He alone can do it for you. Today is your day to arise and walk. You have the power if you believe in Jesus Christ who rose from the dead.

You probably have, just like myself, found yourself walking into convenience stores near some corners and even just at a stop at a red light in some towns have encounter a person in a wheelchair or crippled for some reason. There are some things we do not have the power to do in our own strength. But the God of a second chance, the God of healing power and miracles can change things in an instant.

There are many people who do not have the eternal hurt, or the injury that is visible before our eyes. But inside, they have a crippling mentality that is even worst. That mentality of religious battles and principalities keep them from accepting Jesus as Lord of their life.

I watched a man on television preaching the gospel with a scarred face and legs that were not visible because he had a car accident that severed them. So now his life is without legs. But he does not go around sad and acting like he has no hope. Instead, he gives all that he has to service for Christ. He inspired me to a new level of thinking.

Believers all over the world should see this man who has the tenacity to walk in faith and be healed in mind and soul and spirit. Him. He believes that Jesus is his Lord and there is no other like this is your time for healing. Keep the faith and walk in it. Believe that God can remove any crippling situation in your life. Stop allowing the old past of sin to speak barriers and brokenness in your life. Instead listen to what Jesus said, arise and walk. Your sins have been forgiven.

GALATIANS 5:21-26: "But the fruit of the Spirit is love, joy, peace, longsuffering, kindness, goodness, faithfulness, gentleness, self-control. Against such there is no law. And those who are Christ's have crucified the flesh with its passions and desires. If we live in the Spirit, let us also walk in the Spirit. Let us not become conceited, provoking one another, envying one another."

You have to have patience in just about all the things you do especially for the home. More importantly today, you have to have patience to walk in faith in God. If you are confident in God you do not have to give in to anything in this world. What will take you over in this life and the life to come is the possession of the fruit of the spirit.

The scripture says, *"But the fruit of the Spirit is love, joy, peace, longsuffering, kindness, goodness, faithfulness, gentleness, self-control,"* (Galatians 5). What a combination to live with. When you express a fruitful lifestyle to God, He knows. He wants us to live with other people around us so that they will the power of Jesus love and touch. These fruit are a must in this lifetime if you want to be successful.

Patience wins no matter what the obstacle or barrier may be. If you are sketching something on a canvas for a painting project, you must be patient with all the tenders touch and designs for your painting. You are an artist with expert creative thoughts and you want to apply it. Did you know that you have the ability to sketch in the next super million-dollar convention at the art center.

PASSOVER FOR YOUR CHILDREN

EXODUS 12:13-17: "Now the blood shall be a sign for you on the houses where you are. And when I see the blood, I will pass over you; and the plague shall not be on you to destroy you when I strike the land of Egypt. 'So this day shall be to you a memorial; and you shall keep it as a feast to the LORD throughout your generations. You shall keep it as a feast by an everlasting ordinance. Seven days you shall eat unleavened bread. On the first day you shall remove leaven from your houses. For whoever eats leavened bread from the first day until the seventh day, that person shall be cut off from Israel. On the first day there shall be a holy convocation, and on the seventh day there shall be a holy convocation for you. No manner of work shall be done on them; but that which everyone must eat—that only may be prepared by you. So you shall observe the Feast of Unleavened Bread, for on this same day I will have brought your armies out of the land of Egypt.

Therefore you shall observe this day throughout your generations as an everlasting ordinance.'"

The Exodus is one of the most important events in Jewish history when comes to God's people. The Exodus is when God freed His people from the slavery and bondage of Egyptian taskmasters. Before God has set the Israelites free from Egypt, He had commanded them to eat the Passover meal.

This time was like no other. God sent not rain or a storm to take care of sin in this land. During this particular time, God had had enough of this wickedness with Pharaoh. God is not someone who plays with others. God is serious and loving and just and merciful. This night would be like rain but instead it would be a death angel pouring out death door to door. People are use to God pouring blessings. In this particular time, they were blessing.

Our children need a downpour today to keep them from falling prey to other people and other sinful lifestyles. Too many teenagers are living to impress other peers in their lives. Peer pressure is one of the leading causes to stumble and not achieve the level and heights that is inside of you. You have the ability to do anything. Our children have to remove their minds from the old traditional setting of standing in place and being idled and even in extreme complacency. It is time to live out dreams. No one can stop you from living your dream. One of the reasons that this is being written is because the enemy wants to carry out his version of this scripture and wipe you out. The only sure way of not being wiped out is to accept Jesus as Lord and Savior.

It is time for fathers in the house to act as priests and mothers as the true help to start marking you homes. Ask God to bless the home. It is time to start identifying and equipping young people who have talent to work hard and be successful.

THE GOD HOLD ON A REJOICING SPIRIT

LUKE 10:18-22: "And He said to them, 'I saw Satan fall like lightning from heaven. Behold, I give you the authority to trample on serpents and scorpions, and over all the power of the enemy, and nothing shall by any means hurt you. Nevertheless do not rejoice in this, that the spirits are subject to you, but rather] rejoice because your names are written in heaven.' In that hour Jesus rejoiced in the Spirit and said, 'I thank You, Father, Lord of heaven and earth, that You have hidden these things from the wise and prudent and revealed them to babes. Even so, Father, for so it seemed good in Your sight. All things have been delivered to Me by My Father, and no one knows who the Son is except the Father, and who the Father is except the Son, and the one to whom the Son wills to reveal Him.'"

God had the authority, and still does today, to send Satan from heaven to hell. He still has all authority to send Satan to the lake of fire in the end and He will according to His word. God is so powerful that everything must bow before Him and everything must worship Him in the beauty of His Holiness. No one is exempt from bowing down. Noah found grace for several reasons and I believe it's important for you and I to know so we can be obedient like Noah was. Noah found grace because he loved the Lord. Noah found grace because of His obedience to do what God said no matter what people around him was saying.

Noah found grace because He listened and heard what God had to say. Noah found grace because it was in God's plan. Lightning comes down fast. It may hit whatever is in the path. This is probably the only time in my life when I am happy to hear about lightning. This lightning is for the sake of getting rid of.

What is so unique about this word is that God said, I give you authority to trample no serpents and scorpions. Gods also gives the power to call down the rain in our lives when we have a dry spell. God is able to make His servants rejoice in the time of evil on the battlefield and evil that attack.

A PRIEST IN THE HOUSE!

Your father is the priest in your house. God is the head priest in your life and house. Everyone in the house falls under His complete authority. Everyone in the house must know that God ordained your father to bless the house. God made the order and it is not changing. You just have to live by His order and know it and love it. He orders our footsteps. He orders the marriage because He alone ordained marriage. He orders everyone in the house. He ordained the seed to be birth.

He knew which child in the house would be the way they are at this very moment. God knew then, and knows now, exactly what people are in need of for their lives. God our Lord knows if you honor your father and mother as Ephesians 6 states. It is a good thing to know that the power of God is in your house. So God has His own strategy for your house.

He placed the man as the head of the house because that is simply His order. He desires to keep order in your house. The moment the order is broken, those that assist in breaking the order has to deal with God. It is God's will for your house to walk in blessings. If you step out of order the enemy wants to come right in and disrupt more. In the Bible Job had a visitation. His entire family was wiped out except his wife. All the children were killed by the enemy's attack.

But because Job continued to trust and walk in the faith of God, he was blessed with more abundance than he ever had. I say this to tell children to obey your father so that it will be pleasing in the sight of God.

In Luke 15, the prodigal son did not recognize the extent of the blessing on his father's life and in the house. The prodigal son left home thinking with arrogance that he could make it on his own and He did not need the blessing and inheritance of his father. But to his surprise, life became complicated and challenging to the utmost, beyond his ability to maintain himself. When you find yourself in a condition that forces you to go to the pig pin and slop around with the swine, known as the filthiest animals on earth, you need to get a new attitude and return to God. Jesus is calling now. You do not have to wait until times get difficult. He deserves the praise now.

What you see in the story of the prodigal son is that the father never lost the ability to shower the blessing of love in his house whether someone left or not. He threw a party celebration for his son's arrival back home. There are people today that need to come back home to the father. He is the priest of the house He answers to the Most High God. He sets the condition for you to prosper as long as you remain under the obedience and truth of God. God's will is on your father's life and your life. I tell you that the Father in heaven will never let you down. He will not turn you away. He will never leave you.

He specializes in love, grace, mercy, salvation, deliverance, blessings, and getting all the glory. With your lost son or daughter, do not give in, do not allow the enemy to take authority you take it. Do not give up; God is working on them right at this moment. God is speaking to them at this very moment. Give them a call and ask them what is God saying to them? Tell them what God is saying to you as well. Make it a family revival. Open the word and tell them what scripture the Lord has shared with you as well at the right time. Then pray together. That will make the enemy flee and get mad about his defeat he just experienced. Your victory is in the Lord Jesus Christ. Jesus, Our high priest is the Lord of Lords and King of Kings. Come back home to the priest at your house and worship the Father in heaven with all your heart.

UNCOVER THE ROOF

MARK 2:4: "And when they could not come near Him because of the crowd, they uncovered the roof Where He was, so when they had broken through, they let down the bed on which the paralytic was lying."

Some places allow you the front entry. But sometimes the crowd can force you to use a different entrance. That is what happened with this paralytic. When you need healing, you need to come up with a positive imagination and a prayer life in Christ. Let the Lord know your desire. He wants you to use your mind and allow the blessing to be poured out. You have much potential in your imagination, just uncover it for God's purpose. You have an imagination that can cause you to make millions. Think about it that is all people need is their positive God given imagination.

In this story, the paralyzed man needed a healing. What was so powerful about these men is that they were not about to let anything get in their way. They had already made up their minds that there was a way to get healing. They used their imaginations to get to the roof of the building Jesus was inside of to let the man down to Jesus. These men must be considered God sent!

We live in a society that has many people who have need of healing. The enemy has paralyzed many lives. They also remain paralyzed because men and their families have not accepted Jesus as Lord and Savior. Today is your day to uncover your imagination and uncover the roof, and uncover your heart to let Jesus inside. He will keep you eternally in His hand. If you are around crowds, leave the crowd and go and get saved by Jesus Christ, the son of the Living God. You will never have to be paralyzed again because your spirit and you belong to God and no one else.

When I played football, I ran hard and strong over the defenders and had the potential like so many others to play professional football. But one day something happened to me in football practice on a rainy and muddy day. I was tackled by at least five defenders, which piled on me. They did not realize that my legs had twisted. I left that day with a hip pointer. I had to sit out of the games for a while until I healed properly. In my mind, I lost a little confidence and a little spark because I felt paralyzed. There was no need for me to feel that way. I just told myself that. I come to tell you that you never have feel that way.

Today, if you feel like the enemy has paralyzed you from head to toe and even a broken hip can't keep you from running for the Lord. Call on the name of Jesus for healing. Call on Him to help you to run for His purpose. Call His Holy and righteous name. He will be there to remove the scales that once had you paralyzed.

GOD GIVES THE INCREASE

1 CORINTHIANS 3:5-7: "Who then is Paul, and who is Apollos, but ministers through whom you believe as the Lord gave to each one? I planted, Apollos watered, but God gave the increase. So then neither he who plants is anything, nor he who waters, but God who gives the increase."

The focus must be kept on God. When we take our eyes off the prize, then we begin to sink and drown in our own spiritual abilities. Neither Paul nor Apollos gain the credit for service for the Lord. Everything we do and what they did must be to glorify His righteous name. In their preaching, it had to be the Lord who blesses with the power of conversion and conviction.

It has to be the power of the Holy Spirit who reveals carnality and those who are in need of being spirit filled. The Apostle Paul was tasked with giving the word even to those who were babes in Christ and carnal in mind. The scripture says, I fed you with milk and not with solid food, for until now you were not able to receive it, and even now you are still not able. But in Christ, men of God don't give up. Men might be able to identify weaknesses and what the enemy means for bad. But God always steps in. You see your salvation is not dependent upon these two men. But it is dependent upon God, the one who gives the increase.

Churches are not successful because they have great preachers. Churches are successful because the Holy Spirit shows up and does the work that God requires for His glory. Worship is not happening unless the Holy Spirit leads the congregation. Praise from the heart is not going forth unless the Holy Spirit ushers it through the sanctuary and the people. Sure God has work for His Saints, but we must remember we plant and water, as God requires of us. But God gives the increase. God gives the increase because only He can sanctify. God gives the increase because only He can justify. God gives the increase because He owns the cattle on a thousand hills. God gives the increase because He is the Creator of all things. He knows just what to do with whom He chooses. God gives the increase in any way He sees fit. If He wants 100 or 1,000 new members in one church on one set day, He can do it. If He wants 10,000 or 20,000 new members two setting He can do it. God builds the church not man. God grows the church and sustain its blessings.

The scripture is clear in *Psalms 127:1, except the Lord build a house, they labor in vain that build it; except the Lord keep the city, the watchman watches but in vain.* He has His hand on the pulse of all service and servants. He knows what will prosper to give Him glory.

When I was a young boy, I use to think that the man in the pulpit was God's man and He made it happen. It took me to learn of His word and become a minister in His grace to learn of Him and serve Him according to His will. Today, allow the Holy Spirit to minister to you.

Know that He will enter the heart of man and reveal His love to you right now. He will help you to grow in the faith regardless of what happened in the past. Jesus Christ loves you and always shines His tender mercies and grace on your life. Blessings be unto His Holy Name.

KNOW HIM FOR YOURSELF

PHILIPPIANS 3:10: "...that I may know Him and the power of His resurrection, and the fellowship of His sufferings, being conformed to His death."

When you get into His word, when you get intimate into His word, He will commune with you and your fellowship will become habitual. Your relationship will be stronger that ever before. You will begin to delight yourself in the Lord. You will know Him and experience a glimpse of His resurrection. You will experience even more than you can imagine. An experience with the Lord is more than enough. It is a life of fulfillment. You will never want anything outside of His perfect will and touch for your life. Know Him for yourself.

Scripture says, "To know Him and the power of His resurrection." Imagine knowing Him! Your heart changes when you know Him. More blessings come when you know Him, love flows better when you know Him, life changes for the better when you know Him, and your life changes with abundant blessings ready to enter your life. Now that is a thought! When you commune with God in prayer you might as well get ready to breakthrough because now you are in the right place and position.

I would not want to know anyone better than God. You need to make Him your number one priority to know. You can know someone with the highest education, but they cannot get you into the kingdom of heaven, they cannot get you into salvation, they cannot bless you like Jesus does every day. Knowing someone means you had to get a closer perspective of them. Knowing someone means you know a lot about him or her. You know about their family, you know more personal information. When you go to the doctor, the doctor really does not know your heart but he knows your organs and how to diagnose you. He knows how to treat you with the best medicine. The doctor gets intimate with your case because it could mean life or death in the balance.

That is exactly what Jesus wants. He wants us to get to know Him intimately. Our lives are in the balance for a place in heaven. People need to get to know better than knowing their spouse. Jesus will always be there. In the midst of a storm, He is there. When you go through a marital storm, He is there to rescue you. I always go back to the day that God illuminated His word for me. He made the scriptures come alive and burn in my heart. It was John 1:1-12. He made Himself come down from Heaven to live among His people and bless them.

God just loves when we want to know Him. It is when we take the time to fellowship with Him is when we know Him better. The more you study His word, the more you get in touch with God. He is the word according to John 1:1, in the beginning was the word and the word was with God and the word was God. How can this be? He is God. No one can fully express all of God. He calls the shots. No human in society calls the shots. They may have a role, but they do not call the shots. Otherwise, they would be false gods. No one wants that to happen because it is an abomination to God. When you get to know Him and the power of His resurrection and the fellowship of His suffering, you will be blessed. One thing He does is destroy demons entering into your life.

In 1997, the enemy came into my house and we had a show down. I was just born again, the second time so many years later. He came in to rise up against my family and me. He wanted everyone destroyed in my house. The enemy wanted my wife destroyed and he wanted my career destroyed. The enemy wanted the family to hate instead of have peace. Peace that surpasses all understanding will guard your hearts and minds in Christ Jesus.

Get yourself a new place where you can meet God and talk to Him. Get to know your redeemer and worship Him in the beauty of holiness.

GOD KNOWS YOUR SPIRIT

2 Corinthians 10:12-13: "But they, measuring themselves by themselves, and comparing themselves among themselves, are not wise."

God is the one who does the true measuring of a man. One of God's key missions of the believer is to help one another in love. Love a brother like a brother because a brother will tell you the truth. A brother will help you overcome shortcomings. But first things first, you must ask God to remove the scales from you own eyes. It is just like Matthew 6 says—remove the beam or plank from your eye so you can see as well.

You do not have to settle for what anybody says, you should get the advice from the Holy Spirit. Your trust should always be in the Lord. He will guide your decisions for you. Trust the wisdom of God.

I particularly take interest in this because of the way our society has shape itself under the enemy's umbrella. There is too much false pretense and false advertising and strange commercialism by people who want to get ahead, but misuse what they have for gain. I always tell my children one key statement. Do not sell yourself to the devil because of someone else's perception and opinion of you. They do not hold the key to heaven, nor the key to hell. I am sure they really do not want to hold hell's key. I believe it is valuable to train your children to know that they have a mind and no one controls their mind except they give it to Jesus, the author and finisher.

Look to God for all your answers. Never look to see who is measuring you because they have no power to put you before the throne of God. Our Father in heaven measures you and knows all things about you. He can review your entire life in a flash of a second and allow you to see it. We serve a mighty God, who is all omnipresent, sovereign and omnipotent. He is everywhere. He is the God who can tell you all about you. Be careful not to Judge as written in Matthew 7:7.

About the Author

Joseph Harris is currently a resident of Texas. He is retired from the United States Armed Forces. He is the founder of Christian Worship Outreach Center Ministries. His mission is based on Matthew 16 and Matthew 28. Nevertheless, His focus and foundation is the word of God as the Holy Spirit guides him and this ministry. His goal is to help others receive Jesus Christ as Lord and redeemer in their lives. His prayer is that everyone come to Jesus and become His servant with a transformed mind and heart pleasing to God. He prays that every family comes to the saving knowledge of our Lord and be equally yoked in the spirit. May God be the center force of your life and homes. Phil. 2:5, Col. 1:18-20, Eph. 2:8, Eph. 6. Stand on the word Of God for His love is eternal, never ending in your life.

www.ingramcontent.com/pod-product-compliance
Lightning Source LLC
Chambersburg PA
CBHW050120170426
43197CB00011B/1657